S0-ABS-211

CANADA'S KING

An Essay in Political Psychology

CANADA'S KING

An Essay in Political Psychology

Paul Roazen

Mosaic Press

OAKVILLE, ON - BUFFALO, NY

Canadian Cataloguing in Publication Data

Roazen, Paul, 1936-
    Canada's King

Includes bibliographical references.
ISBN 0-88962-667-7

1. King, William Lyon Mackenzie, 1874-1950 - Psychology. I. Title.

FC581.K5R58 1998   971.063'2'092   C98-931058-2
F1033.K5R58 1998

No part of this book may be reproduced or transmitted in any form, by any means, electronic or mechanical, including photocopying and recording information storage and retrieval systems, without permission in writing from the publisher, except by a reviewer who may quote brief passages in a review.

Published by MOSAIC PRESS, P.O. Box 1032, Oakville, Ontario, L6J 5E9, Canada. Offices and warehouse at 1252 Speers Road, Units #1&2, Oakville, Ontario, L6L 5N9, Canada and Mosaic Press, 85 River Rock Drive, Suite 202, Buffalo, N.Y., 14207, USA.

Mosaic Press acknowledges the assistance of the Canada Council and the Dept. of Canadian Heritage, Government of Canada, for their support of our publishing programme.

THE CANADA COUNCIL | LE CONSEIL DES ARTS
    FOR THE ARTS | DU CANADA
    SINCE 1957 | DEPUIS 1957

Copyright ©1998 Paul Roazen
ISBN 0-88962-667-7

Printed and bound in Canada
Cover design by: Amy Land

MOSAIC PRESS, in Canada:
1252 Speers Road, Units #1&2,
Oakville, Ontario, L6L 5N9
Phone / Fax: (905) 825-2130
E-mail: cp507@freenet.toronto.on.ca

MOSAIC PRESS, in the USA:
85 River Rock Drive, Suite 202, Buffalo,
N.Y., 14207
Phone / Fax: 1-800-387-8992
E-mail: cp507@freenet.toronto.on.ca

MOSAIC PRESS in the UK and Europe:
DRAKE INTERNATIONAL SERVICES
Market House, Market Place,
7Deddington, Oxford. OX15 OSF

Table of Contents

Other Books by Paul Roazen

Freud: Political and Social Thought

Brother Animal: The Story of Freud and Tausk

Sigmund Freud (editor)

Freud and His Followers

Erik H. Erikson: The Power and Limits of a Vision

Helene Deutsch: A Psychoanalyst's Life

Walter Lippmann, The Public Philosophy (editor)

Encountering Freud: The Politics and Histories of Psychoanalysis

Louis Hartz, The Necessity of Choice: Nineteenth Century Political Thought (editor)

Helene Deutsch, Psychoanalysis of the Sexual Functions of Women (editor)

Victor Tausk, Sexuality, War, and Schizophrenia: Collected Psychoanalytic Papers (editor)

Helene Deutsch, The Therapeutic Process, the Self, and Female Psychology: Collected Psychoanalytic Papers (editor)

Meeting Freud's Family

Walter Lippmann, Liberty and the News (editor)

How Freud Worked: First-Hand Accounts of Patients

Heresy: Sandor Rado and the Psychoanalytic Movement (with Bluma Swerdloff)

For Eric and Sonia

"You'd better face it, Boy; Mackenzie King rules Canada because he himself is the embodiment of Canada – cold and cautious on the outside, dowdy and pussy in every overt action, but inside a mass of intuition and dark intentions."

-Robertson Davies, *The Manticore*

List of Illustrations

Dr. Adolf Meyer in 1913
The most influential psychiatrist in twentieth century North American history, who saw King for clinical consultations in 1916. The symptoms, such as those of electrical influence, could sound humanly bizarre and psychiatrically worrisome.

Alan Mason Chesney Medical Archives

Alan Mason Chesney Medical Archives

The Phipps Clinic in 1916
The pioneering psychiatric facility at Johns Hopkins which Meyer headed.

Dr. Lewellys Barker in 1900
The Canadian neurologist at
Johns Hopkins who referred
King to Meyer. King stayed
permanently in touch with
Barker and kept his picture
in his study at Laurier
House.

Alan Mason Chesney Medical Archives

Dr. Adolf Meyer in 1940
Although Meyer has been
one of the founders of
psychoanalysis in America,
by World War II he was
considered a critic.

Alan Mason Chesney Medical Archives

photo by: Katrina B. Valenstein

Sigmund Freud
Freud remains the single most important psychological theorist of this past century. This bust was made shortly before his 1939 death in London, England. Bust by Peter Lamda

National Archives

President Roosevelt, Prime Minister King & Prime Minister Churchill in 1943
King, Canada's longest serving Prime Minister, remains known in the United States because of his World War II leadership.

W.L. Mackenzie, 1834
King's maternal grandfather.
King's mother was born during her
father's exile in America.

National Archives

**Isabel Grace Mackenzie
King in 1885**
King's mother. Her
younger son Max pro-
posed that certain kinds
of mothers evoke an
oedipal response in their
sons.

National Archives

National Archives

Mackenzie King (left) with his brother Macdougall and his father in 1899
This was an intimate old-fashioned family, and their letters to each other constitute an important social document.

(National Archives)

John King
King's father, a lawyer and teacher, who helped on certain key decisions in his older son's career.

x(g)

National Archives

Mr. and Mrs. John King with their son Mackenzie in 1911
By now King had been well-landed in his political career, but about to lose his seat in the House of Commons.

National Archives

Isabel Grace King, from a painting by J.W.L. Forester
She was a serious reader in addition to being the mother of four children. She was ambitious for her older son.

Mackenzie King in 1914
While out of elected political office he was working for the Rockefellers in the United States even after the outbreak of World War I.

National Archives

Charles William Elliot
One of the great pioneering presidents of Harvard, he became a patron of King and was the key to his association with the Rockefellers.

National Archives

National Archives

John D. Rockefeller, Jr. in 1915
His father had a reputation as one of the worst of the industrialist bandits. Rockefeller Jr. and King became close friends.

(Below)
Sir Wilfred Laurier and Mackenzie King in 1915
Sir Wilfred and his wife were among many who tried to find a wife for King. King always remained loyal to Sir Wilfred's political legacy.

National Archives

National Archives

Front row left to right: **F.A. McGregor, Mackenzie King, and John D. Rockefeller Jr. in Colorado in 1915**
McGregor was King's private secretary. The strike at Ludlow was one of America's worst, and a public relations disaster for the Rockefellers.

(Right)
Mackenzie King and John D. Rockefeller, Jr. in Washington D.C. in 1915
King helped Rockefeller make a better political impression before congress.

National Archives

National Archives

National Archives

(Above)
Mackenzie King's cottage at Kingsmere in 1916
While staying at Kingsmere, King was so unhappy that he decided he needed to seek professional help.

(Left)
Mathilde Barchet (nee Grossert) in 1916
She was the nurse King had once been in love with as a graduate student at the University of Chicago. She and her husband were living in Maryland where King visited them in 1916.

(Right)
Mackenzie King and his brother Max in Colorado
Max had gone to Colorado because of his tuberculosis, but still the illness succeeded in shortening his life.

National Archives

(Left)
Mackenzie King in 1919, Leader of the Liberal Party
When King succeeded as Laurier's successor he felt his entire family as living presences.

National Archives

(Right)
King and his dog Pat at Kingsmere
King had expanded from his cottage to make a great estate. His attachment to his dogs is well-known.

National Archives

x(m)

National Archives

Mackenzie King on his 75th birthday in 1949
In retirement King was ill, lonely and sad.

Prologue

Any author has difficulties living with each biographical subject. Undertaking a biographical inquiry amounts to inviting a long-standing guest into one's study. Most biographers become so enmeshed in the lives they are working on that it requires an emotional reliving of another's experience to succeed in such a historical project. It should be helpful especially to admire the person chosen to write about, if not for outstanding personal qualities then for the place in history that he or she occupied. A favorable, positive appraisal can assist in keeping one going over the necessary hard-slogging. Otherwise, as has happened to a professional acquaintance of mine working on a multi-volume examination of Josef Stalin, the biographer can come to feel victimized by his tyrannical subject. The example of a terrible dictator may be the exception that proves the rule, which leads away from examining anyone's life whom one cannot identify with.

Some books do need to be written for a moral purpose of condemnation, and others for the sake of belittling. It is easy to imagine how certain reputations can get so inflated that it becomes tempting to prick such a balloon; in circumstances like that the biographer remains certainly in charge, but it requires a special sort of moral fervor for an author to sustain a full-scale debunking. Still the gratifications in all biographical work are few enough so that in most instances biographers like to think of at least the prospect of hanging a new photograph on the wall.

Sigmund Freud, a modern master at understanding conflicting emotions, wrote about the psychology of how biographers feel, acknowledging the reasonableness of the human need to "add...to the fathers, teachers, exemplars whom we have known or whose influence we have already experienced." Freud also saw the complex underside to such explicit and conscious admiration:

The biographer's justification also contains a confession. It is true that the biographer does not want to depose his hero, but he does want to bring him nearer to us. That means, however, reducing the distance that separates him from us; it still tends in effect toward degradation. And it is unavoidable that if we learn more about a great man's life we shall also hear of occasions on which he has in fact done no better than we, has in fact come nearer to us as a human being.

Freud concluded, at his most papal, that "nevertheless" he thought "we may declare the efforts of biography to be legitimate." He was taking it for granted that in the nature of the case there will be what he called an oedipal component to biography-writing:

> Our attitude to fathers and teachers is, after all, an ambivalent one since our reverence for them regularly conceals a component of hostile rebellion. That is a psychological fatality; it cannot be altered without forcible suppression of the truth and is bound to extend to our relations with the great men whose life histories we wish to investigate. [1]

As Freud wrote these dispassionate words in 1930, he was thinking about others being subjected to biographical scrutiny. But when, only six years later, a loyal follower of his own, who also happened to be a talented novelist, wrote to Freud asking permission to write his biography, Freud reacted with spontaneously eloquent horror. He shot back that he was

> alarmed by the threat that you want to become my biographer – you, who have so much better and more important things to do, you who can establish monarchs and who can survey the brutal folly of mankind from a lofty vantage point; no, I am far too fond of you to permit such a thing. Anyone who writes a biography is committed to lies, concealments, hypocrisy, flattery and even to hiding his own lack of understanding, for biographical truth does not exist, and if it did we could not use it.
>
> Truth is unobtainable, mankind does not deserve it, and in any case is not our Prince Hamlet right when he asks who would

escape whipping were he used after his desert? [2]

Whatever Freud's popular reputation may be like nowadays, such subtle words written off the top of his head should indicate that he was no slouch either as a writer or a psychologist. From my own point of view, having already had the experience of undertaking more than one biographical endeavor, I appreciate that no matter how sterling a character the selected individual may turn out to have had, there are bound to be rough spots in any such research relationship, occasions on which the object of study behaved disappointingly. The greater our emotional commitment the more we are apt to expect humanly, which means that the consequent disillusionment will be proportionately greater.

So there must be some kind of magical glue, usually made up of more or less non-rational feelings of hero-worship or perhaps group loyalty like patriotism, that keeps the biographer firmly attached – in spite of everything that could be disruptive – to what he has decided to write about. Without some such emotional bond the distractions of everyday life can doom the most promising biographical quest. For even after a book gets finished, the process of re-thinking a life history does not cease, assuming the initial emotional investment has been a substantial one. A biographical choice may not be as momentous as a marriage but nevertheless ought not to be undertaken lightly.

In the case of Mackenzie King, who served as Prime Minister longer than anyone else in Canadian history, I have been thinking of publishing a study of him for over a decade now. And yet what has held me to him has not been any particular affection for him as a man, although at times I have felt him to be seriously misunderstood. Nor have I experienced any special loyalty to the political causes for which he struggled; still the seemingly perpetual constitutional crises of recent Canadian history, as in the Quebec referendum of 1995, were unknown in King's time of prominence, in no small part due to his exceptional skillfulness as a leader.

My main attraction to King was that I knew he presented a historical puzzle, in that he was one of Canada's most powerful political leaders who at the same time seems to have possessed such a variety of personal quirks as to appear to defy common sense explanations. To the extent that King is remembered at all today, a few people now seem to think that he governed Canada literally with the help of a crystal ball, although that particular oddity is a falsifiable myth.

Nonetheless what has primarily kept me attached to King has been the specific problem of how someone could be as privately eccentric as he unquestionably was, and yet at the same time without challenge one of the greatest political success stories in Canadian history.

Then I happened to discover a fascinating psychiatric file on King from 1916 which casts a special light on his character and beliefs. Diagnostic terminology has changed a lot since that long ago era, but the main issue remains that King's presenting symptoms were so bizarre as to be hard to comprehend without something more than the garden-variety psychology of normality. In the textbook clinical literature his problems are usually discussed in the context of the concept of schizophrenia, yet there is clearly something amiss with using any label like schizophrenic on someone as notoriously politically accomplished as King. Still, King's particular 1916 difficulties were so strange as not just to elude everyday categories of thinking, but will be hard for even sophisticated historians and political scientists to follow. If nothing else, King's psychiatric records illustrate how there was something about him that resists our following his strange ways of thinking. Perhaps this will also help explain why, in contrast to the Canadian reaction to the death of other former prime ministers, there was a relative lack of public mourning at King's 1950 passing.

It was at the suggestion of officers of the Rockefeller Foundation, when King (at the age of forty-one) was working for them in the States during World War I, that he consulted a Canadian neurologist in Baltimore, Maryland, who in turn sent King to the most famous North American psychiatrist of the time: John Hopkins University's Adolf Meyer. Earlier King had seen other physicians about his various "nervous" afflictions. Although any psychiatric material, hard though it be to interpret in hindsight, cannot be expected to wave a magic wand over all the most perplexing aspects of King's biography, it does not take much such detailed evidence of symptomatology to put in a fresh light what has come to be known about this mysterious man. Each of us have symptoms, but modern psychology has taught how they represent structured emotional conflicts which are characteristic of our personalities as a whole. Interpreting the kind of material about someone like King that psychiatry has to offer may be harder for traditionally trained historians than they might expect; it is not easy to use clinical diagnoses within a historical context, unless one wants to stigmatize political actors by means of psychopathological labelling.

And political scientists, who tend to focus more or less exclusively on the rational acquisition of power – such as who gets what, when and how – can be even less open than historians, who at least in principle acknowledge that past history-writing has had to assume a built-in theory of human nature.

Readers are entitled to a conceptual itinerary of what follows. The Introduction deals with the methodology of relating psychology and politics, and in particular explores the central role of Freud's thought. It is indicative of how Freud became, in W. H. Auden's words, "a whole climate of opinion"[3] that not only the doctors King saw relied on psychoanalytic thinking, but friends and relatives of King applied Freudian categories to help understand him.

King's emotional life, as well as his political standing, is the subject of Chapter 1. Next I have examined the psychiatric career of Adolf Meyer. Starting with Chapter 3 it is possible to follow a narrative account of what happened to King in 1916. Chapter 4 focuses on the specific symptoms King had, and Chapter 5 deals with the brief hospitalization. King's extensive diary is throughout a key document, but Chapter 6 provides an account of what can be learned from examining King's correspondence with friends and relatives. Chapter 7 deals finally with the conclusions that I think can be validly drawn.

Toward the end of my thinking about King, after weighing and evaluating what this fresh psychiatric documentation can do to help us understand key aspects of his life, I decided to return to his grave in Mt. Pleasant Cemetery in Toronto, where I had lived for many years. Almost from the outset of my interest in King a Liberal friend, knowledgeable about King, helpfully volunteered to take me there to show me the spot. But the cemetary itself, first established in 1876, makes up a huge tract of over 200 acres, ranging east-west between Bayview Avenue and Yonge Street, bounded on the north by Merton Street and on the south by Moore Avenue. My second visit there, this time on my own, was designed to pay my respects to the man who had been such an absorbing puzzle for me, at the same time as I went to say a good-bye to the various drafts of manuscripts that I had developed over the years.

So it was not surprising, given how long ago I had first been there, that I could not easily find the place I was looking for. I remembered that King had been buried surrounded by almost all the rest of his immediate family. Mt. Pleasant Cemetary is now so centrally located, given how the city has grown since the late nineteenth century, that people often go there for walks, cycling or jogging. I was not surprised that no one I chanced to ask for directions knew how to find the grave I was looking for.

There is, however, deep within the cemetary grounds an efficient-sounding central office, and it turns out that everyone buried in that vast area is supposed to be listed on an up-to-date computer giving the exact location – the plot, section, and lot – of the person one might be inquiring after. I would not expect most Canadians to be now aware even in what city Mackenzie King is buried, or be surprised if Torontonians themselves are also ignorant of the matter. But the woman conscientiously working at the computer of the Mt. Pleasant Cemetary office could not seem to find Mackenzie King's name in her elaborate system. Nor did she know, when I specifically asked her about it, who he had been.

Finally, in a desperate last-minute guess about how to find the grave, I thought of King's father's name, John, since that seemed rather more straight-forward than the possibilities of mis-spelling Mackenzie. Although there turned out to be more than one John King interred there, only a single John King had died in the right year of 1916, and therefore I got the information with the directions enabling me to succeed in finding the whole set of family graves.

What does it say about King, and possibly Canada generally, that such a situation could arise? Recently it has appeared that Mackenzie King's reputation may be at last starting to be on the rise once again; at least an excellent and widely-sold recent book has called King "the greatest and most interesting of Canada's prime ministers."[4] And King's picture does appear today on fifty dollar Canadian bills. I suspect that it is going to take more than one book-length study to re-establish King's standing, and perhaps there is a more general problem, aside from the special issues connected with what has happened to King's status, obstructing the way his memory gets treated. Canada remains a country relatively without heroes; it cannot boast of a universal genius, like Thomas Jefferson, among its founders, or even a Washington, not to mention Abraham Lincoln and Franklin Roosevelt later on.

I do not anticipate that this particular examination of King's political psychology will accomplish a full-scale re-evaluation of his role in Canadian politics. But I think that the more general problem of the psychology of political leadership, and how we understand the dynamics of the ways in which high public officials think, can be enhanced by the example of Mackenzie King. Just as I did not pursue this inquiry with any purposes of glorifying King, neither did I set out to diminish him; it has long been my conviction that the psychology of leaders can benefit from the special sorts of understanding that comes from modern psychiatric thinking. The terminology we tend to use nowadays – including such words as "unbalanced," "lunatic", in addition to such praise as "well-adjusted" or "normal" – implies some broad theories of mental functioning, even if we do not readily acknowledge the conceptional commitments underlying our snap judgments. In Mackenzie King's case no abstract speculative theorizing should be necessary, except that which arises out of the concrete psychiatric data provided by his 1916 file. But it takes some perspective in order to understand how to evaluate any such material to be sure that it gets adequately heard without being sensationalistically mis-used.

Introduction:
How Psychology Relates to Politics

I had been living in Canada for only a couple of months, after moving from the States in 1971, when an eminent Canadian historian first alerted me to the reasons why he thought I should be especially interested in the career and character of Mackenzie King. Sophisticated Canadians are aware of how little Americans can be expected to know about their country before living there. One popular text I consulted at the time, in order to orient myself in a new setting, well summarized the general state of King's reputation then: "An un-prepossessing, pudgy little man who remained a bachelor and was almost psychotically devoted to his mother's memory, King is the most enigmatic personality of Canadian political history."[1]

What has happened when it becomes possible for a mainstream historian to say that King was "almost psychotically" involved with his mother's memory? Even aside from the alarming-sounding terminology, all biographies have to involve a more or less implicit psychology. As our conceptions of human nature have altered, and been inevitably influenced by modern psychological systems of thought, the kind of behavior that will be made the subject of biographical interpretation will also alter. Nowadays a biographical study will be less likely to ignore the existence of symptomatology, whether it be of a neurotic or even a more disturbed sort. Psychoanalytic thinking has attuned us to the meaningfulness of kinds of thinking which in an earlier time might have been discarded as simply unrealistic or eccentric.

My own professional background and training had been in political science, though my specialty was doing research about the psychoanalytic ideas of Freud and his followers. Some people think that Freud's work was full of over-heated Viennese sexuality, and that his contribution to Western thought can be categorized as some kind of invitation to promiscuity. Even a cursory familiarity with his writings, though, on a subject such as biography-writing itself, should indicate how complex Freud could be. It is true that he, around the turn of the twentieth century, specifically indicted the bad consequences of dammed-up sexuality, and how instinctual frustrations can be distorting to personality development. But only a grotesque mis-reading of him can miss just how broadly he came to define sexuality, or how civilized a set of moral restraints he took for granted. Freud expected a lot of people, at least those he thought were worth-while enough to benefit from the kind of approach to human troubles that he himself was embarked on.

At times it is true that Freud could be extravagant about his own findings and theories. After he had proposed a three-part conception of personality, comprising what he called the "id," the "ego," and the "super-ego," Freud could jump too quickly from understanding the psychology of the individual to conjecturing about human history as a whole. As he wrote in 1933, only six years away from his own death in old age, Freud proposed that:

> the events of human history, the interactions between human nature, cultural development and the precipitates of primaeval experience (the most prominent example of which is religion) are no more than a reflection of the dynamic conflicts between the ego, the id and the super-ego, which psychoanalysis studies in the individual – are the very same processes repeated upon a wider stage.[2]

One wishes that Freud had been more cautious, for his way of thinking has often been too-quickly tarred by the propensity for extravagant claims to be made in behalf of his outlook.

Yet it would be hard to over-estimate either the significance of Freud's impact, or how he continues to loom over the modern consciousness. One famous literary critic considers Freud the single greatest modern thinker: "No 20th century writer – not even Proust or Joyce or Kafka – rivals Freud's' position as the central imagination of our age."

> Freud was one of the greatest Western speculators, and was certainly the most suggestive myth maker of the last century.

Asserting that his new science was firmly grounded on evidence, on practice and observation, Freud nevertheless imagined a new map of the mind, or else he discovered ways of mythologizing a Western map of the mind that had been developing for some centuries. Seeing himself as making a third with Copernicus and Darwin, Freud actually may have made a fourth in the sequence of Plato, Montaigne, and Shakespeare. The neurologist who sought a dynamic psychology seems today to have been a speculative moralist and a mythologizing dramatist of the inner life.[3]

Freud may have been too bold in his own biographical reconstructions, and his book on Leonardo da Vinci[4], or his collaborative study (with William C. Bullitt) on President Woodrow Wilson[5], might have exceeded the grounds which seem to us today justifiable. Like all pioneers Freud was an enthusiastic advocate of his own theories; not unlike Karl Marx, Freud felt he had a special intellectual mission to accomplish in imposing on world thought his own conceptualization. But Freud's version of the Oedipus complex, for which he is perhaps most famous, was more complicated than might appear at first glance. At times it became almost a metaphysical notion, which is how it had to come up also in connection with biography writing. Freud was proposing that infantile attachments to the parent of the opposite sex can endure throughout adulthood, and that these feelings – without being stigmatized as mad or psychotic – have to endure unconsciously, beyond our rational awareness. And Freud was suggesting that opposite emotions, animosity underlying conscious devotions, may too play their role.

With someone like Mackenzie King, so successful in everyday life, I would have thought there was some special impropriety in invoking psychopathological terminology to describe him at all. At least my own inclination would be not to try to reduce anyone down to their possible pathology. Symptoms can be a reasonable beginning to talking about character structure, but no one who ever lived was without problems. And the key issue is how people manage to cope in spite of great stress, and the extent to which they make use of frailties to attain their accomplishments. Freud popularized the notion of sublimation, which links the best in us to our worst, but once again that is a concept of his which is as widely used as it is easily mis-understood. In my experience it is only callow readers of Freud who are confident of the implications of what he meant.

In the instance of Mackenzie King, it is not just present-day historians, influenced by the Freudian revolution in ideas which has shaped our contemporary consciousness, who have been apt to use diagnostic categories on him. His own younger brother was a practicing physician who died prematurely but was, like King himself, an author, and one who happened to write a posthumously published book called *Nerves and Personal Power* (1922). This obscure text, which casts some light on the prime minister's psychology, has been up until now ignored as a possible source of information. Mackenzie King, as we shall see, wrote a personally revealing introduction to his late brother's volume.

King's brother Macdougall was not only familiar with a work like Freud's famous *Psychopathology of Everyday Life* (1901), but Macdougall also explicitly wrote about the existence of oedipal feelings, and how they could explain "nervous" symptoms rather like those of his already eminent sibling. When Freud himself wrote about biographical heroes, he may sound from today's perspective as excessively a male chauvinist, since he did not for instance mention women as possible models; whatever Freud may have failed to understand about women, it need not be surprising if he was inevitably a man of his own times. He approached female psychology with a set of blinders which have subsequently needed correction, and there is a considerable literature on this subject. But the theory of the Oedipus complex does necessarily involve mothers as well as fathers, even if Freud's own conception of mothering may have been unduly idealizing. If this was evident by the time of Macdougall King's 1922 study, I would guess that it should be attributable to how much younger than Freud Macdougall was, in addition to the different mores in the new world rather than what would have been characteristic in traditional European culture.

Macdougall King, familiar with some of his brother's most intimate medical problems, took explicit aim at what he saw as "a result of excessive and misplaced sympathy...to be seen in what is described by Freud as the Oedipus complex."[6] We will be discussing some hypotheses about the kind of mother the King sons may have experienced. In the light of what Macdougall King was talking about in 1922, I do not think it inappropriate for us now to use Freud's categories, as best we can, to untangle some of Mackenzie King's specific problems. It could look out of place, or anachronistic, to impose on Mackenzie King a system of ideas wholly alien to his human experience. But his brother's writings imply something specific about how their mother might have mobilized in her elder son feelings which became interferences in his life as a whole. What Macdougall had to suggest, as expressed in what I propose can be seen as the disguised form of his textbook discussion, is of course only part of the story, to be supplemented by other evidence as well. Just as no one like Mackenzie King should be understood solely in the light of his emotional difficulties, it would be unfair to blame any one person for the way he turned out. One of the most unfortunate aspects of the uses of Freud's ideas has been the extent to which they have been employed in a moralistic or accusatory way.

So it is not just what is currently fashionable which requires us to look in Freud's direction for the sake of untangling, as best we can, the mysteries of what motivated Mackenzie King. As we shall be discussing, the psychiatrist who saw him in 1916, although sophisticated about psychoanalysis as it existed at that time, was by no means an uncritical advocate of Freud's own point of view. At least psychoanalytic thinking gives one a reasonable place to start, and is in keeping with Macdougall King's reasoning; without being a special partisan of Freud's, he also recommended some of Freud's writings to his older brother, and we will find King himself explicitly referring to having had "Freudian" dreams.

As best we can it will be necessary to look at the 1916 diagnoses of King in the light of what we think nowadays. But oddly enough it is less likely that we will do retrospective damage to the authenticity of historical material by relying on Freud's thinking than if we were to substitute some completely alien, even if apparently up-to-date, perspective that might be popular now. It would be in accord with Freud's theories to assume that we can attribute psychological meaning to Mackenzie King's 1916 symptomatology, as well as to any dream material he may have given us. In any event, historians and political scientists have been making use of Freud's broad outlook on King, without knowing about his 1916 difficulties, so that to look at him in a psychoanalytic light does not imply any professional arrogance on the part of psychoanalysts themselves. It is true that psychiatrists seem to have a know-it-all propensity, whatever school of thought they may belong to, and such unfortunate tendencies seem to persist even today. But when dealing with material as complex as that presented by Mackenzie King's life, I think it behooves us to make use of every interpretive angle that we can lay our hands on.

My own special combination of interests is not a usual one, although Freud did succeed in having an immense impact on all the modern social sciences. The world of politics appears at first glance to exist far apart from the concerns of psychology. Political struggles involve public issues that center on controversies about power, influence, and prestige. At least since Machiavelli wrote in the early sixteenth century, observers of political conflicts have been relatively unashamed to keep a kind of score-card of public careers, tracking how individual leaders might be waxing or waning in their reputations.

Political disputes do sometimes take place behind closed doors, but such negotiations are increasingly conducted as if they can be apt to be exposed to the full glare of publicity; today the media try to watch the comings and goings of high officials with a close interest that, to those of us not accustomed to living in that kind of fish-bowl, appears appalling. It is not just that any minor slip-up, connected for example with alcohol, sex, or money, to think of only a few of the variety of sins that the flesh is prey to, get magnified in the press. One can reasonably wonder whether today, unlike the case for instance with President Franklin Roosevelt's tragic affliction by polio, much more attention would not be given to all the problems associated with his partial paralysis. It is hard to imagine, for those of us who have the privileges of privacy that go with not being in politics, how people in public life put up with the loss of anonymity which accompanies the positions they hold. Certain kinds of people do enjoy being the center of attention, and when Mackenzie King for example was out of office he was likely to feel at loose ends. One wonders, though, how he would deal with the kind of intense scrutiny to which leaders are now commonly subjected. President Richard Nixon even had Daniel Ellsberg's psychiatrist's office burglarized in the hope of finding some personal "dirt" to balance the leaking of the Pentagon papers.

Psychology, in contrast to the ruthless publicity of politics, has to do with those intimate matters that are the knowledge of our most secret selves. Freud made it the "fundamental rule" of all psychoanalytic treatment that patients provide their free associations, with-holding no thoughts, no matter how random, from the psychoanalyst's consulting room. Freud's idea was that implicit in even the most chaotic-seeming reflections on the patient's part the analyst should be able to discern patterns of hidden meaning.

Freud was proceeding on the basis of what he always thought was his most momentous achievement, starting with his 1900 insistence that dreams have a disguised significance. It is now known, as it was not yet in Freud's lifetime, how each of us spends several hours a night dreaming, even though we recall afterwards at best only a fraction of those confusing dream thoughts. There is even now experimental evidence of how personally disorientating it can be to be deprived of dreams. Since we follow dream stories with our eyes, so-called Rapid Eye Movement – or REM sleep -- is now seen as a distinct entity. (Deprivation of normal waking sensory perceptions, thanks to blind-folding or ear-plugs, has even been used as a weapon of political inquisition, as for example the British did for a time while interrogating IRA suspects. One of the grounds for putting a stop to the British practice was psychiatric testimony that nobody could be sure of the long-term bad consequences of such emotional disorientation.)

Even before modern science had been able through electronic means to explore the full extent of our dreaming, Freud remained prophetically confident that human beings engage in a considerable degree of self-deception; we both remember and forget our dreams, according to Freud, for a purpose. With the model of dreaming and our forgetfulness in mind, Freud used the selectiveness of human memory to establish the extent to which people disguise from themselves their own motivation. So that his psychology was designed to deal with aspects of human behavior which take place not only outside the glare of publicity, but even beyond the private understanding of the people most directly involved. Freud's work on the psychopathology of everyday life proved propagandistically most persuasive in promoting the impact of psychoanalysis, and Macdougall King was one of the many to be so influenced. According to one story it was on Freud's only trip to the United States in 1909, when he received an honorary degree from Clark University, that he noticed a cabin steward reading *The_Psychopathology of Everyday Life*, and then Freud realized how he had succeeded in conquering the public imagination. Freud's work in this area proved so widely accepted that the reality of so-called Freudian slips, both of speech as well as of the pen, has long before now entered into our ordinary conversation.

Freud generalized that meaningfulness could be attributed not just to dreams, as well as such apparent trivia as slips of the tongue, but he sought to try to understand those stable conflicts that he called neuroses. Individual neurotic symptoms can be understood, Freud held, on the model of the compromise formations that underlie dreams.

For many years Freud argued that the severe mental illnesses we now call psychoses were merely "narcissistic neuroses", a term that has long since gone out of fashion; Freud meant that narcissistic neurotics were to be distinguished from those capable of establishing enough of a human relationship with an analyst ("transferences") to be treatable by the kind of rational interpretations that an analyst could offer. But by the 1920's Freud was conceptually finally distinguishing between neurosis as opposed to psychosis, and this distinction will be a key problem in approaching the psychiatric data about Mackenzie King. (The reader will remember how readily a historian could write about King being "almost psychotically devoted to his mother's memory....")

However Freud's terminological thinking may have altered with the passage of time, and in the face of criticism that he was being too ambitious about the therapeutic scope of his system of theorizing, he had almost immediately after first proposing his interpretation of dreams gone on, long before World War I, to declare that he had discovered the realm of the "unconscious." Freud meant by that term that there are areas of our thoughts and desires that we deliberately conceal from our conscious self-awareness. We supposedly disguise our own motives because we have impulses that conflict with other aspects of our sense of ourselves; without some such self-blinding we would have to face up to disharmonies that would be painful to have to bear. In principle Freud proposed that it was the analyst's job to present unwelcome insight. Patients would supposedly accept such interpretations for the sake of maintaining the help implicit in a therapeutic relationship. Freud also saw himself, as in what he had to say about biography-writing in particular, as generally lecturing mankind, and he held out a fresh version of how life could be experienced. He would also come to denounce religion as an unnecessary neurotic crutch. But right from the outset, when at the turn of the century he first proposed his theory of dreams, he was quick not only to explore the implications his "discovery" about dreaming had for a general theory of psychology, but he soon proceeded to found a new profession that he called psychoanalysis.

Freud's own specialty had originally been in neurology, which in the world of old Vienna was a field professionally separate from psychiatry. It is an open question how many genuine neurological patients there were to go around, and neurologists have often treated "nervousness" as well as nerves. Freud was in principle, as we have discussed, standoffish towards psychosis, the traditional preserve of the psychiatrists who then saw only institutionalized patients, usually as custodians. Even today it has been estimated that mental health "experts" probably see only a tiny fraction of patients who are emotionally ill as primary caretakers (including general practitioners, parish priests, and nurses) are left to deal on a practical basis with most of the potentially suffering population.

Freud chose to work with individual people in his office on a one-to-one basis. His clinical practice rested on the hope that he knew how to relieve human torments. He saw clients for fifty-minute sessions, six days a week, at first for periods lasting several months; but by the 1920's and 1930's he was as a matter of course treating patients for periods that often lasted over a number of years. Despite how in principle he ruled psychotics out of the realm of psychoanalytic treatment, he sought to understand psychotic thought-processes, and even could encourage certain of his disciples to try to adapt his treatment-setting for more disturbed people than run-of-the-mill neurotics. We now know that Freud could make his share of diagnostic mistakes, and neurotic facades could turn out to be defenses against far more deeply rooted disturbances; relief of a neurosis could pave the way for even more painful human troubles. Initially in the 1890s, when he thought he was treating so-called hysterics, Freud had relied on the technique of hypnosis; that is the historical origins of his recommending that his patients lie down on a couch. For a variety of reasons, some admittedly personal and others of a more scientific nature, Freud gave up on hypnotizing people in favor of free associations.

According to Freud's formal requirements, therefore, psychoanalytic patients were supposed to bring their thoughts without conscious censorship; in return, Freud proposed to offer enlightenment and rational understanding in order to dissolve emotional conflicts through the insight made possible by the analyst's detachment. Distance was, Freud thought, the ideal way of overcoming emotional distress. It might be temporarily necessary for patients to grow worse, as they re-experienced early childhood conflicts in their relationship with the analyst. But Freud was confident that in the long run the power of reason would win out, at least with those patients he deemed "worthy" of benefiting from his form of treatment. Psychoanalysis was in Freud's view by no means designed for everybody, but for those superior few who he hoped would form the vanguard of future ethical models of how to live. Although he warned against relying on the impact of "suggestion," or the rapport with the therapist, instead of insight, in practice he does seem to have sought converts among his adherents.

As early as 1902 he had started establishing a school of his own, so that disciples of his were soon following his precepts as well as the informal example he set. His followers were not just in central Europe but he increasingly attracted supporters across the world. By 1916, when Mackenzie King sought psychotherapeutic help, Freud's way of thinking was one of the most prominent and progressive-seeming, although critics had all along stressed the limitations of Freud's outlook. By the end of World War I, Freud had achieved real fame; Freud's 1938 fate in Vienna, once Hitler had annexed Austria, had been notable enough to be front-page news in Toronto's *Globe and Mail*[7]. At the time of Freud's 1939 death in London, England, where he had fled because of the Nazis, psychoanalysis was an established profession throughout advanced industrialized countries.

Today there are many rivals to the Freudian perspective, but no single person has matched his stature in the history of twentieth century psychology. From philosophical treatises to manuals on child-rearing the impact of psychoanalysis has been immense. Even where Freud is no longer deemed therapeutically pertinent, his principles are widely used even if not always properly understood. Repeatedly Mackenzie King's life and career have been described by key categories which would be inconceivable without Freud's work.

An incongruity in trying to use Freud's ideas to understand a political figure is the way in which he taught that it was not the job of a therapist to intervene actively in the real lives of people, though in practice he could be far more interventionistic with patients than his own stated principles may imply. But his psychoanalytic approach meant that he was not proposing to do more than dissolve conflicts, with the conviction that people knew best how to set their own priorities. He was not recommending that analysts try to alter the realistic situations in which clients who came found themselves. Freud set out to work with inner realities, like dreams, fantasies, and expectations; he aimed to reorganize the subjective outlook of his patients. And so he rarely took any part in day-to-day social and political activities. Even after all these years Freud's successors have continued to follow his model pretty closely; they have by and large concentrated on their clinical work with isolated individuals, and scarcely ever mixed in with large-scale matters connected with external political realities.

A long tradition of left-wing thinkers have dismissed psycho-analysis as a decadent form of soul-searching. Starting with Lenin himself, he was reputed to have maintained:

> The extension on Freudian hypotheses seems "educated", even scientific, but it is ignorant, bungling. Freudian theory is the modern fashion. I mistrust the sexual theories of the articles, dissertations, pamphlets, etc., in short, of that particular kind of literature which flourishes luxuriantly on the dirty soil of bourgeois society. I mistrust those who are always contemplating the sexual questions, like the Indian saint his navel. It seems to me that these flourishing sexual theories which are mainly hypothetical, and often quite arbitrary hypotheses, arise from the personal need to justify personal abnormality or hypertrophy in sexual life before bourgeois morality, and to entreat its patience. This masked respect for bourgeois morality seems to me just as repulsive as poking about in sexual matters. However wild and revolutionary this behavior may be, it is still really quite bourgeois. It is, mainly, a hobby of the intellectuals and of the sections nearest them. There is no place for it in the Party, in the class conscious, fighting proletariat....[8]

(The whole tradition of American behaviorist psychology, exemplified most recently by B.F. Skinner, would be no less hostile to Freud's point of view.) *Pravda* reprinted these remarks of Lenin after his death. Despite Lenin's position psychoanalysis was in fact a flourishing movement in the Soviet Union during the 1920s, and Trotsky took a far more open-minded approach toward the signifi-cance of all Freud's teachings.[9]

Marxists have been divided about what to do with Freud. On the one hand someone like the British leftist John Strachey could dismiss Freud in 1933 on the grounds that "for all his great intellectual powers," he remained "the last major thinker of the European capitalist class, unable to step outside his class limitations." Strachey saw Freud's *Civilization and Its Discontents* (1930) as an expression of "nihilistic pessimism". The Hungarian Marxist Georg Lukacs, who lived for a time in Freud's Vienna, was also damning: "I can say that I have never felt frustration or any kind of complex in my life. I know what these mean, from the literature of the twentieth century, and from having read Freud. But I have not experienced them myself." I find positively frightening some of Lukacs's further remarks: "What preserves me is that I have no inner life. I am interested in everything except my soul."[10] (Mackenzie King's own kind of religiously-inspired introspectiveness might have seemed to Lukacs as a typical sort of reactionary form of reasoning, as retrograde as Freud's psychoanalysis.)

Part of what energized Lenin's critique, and that of Lukacs too, was that within Marxist socialism there has been a long history of theorists eager to unite Marxist concepts with those of Freud. Alfred Adler, one of Freud's first students, was also a socialist, who went on to found a school of "individual psychology" apart from Freud's own.[11] A whole list of later thinkers – including Wilhelm Reich, Erich Fromm, Theodor Adorno, and Herbert Marcuse – has tried to link Marxist insights with Freudian ones.[12] How successful any of these attempts at synthesis have been is a controversial question, but they are undeniably a notable part of the intellectual history of the past century.

Freud thought he could proceed independently of the Marxist stream of thought. Instead of starting from Marx's premise of the inevitability of class conflict, and the power of social situations to determine thought processes, Freud had a different – but equally consistently worked out – point of departure. He worked on the understanding that the long period of childhood dependency, the time when we have to rely on the adults around us, is unique to the human condition, leaving each of us as grown-ups prey to the weakness of returning to characteristically childish ways of coping. He understood neurosis to be the permanent power of infantilism in us. He held that we are all capable of falling back, no matter what our advanced ages or apparent maturity, on patterns of reacting to others that are appropriate to childhood; and he set out to highlight the role in our lives of such neurotic propensities. Psychoanalysis insists on the key significance of the infantile factor in explaining human conduct. Freud even proposed that it was desirable for his form of therapy to aim at inducing temporary regressions in patients. He claimed to seek to mobilize non-rational reactions in patients, which he called transferences, for the sake of making it easier to demonstrate to them the persistence of early childhood attachments.

Although Freud took a good while to admit it publicly, certain patients did dramatically worsen in his form of treatment. Therapeutic failures led to the invention of a special concept to explain them – the idea of a "negative therapeutic reaction" was devised to describe such set-backs.   Supposedly there was nothing amiss in Freud's recommended therapeutic setting; the problem reputedly resided in the existence of guilt feelings on the part of the patients, leading them to deteriorate rather than benefit from the analyst's proposed insights. However defensively Freud may have reacted to reports of the failure of patients to thrive, and he himself had his share of disappointing experiences, it became privately known that there were distinct dangers implicit in how Freud recommended neurotics be treated. For example, in a passing comment which will bear directly on how cautiously Mackenzie King was approached clinically, one of Freud's loyal students maintained in 1945 that "the danger always exists that the analytic procedure, by straining the patient's conflicts, may force the patients into a psychotic episode."[13]

Freud himself tried to claim to be unafraid of the dangers of arousing issues best left alone. His reasoning was, in his own terms, impeccable, even if a later generation of analysts might be skeptical at his own logical rigor. In 1937 he addressed a key question that had been bothering outsiders all along:

> The warning that we should let sleeping dogs lie, which we have so often heard in connection with our efforts to explore the psychical underworld, is peculiarly inapposite when applied to the conditions of mental life. For if the instincts are causing disturbances, it is a proof that the dogs are not sleeping; and if they seem really sleeping, it is not in our power to awaken them.

After having decisively, or so he thought, dealt with this matter, Freud knew that "this last statement does not seem to be quite accurate," and he immediately went on to fulfill the call "for a more detailed discussion."[14]

Despite how he might qualify his objectives, it has to remain permanently striking how he boldly stood for the aim of rational self-understanding; he thought that psychoanalysis could help dissolve neurotic emotional rigidities through the power of reasoning and enlightenment. The public, including Mackenzie King himself, has often misunderstood Freud's aim because of how extensively he wrote about sex. But much of what Freud meant in discussing sexuality had to do with his conviction about the endurance in neurotic adults of the pleasure-seeking which is really appropriate to young children. The breadth of his conception of sexuality, including much more than the adult genital behavior which someone like Lenin singled out with distaste, has too often obscured the extent to which it was human self-division, and the torments which leave us at odds with ourselves, which were his special concern.

Freud was certainly eager to "apply" his insights outside a clinical setting, and he wrote about the origins of civilization as well as the problem of religious belief. But he was inevitably relying on the social thinking of his youth, and someone born in 1856 was bound to sound, by later twentieth century standards, limited compared to subsequent anthropological and sociological modes of reasoning. As much as Freud wanted to extend the impact of his special way of thinking, he retained an exceptional disdain for philosophizing. Although as a young man he had been tempted to take a second doctorate in philosophy, he wanted his psychology to be accepted as a science, and not confused with abstract speculative systems. Doubtless he would be irritated by how North American librarians consigned all his work, and that inspired by his teachings, to be catalogued under the rubric of philosophy,[15] but then he also might have felt confirmed in his prejudices against New World inadequacies.

The upshot is that psychology and politics would appear to be as different subjects as one might imagine. Of course there are now many different schools of psychological thought; under Communism in eastern Europe it was Ivan Pavlov who flourished, although with the collapse of the Soviet empire Freud has been making a distinct comeback there. Different political regimes do encourage special sorts of psychological thinking.

Freud has succeeded, if only because of his unique powers as a writer, to dominate the way we think about people, even as his own specific techniques are often not considered appropriate today. His recommended use of the couch, or the length of treatment, and how neutral or detached therapists should be, may be frequently set aside now. But certain of his key ideals have lastingly endured; he sought by interpretations to treat people who were in trouble, without relying on organic means or physical means of therapy. In 1936 Freud surprised one of his students by briefing remarking: "Constitution is everything,"[16] a comment which implied his usually unspoken belief in the overwhelming significance of the non-psychological elements to how patients fared.

Much of the confusion about what Freud stood for stems from how complicated his ambitions were. For he could stoutly deny that his form of treatment resembled in any way the kind of old-fashioned direction associated with his initial use of hypnosis, even at the same time that many have insisted on the hidden suggestive elements, and implicit advice-giving, of all forms of psychotherapeutic treatment. Some of Freud's notable dissenting pupils tried to spell out the significance of the synthetic or directive elements that Freud chose to take for granted. Mackenzie King was to be among those patients explicitly looking for outside guidance, at least during a particularly troubled period in his life.

However Marxists might have liked to use Freud's thinking to re-order society in a utopian way, psychoanalytic psychology starts by concentrating on the almost infinite capacity we have for messing up our lives. It was characteristic of Freud's approach to assume that the external world, and the circumstances of outside events, can be held to be a constant; and within those outer boundaries, taken as givens, he sought to understand how we bring about, against our conscious wills, personal difficulties which are distinctive for us.

When he turned his attention to neurotic "symptoms", such phenomena were signs that people were conflicted. A relative absence of neurosis was to Freud an indication of being less than fully civilized; an Oedipus complex was for Freud an expression of inherent superiority, and he is said to have once disdainfully dismissed a patient on the grounds that he had "no unconscious!" – the worst possible indictment Freud thought he could level at anyone. Oedipal feelings, and neurosis itself, were an indication that people internalize conflicts, a sign that they know how to bear suffering, as distinct from the "good-for-nothings" of this world who are less capable of such stoical capacities. Freud thought he could assist the exceptional in handling their problems. Any evidence of the existence of self-defeating trends became for Freud grist for the psychoanalytic mill. He intended to persuade us that we have underlying and hidden motivation, which ultimately can be traced back to childish aspirations, and should be considered the root sources to that which interferes with successful day-to-day functioning.

In contrast to Freud's psychoanalysis, which deals with outsiders who are up against it in one way or another, political science is concerned with those people who triumph in extraordinary ways. The study of politics is an account of how it is possible to become outstandingly successful, instead of psychology's focus on how we can foul up. In contrast to thinking in terms of unconscious psychodynamics, political scientists are apt to think about the significance of the various roles reality places on us. So that the pressure and demands of political office, for instance, get cited, along with the practical logic of certain concrete situations met up with; these are the types of factors that get called upon by students of politics to explain how certain leaders have conducted themselves.[17]

Freudian psychology, on the other hand, reminds us how we can be our own worst enemies, even in ways which we ourselves do not adequately understand, because of the persistence of infantile tendencies in our adult make-up. Political scientists are apt to invoke unconscious factors when a political leader somehow surprisingly behaves in a way which seems irrational; so Woodrow Wilson has been recurrently studied because of the degree to which his intransigence or illnesses led to his failure to get the League of Nations approved by the U.S. Senate. Mackenzie King, in contrast, has appeared to be almost endlessly masterful. Politics is regularly understood as a matter of the public conquest, observed by journalists and later on historians, of problems touching human issues that become worthy of being considered news, in the daily press as well as history books.

It has not helped advance the cause of building stable bridges between psychology and politics that a famous analyst like Ernest Jones could once be imperialistic enough to ask: "How many years will pass before no Foreign Secretary can be appointed without first presenting a psychoanalytic report on his mental stability and freedom from complexes?"[18] Any such proposal should immediately raise questions of who would be able to watch over such idealized guardians, when the more limited issue ought to legitimately be what psychiatrists and political scientists can learn from one another.[19]

As different as psychology and politics assuredly are, for me they have long been intrinsically inter-connected. The inevitable success-orientation of political science seemed to me well-complemented by psychology's special attention to failure and malfunctioning. People seek power for special sorts of motives which still would benefit from clarification. The study of political life ought not to be restricted solely to the triumph of the big battalions, since examples of oppression are every bit as much a part of political life as the achievement of overcoming obstacles. In fact people tend to perpetuate their own subservience, and this aspect of life can be illustrated by the heritage of both colonialism and racism, to take only two kinds of problems whose persistence flies in the face of any optimistic concentration on the road to so-called progress.

My particular professional background was in political philosophy, which meant I had studied the writings of great thinkers like Plato and Aristotle in ancient Greece, as well as Machiavelli, Hobbes, Rousseau and others in modern times. From the beginning I approached Freud's writings, and psychoanalytic thought in general, as an aspect of examining intellectual history. My assumption at the outset was that Freud would be a figure of lasting stature in the world of ideas; so for over thirty years I have been concerned with all aspects of the ways in which the movement of thought that Freud initiated has affected how we think about the broadest matters of a social and ethical nature, as well as more narrowly political matters. Someone like Rousseau dealt momentously with the paradox of "forcing" people to be "free", an enterprise which I thought would have to be considered similar to Freud's own therapeutic intentions. For he was proposing that the structure of the psychoanalytic setting, to which patients temporarily had to submit, could ultimately lead to human emancipation.

From the beginning of my publications about Freud I did not assume that the task ahead of me was simply one of propagandizing a psychoanalytic perspective. There have been all too many like Jones who have proposed a kind of intellectual trade union expansion, which feeds on the public's naive expectations of what experts in the so-called mental health field can be expected to know. I did believe that too much of social science took a theory of human nature for granted, without adequately spelling out what motives might be psychologically plausible. Subjects like cultural anthropology, and history too, have been notably receptive to trying to respond to changing preconceptions about what might be humanly conceivable as explanations.

Therefore, I have long thought that Freud, along with some necessary revisions to his thinking, had founded a tradition of depth psychology, going beyond surface motives, that had something to teach. But I also was convinced that psychoanalytic theorizing was necessarily filled with evaluative components of an ethical nature, and that Freud's profession could benefit from a broader contact with the kinds of questions that students of society are prone to ask. Freud can be useful in that historical narratives inevitably contain psychological suppositions which are scarcely ever spelled out; but on the other hand clinicians are apt to take their moral values too much for granted. Social scientists too often presume that motivation is self-evident; but then clinical encounters require choices of value which are, from an outsider's point of view, subject to critical challenge. For me, then, the relationship between psychology and politics was very much a two-way street.

It has been widely agreed that every past social philosopher has proceeded by means of a more or less explicit set of conceptions about human nature. The kinds of questions that get repeatedly asked can be boiled down to ones like: to what extent are people naturally aggressive, or to what degree do they have on the other hand a natural propensity toward being altruistic and compassionate for the suffering of others? These may seem like simplistic sets of opposite tendencies to be examining, and in the end pose questions which are unanswerable one way or the other -- yet real nonetheless. Behind even the most elaborately constructed philosophic systems lie some such basic core of ultimate concerns.

It is a defect in Freud's own approach that he was so determined to stay at arm's length from philosophy on the grounds that what was moral or decent had to be considered merely a question of self-evidence. In some sense ethics can never be proven but only defended on intuitive-like grounds, yet Freud tried to isolate his school of thinking from anything that might possibly resemble traditional religion's kind of mission. At the time Macdougall King was recommending Freud's work to his troubled brother, neither of them may have realized the full import of Freud's attack on organized religion which largely lay in future publications. Under the banner of atheism, and wrapped in the hopefulness of science, psychoanalysts were able like Marxists to endorse their own secular species of religion.

Freud's contribution to the age-old philosophic dialogues lay partly in his having offered a theory of what people are like which was supposed to be derived from series of clinical engagements. Freud to be sure felt himself to be a secure part of Western thought, and he was more familiar with earlier writers than he sometimes liked to acknowledge; but if we take Freud at his word he tested his ideas on the basis of medical interactions with patients who came to him in need of therapeutic help. (That he was fallible, even given to self-deception, should go without saying.) He ultimately concluded that medical qualifications were superfluous to the practice of analysis, and that trained non-medical ("lay") analysts were suitable for membership within his profession; but he insisted over and over again that he had created a science which was capable of being independently verified apart from his personal role in having created it. He did rely on his personal dreams, for example, as key evidence in behalf of his theories, but he also firmly sought to distance what he called his "discoveries" from the idiosyncracies of his own character. Psychoanalysis has been used, even starting while Freud was still alive, for a variety of religious purposes, and in behalf of a series of different ethical objectives. To the extent that others after Freud have been able to use his approach to arrive at conclusions at odds with his own, then he did in some sense succeed in his ambitions as a scientist.

At modest moments Freud acknowledged the artistic side to psychoanalysis rather than its scientific components. As much as Freud sought to create a neutral therapeutic technique which could be passed on to others for use with patients, among his intimate pupils he pointed out just how important the personal elements of the analyst's character were to the success or failure of every clinical encounter. (Jung was ahead of Freud here.) As Freud was once quoted as having observed, "More important than what one does is what one is."[20] Such a verbal concession pulls the rug out from under much of what Freud elsewhere published about his form of technique. We now know more about the ways in which the personal characteristics of an analyst, including personal quirks as well as ethical values, get not only communicated to patients but are at least as effective therapeutically as any conscious interpretations offered by the analyst to help explain an individual's life history. The human relationship between therapist and patient remains an intangible but vital constituent of all therapeutic change.

Psychoanalysis has too often been treated as a science embodying a technique which can enable even the clumsiest to come up with unusual insights. While Freud did talk and even write about the necessity of tact, old world manners are elusive to today's young practitioners. It is reasonable that the whole subject of Freud, entirely apart from the kind of ideological objections raised by Marxists for instance, has sounded alarm-bells in the mind of fair-minded observers. Too many partisan efforts have appeared under the rubric of "applying" either Freud's ideas or the concepts of some of his disciples. So that impartial onlookers with a concern for the least biassed history-writing are entitled to be wary of what has often looked like psychoanalytic zealots proselytizing in behalf of their beliefs.

In spite of all the professional obstacles in the way of making good use of understanding politics by means of relying on psychological concepts, I proceeded with the conviction that our notions of what it is to be human are bound to influence how we reason. And therefore as an aspect of my learning more about how psychotherapists think and make use of their ideas in practical work, after completing my Ph.D. dissertation on "Freud and Political Theory" I sat in on clinical case presentations at a research mental hospital over the course of an academic year, which was back in the mid-1960s.[21] I then wanted to learn about psychoanalytic psychiatry by observing how these ideas got implemented in practice. Witnessing patients being interviewed by senior therapists, for the sake of instructing beginners, was an unforgettable experience, and I can recommend any similar exposure to those who might want to pursue work in this area. Concrete clinical dilemmas stay etched in one's mind long after different theories have changed in fashion.

In recent years more biologically oriented psychiatry has been in the forefront, at least in North America. Starting with the use of tranquillizers psychoanalysis's reliance on rational insight as a therapeutic tool has come to seem unduly idealistic. There are a number of new ways of quickly helping people in trouble, and the variety of fresh drugs has to be considered impressive. But no matter how striking the advances that have come from within biological psychiatry, it is still the case that Freud's work will endure to the extent that he rightly focused on the prime importance of the human interaction between therapist and patient.

In the era of Mackenzie King's acute difficulties, the prevalent imagery was to talk about the existence of brain "toxins," and there is today a renewed interest in that line of reasoning. But the persisting areas of mystery and ignorance are still being covered over by mythologizing associated with biology. And the whole effort at the classification of mental problems, which was also especially prominent at the time Freud first set out to work, has been reawakened if only for a special contemporary reason: insurance companies demand to know what they are paying for, even if bewildered clinicians often feel they are spinning a diagnostic roulette wheel in order to settle on a given named disorder.

Even as I was first seeking to learn about the clinical dimensions to Freud's psychology, including both its drawbacks and advantages, I was always doing so as a social theorist. In the 1960s I interviewed a number of people who had known Freud, as part of my effort to understand him within intellectual history; this work did bring me in contact with a wide variety of therapists. I was not yearning to practice psychotherapy itself, but rather to make use of psychological concepts in my own research. And one key aspect to all my previous concerns has had to do with how psychoanalysis changed the way in which we approach biographical studies. I have naturally wondered how Freud's views have influenced the way we construct life histories of people taken from the past.

Despite all the unfortunate distortions to which psychological-mindedness has been associated, it is I think incontestable that in the understanding of any life history there are bound to be gaps in material, or contradictions in emotional reactions, which seem to crave psychological interpretations. It hardly requires an experienced clinician to spot areas in a life – early childhood, intimate adult relationships (or, as in Mackenzie King's case, their paucity), to take some obvious examples – which benefit from a psychoanalytic perspective. In Mackenzie King's life his relative isolation from "normal" human contacts may seem most striking. Popular biographies have in fact absorbed the significance of psychology, and if one were to make a study of major biographical efforts which either were widely hailed critically or successful on a commercial level, abundant illustrations would appear of the impact of the Freudian revolution in ideas.

A central problem has been that psychoanalysts, including Freud himself, have been prone to use psychology reductively; the temptation has been to look for weak spots in leaders, employing psychology as a away of highlighting disguised infantilism. One of the reasons that psychology has had a dubious reputation among independent scholars is that Freud's concepts seem to be too easily mis-used for purposes of polemical political warfare. These ideas about hidden human motives can be invoked in order to tarnish those one does not approve of or admire, and the scientific-sounding language can become a smoke-screen for unspoken moral preferences. An ounce of historical evidence can be too readily exaggerated, by means of psychoanalytic chains of reasoning, to add up to at least a pound of speculative conjecturing. Yet so influential has the impact of Freudian thinking been that a political biography that failed to go into psychological inquiry would be apt now to be considered as superficial and lacking in a needed dimension of exploration. In the course of describing how Prime Minister Brian Mulroney's Meech Lake and Charlottetown negotiations were conducted in the light of Mulroney's predecessor in office, Pierre Elliott Trudeau, a historian has recently insisted that King would have been "too smart and too psychologically well-adjusted to have felt any need to prove himself a better man than Trudeau."[22] (One suspects here a relish in turning the tables on conventional Canadian wisdom as King becomes a standard of normality.)

As dubious and critically-minded as one ought to be about how uncritically psychology has sometimes been made use of, by analysts as often as by political scientist and historians, the problem of biography-writing has to remain especially important since the past does get communicated to the present largely through accounts of the life histories of prominent individuals. The narrative stories that we now read about our leaders have been unquestionably influenced by the effects of psychoanalytic ideas. Excesses in this direction have meant that we have sometimes learned more about the sexual or drinking habits of high officials than may seem warranted in order to evaluate their political performances. But I think that thanks to Freud's teachings, whether or not we approve of these sorts of disclosures, it is now evident how experiences from early childhood, as well as adult personal emotional conflicts, have to be more central to our understanding of public figures than would once have seemed to be the case.

Intuitive writers have over the centuries known much of what later got highlighted due to the effects of Freud on twentieth century biographical studies, and they offered unforgettable accounts of the political character of individual leaders. But it is only in our own time that it has become a matter of course to think of a public figure's private peculiarities bearing on our understanding and appreciation of particular political accomplishments. Still, the exact linkages between private and public life remain mysterious and controversial, and little agreement exists about how one should discuss the connections between the individual and society.

When I first came to Canada I was as ill-informed about that country as most new immigrants. But all the special complications to Canada had to lend it a special magic. Canadian culture was noticeably different from the America I had grown up in. For example, even psychoanalysis had its own special Canadian patterns. Freud's British disciple Jones was in Toronto before World War I, and looked down his nose at the local inhabitants; as Jones wrote Freud (who had his own prejudices against the New World) in 1908:

> The people are 19 parts American, and one part Colonial, therefore are very insulted if called Americans...They are a stupid race, exceedingly bourgeois, quite uncultured, very rude, very stupid and very narrow and pious. They are naive, childish and hold the simplest views of the problems of life. They care for nothing except money-making and sport, they chew gum instead of smoking or drinking, and their public meetings are monuments of sentimental platitudes. They are horror-struck with me because I don't know the date of the King's birthday, for they take their loyalty like everything else in dead seriousness and have no sense of humor.[23]

Jones' stay in Toronto was an unhappy one, and doubtless the Torontonians sensed his arrogant air of superiority. It was not until well after the Second World War that psychoanalytic training really got going in Canada, and Montreal was ahead of Toronto in this area. Until then Canadian analysts had to be trained abroad – in England, France, or the States.

Yet although psychoanalysis has been relatively new in Canada, it quickly acquired distinctive features. The provincial health insurance programs have been extraordinarily generous in subsidizing psychoanalytic treatment, and as a result patients have kept on undertaking Freud's recommended therapy long after it went out of fashion in America. But Freud's general ideas have been more apt to be balanced by Jung's work than would be the case in the States, and I think this has to have been due to the special role religion has played in Canada. (Jungian categories come up rather strikingly, for instance, in the award-winning Clarkson-McCall Volume I of *Trudeau and Our Times*.[24]) While Freud was almost wholly negative about religious thinking, Jung's own tolerance toward religion meant that his orientation fit in well with certain characteristically Canadian perspectives.

Once I had come to Canada I quickly came to understand, thanks to the Canadian historians that I knew, that a special enigma did indeed surround the life of Mackenzie King. On the one hand it was assumed on all sides, at least among students of Canadian politics if not the public at large, that King had been an immensely accomplished Prime Minister. Being a foreigner allows one liberties that might tax native loyalties; so I could make friends with liberals, conservatives, and socialists, without compromising my integrity since homegrown allegiances were not at risk. King might not have succeeded in arousing enduring political or personal followers, but he had left a legacy of genuine respect for his capacities as a leader that was broad and cut across the usual boundaries drawn by members of the various political parties.

By today Canada's federal unity seems under more pressure than at almost any other time in its history; the separatist movement in Quebec continues to threaten to break apart the country's fragile coherence. Even back in the early 1970s King seemed notable for his multiple political triumphs. He had governed in the 1920s following fractious national difficulties during the First World War; he was Prime Minister during part of the Great Depression of the 1930s, and also surmounted the specially divisive possibilities that beset Canada during World War II. King was not only a public leader for over four decades, but succeeded in being Prime Minister longer than anyone else in British Commonwealth history.

In the light of King's contemporary standing the 1916 psychiatric file on him casts a special light on his character and beliefs. Although Adolf Meyer is today unknown to students of King's political career, he still stands as the most important single figure in the history of North American twentieth century psychiatry. Meyer not only kept notes of his interview with King, but the hospital records include the various doctors' comments to each other. And King's massively detailed diary entries contain his own version of the physicians' attitudes toward his difficulties, as well as his responses to their diagnoses.

As far as I know this is a unique instance of being able to compare and contrast a therapist's reaction to that of a patient. In addition, King's correspondences fill out further parts of the story, since he was remarkably candid with certain of his friends. The tale can also be amplified by what King wrote his physician brother, as well as his mother, about his psychiatric encounter. None of this material, however, can be taken to speak for itself; psychiatric evidence cannot, any more than other historical material, simply be accepted at face value and without interpretive glosses.

My intention is to use this 1916 documentation in order to explore the nature of King's psychology, and how his personality bears on his political career. The whole issue of the psychology of political leadership is not adequately understood, although it was first notably raised as long ago as 1930 by Harold Lasswell.[25] In King's instance his achievements would seem to have stemmed from a constructive use of his psychopathology. It is noteworthy that someone so privately odd could nonetheless function so superbly in a modern democracy. If his 1916 problems, which in some form probably persisted throughout the rest of his life, did not turn out to be a political deficit, it was because his genuine assets were so large. "Mackenzie King was not a good man or a normal man or a straight-forward man or a likeable man. He was simply a great man at his trade...."[26]

In order to supplement the written records that are available, I have interviewed a number of King's private secretaries, one of his Cabinet members, a former Senator, and some acquaintances of his, in an effort to see what sense they could make of the 1916 medical records. (He was known to them all, by his preference, as "Mr King," because of his acute awareness of the possibility that he would sometimes not be Prime Minister.) King's personal staff was, I think, notably lacking in personal allegiance to him. I am not sure I met anyone who genuinely seemed to like him; on the whole I found it painful to have to interview some of these people, since they found him so easy to hate. However he failed to make them understood as individuals, he excelled at moving them about as in a chess-game.

Although King's attitude toward doctors in general was a known peculiarity of his, the special nature of his Baltimore physicians remained secret. Yet King sent political associates of his, later also suffering from "nervous strain," to Baltimore. Ernest Lapointe, King's key Quebec lieutenant, and also a Premier of Nova Scotia, Angus Macdonald, followed King's example. King as Prime Minister took special steps to safeguard the privacy of his political friends, and the news of their reliance on specialized medical help did not leak out.

The focus of this book is on the full details of the 1916 tale of King's psychiatric consultation. As long as we do not exaggerate the nature of any such evidence, understanding the implications of it can be rich for appreciating the rest of King's career and the nature of politics in Canada. Nowadays, thanks partly to the Freudian impact on our ideas, a North American candidate's private life is so much a matter of public display that privacy gets used manipulatively. Leaders can use private weaknesses as part of a strategy of defusing political criticism by making themselves appear more human. Politicians can make an active disclosure about their tastes and family history in the course of their trying to sell themselves.

For King to have seen a psychiatrist in 1916, however, has to be altogether another matter. He was in the context of his times taking a bold act, although to be sure his decision was precipitated by the perception of others that he was in need of help. King's psychiatric encounter was unusual enough at the time for his friends to have kept it quiet, and historians have entirely overlooked the significance of the incident. And only now that we examine it will that consultation become another piece in the extraordinary puzzle that is King's life.

Chapter 1
The Enigma Deepens

By general consensus Mackenzie King was the most successful politician in Canadian history.* He led the Liberal party for three decades, and was Prime Minister for some twenty-two years. One of King's private secretaries told me that each time King surpassed the record of longevity of other office-holders, King used to have him make a point of keeping the members of the press gallery duly informed of the news. During World War II King shared a place alongside Franklin Roosevelt and Winston Churchill in the historic alliance to oppose the Axis powers of Germany, Italy, and Japan. (That cooperation with Roosevelt and Churchill may now be King's chief claim to fame in the States.) Unlike Churchill, who was turned out of office after the historic triumph, King was able to win re-election following the war. And when King, at the age of seventy-three, finally decided to retire from politics in 1948, he left his party's political fortunes in good order. One test of a leader's talent is the ability to pass on the mantle of power; neither Trudeau nor Mulroney succeeded in this particular endeavor. King's chosen successor, Louis St. Laurent, went on to win election in his own right in 1949. King, lonely and in ill health, finally died on July 22, 1950.

History gets written in a curiously capricious way. For King is no longer widely known in Canada as a great success story, a leader with such acute antennae that he was able to balance the complex shifting forces of political life, and in that way shrewdly best a whole series of opponents. Instead of his being remembered as someone who

1

* According to a 1997 *Maclean's* survey among twenty-five scholars, King came out ranked as the greatest Canadian prime minister. It is telling that *Maclean's* editor admitted to being astonished at King's position.[1]

preserved national unity while managing to win so many general elections, surviving a series of obstacles in an almost uncanny way, King today is primarily recalled by the general public for his having possessed surprising private oddities. It surely says something about our own time that King's monumental political effectiveness could be swamped by the titillation aroused by a series of revelations about striking aspects of his character and beliefs.

For many years a series of books about King had been written for largely partisan political purposes. He was portrayed by party loyalists as a gentle humanitarian with a serious interest in social justice; and it was true that some of King's policies did notably contribute to the creation of the modern welfare state, even if he had to be persuaded against his own cautious skepticism about the advisability of such reforms. But the "spin doctors" of the time went about building up the image of a country squire who loved the peace of the countryside, and King spent a lot of energy creating the retreat of his Gatineau property outside Ottawa known as "Kingsmere." A conservative like Dalton Camp, who readily conceded that King was "the consummate politician," the "most important" one in Canadian history, also felt there had been "a conspiracy to create a myth about him."[2]

In 1944 Emil Ludwig, author of studies of Napoleon, Lincoln, Bismarck, Byron, Frederick the Great, Masaryk, Freud, Wagner, Goethe, Wilson, Stalin, Mussolini, and Franklin Roosevelt, added Mackenzie King to his list of biographical portrait sketches. It is questionable how much Ludwig knew about King, yet uncertain whether it was less than what Ludwig understood about any of his other more famous subjects. But when King was sketching out his memoirs in 1948, it may have been a sign of his vanity that the first chapter title that occurred to him was "My Friendship with Ludwig."[3]

The momentous sea change in King's reputation first began in late 1951 when an eminent and respected journalist, also a Liberal insider, Blair Fraser, published an article in *Maclean's*, which then called itself "Canada's National Magazine." Fraser's piece, entitled "The Secret Life of Mackenzie King, Spiritualist,"[4] became one of Canadian journalism's great scoops. This one article is how the news publicly broke about King's efforts to communicate telepathically with the dead through the help of various spiritualist mediums. Fraser's story was to be the beginning of what turned into a subsequent collapse of King's political standing in Canada.

One former Senator whom I interviewed, who had known both

Fraser and King, said that at the time the startling *Maclean's* article first came out he thought Fraser had gone crazy.[5] King appeared so thoroughly sane and politically knowledgeable that it seemed unbelievable that there was such a different side to King, so unlike the man his admirer had known for years. Yet in a short time my informant thought he had to accept Fraser's findings, and the shock he experienced helps reflect why King's reputation with others began so serious a slide.

King not only attended seances while leader of the Opposition as well as Prime Minister, but he also seriously believed in a wide variety of occult doctrines. (Freud too was rather more fascinated in occultism than his partisans have ever wanted fully to acknowledge,) It turned out that King had maintained a number of special devotions – to his dead mother, and a series of wire-haired terriers all named Pat. King's emotional investments in his sequence of dogs have led to widespread ridicule beyond the diagnostic name-calling associated with his attachment to his mother. According to one unpublished source, at King's summer home "there was an alcove off the library in which King had hung a portrait of his mother. It was his want before going to bed at night to spend a while with this portrait, and while I cannot say that he prayed to his mother, it is fair to say that he prayed *with* her."[6] And at his home in Ottawa "a prominent feature was the portrait of his mother, lighted day and night by a special lamp."[7]

King also thought himself peculiarly closely linked to his deceased political mentor Sir Wilfrid Laurier. Fraser had not known about King's private spiritualist efforts, conducted at his home with the help of intimate friends. The "craziest"[8] of all King's sessions at what he called "the little table" he used for such communicating by means of "rapping" came at the outset of World War II, although it only became public knowledge decades later: King's understanding was that Hitler had been shot dead when in fact it was just at the time when the British were delivering a military ultimatum to the Germans over their invasion of Poland. King, who remained a life-long bachelor, always tried to keep in touch with loved ones (and even Roosevelt after his death) through means which became easy to make fun of, once the full evidence about King's private life was exposed to public scrutiny.

At first some Liberal party officials hit the roof when they initially heard that not long after King's death two British mediums, who at the time they saw King thought he was a New York City parson, intended to publish about their contact with him. Everyone involved naturally thought of their association with a former Canadian Prime Minister as a source of considerable pride. So one prominent Ottawa Liberal was dispatched to London to try to keep the ladies quiet. This representative of King's political successors wanted these women to know that by revealing anything about their relationship with King they were unprofessionally compromising the confidentiality of a client. The loyal Liberal heirs were too upset and angry about the impending damaging publicity to realize how their explicit message conflicted with another one which they were also implying if not formally stating. For to down-to-earth observers like these Liberal officials the idea of communicating with the world of the spirits was a lot of humbug, and those who undertook to help reach the dead, and be paid for it, appeared to be charlatans and quacks. The women in question, who thought of themselves as having undertaken legitimate research into obscure psychical phenomena, understood something of the conflicting signals that the Liberals were giving them, and proceeded to spill at least part of the beans.[9]

In 1952 another prominent journalist, Bruce Hutchison, published his *The Incredible Canadian: A Candid Portrait of Mackenzie King*. According to what Hutchison told me, this memorable book was written quickly; but it retains a convincing-appearing consistency. Although Hutchison had been well acquainted with King for a number of years, at the time King was alive Hutchison had known nothing about King's spiritualist side. So in 1952 it seemed appropriate for Hutchison to be writing about the "mystery" to King's character. As far as Hutchison was concerned, "the central fact" of King's life "was concerned with death." Hutchison proposed that while King was "outwardly the dullest, he was inwardly the most vivid, fascinating, and improbable issue of the Canadian race." By 1988, when I talked with Hutchison, he thought more books had come out about King than concerning Sir John A. Macdonald, one of the chief architects of Confederation and Canada's first Prime Minister. This imbalance in the literature seemed to Hutchison a paradox since he felt Macdonald was so much more colorful and inherently politically interesting.[10]

In 1952 Hutchison had proposed that "psychologists will never cease to disagree about what is most obvious in other men, King's relations with women. A woman, his mother, dominated him long after she was dead." Little did Hutchison know that "psychologists" have still, as of today, scarcely begun the possibilities of their disagreements. But Hutchison was prophetically suggesting that King was inwardly haunted in a way that went beyond regular or customary political analysis. This was a Prime Minister for whom "the imaginary world contained a deeper reality. The real and the imaginary – King moved day by day and hour by hour from one to the other."[11] But what does the "imaginary" consist in? Freud and others after him have taught us that there is a inner logic to the irrational, and that even blatant superstitions have their psychological meaning.

King's enemies had seen him as a schemer capable of endless duplicities. Dalton Camp, for example, singled out "his deviousness, his notorious ambivalence, his ruthless cunning, and plain dishonesty – all of which helps to explain his unique success as Canada's supreme politician."[12] In King's life-time there had been King-haters not unlike the way Pierre Elliott Trudeau later aroused passionate animosities. Disappointments help fuel such emotion-laden convictions. King himself was aware of how he often got perceived, and was taken aback by his widespread reputation for being duplicit.

In Hutchison's judgment King was "always sincere, even in his most misleading moments, for whenever the occasion required it, he could mislead himself and believe almost anything." King's devotion to scripture reassured him about his own integrity. By current standards of behavior it may seem striking how King not only, like President Woodrow Wilson, read the Bible daily, but made numerous marginal notations. King was a writer who took books seriously, and he also enjoyed classical music. According to Hutchison King was a "scholar and mystic" who engaged in "habitual self-deception." Self-blinding is of course the stuff of what Freud's psychoanalysis was designed to help explain. King's self-absorption could help explain his naivete. Hutchison maintained that King was a "great egotist" with an endless supply of "cunning." Comparing King with notable precursors as Prime Minister, Laurier and Macdonald, Hutchison summed up the contrast by saying that "by the public measure of statesmanship King was the greatest Canadian." But "by the private measurement of character, by the dimensions of the man himself, his two predecessors tower over him." Hutchison was, however, begging the philosophic question of how one distinguishes such admirable qualities of private personality. He felt confidently entitled to declare that King had succeeded in building "a personal achievement incomparably larger than himself."[13]

I would question how far the distinction between public and private can in principle be sharply sustained. Yet the conventional wisdom among social scientists is otherwise, as reflected in a recent historian's belief that Macdonald "was unusual among Canadian public figures in not being able fully to separate his private and public lives."[14] The apparently successful division between King's sensible, mainstream public stance, including all his wiliness and waffling, as opposed to his bizarre-sounding inner world, is precisely what makes him so baffling. A political leader's quirks may be not only intrinsically interesting, but I think inevitably help to understand political stands that get taken. The timing of at least one of King's calls for a general election (1930) can be linked to what King thought he had learned through spiritualist sources; this is so even if basically the mediums confirmed him in his own predilections. But in the end it remains the case that a statesman ought to be defined by his statecraft; Hutchison might agree that if King by public standards was anything like "the greatest Canadian," then it has to be questionable if any amount of personal psychological scrutiny should deprive him of his genuine achievements.

In hindsight King-watchers might have spotted signs of how eccentric he could be long before Fraser broke the spiritualist news in *Maclean's*. One of King's frustrated former speech-writers, E.K. Brown, who later became a distinguished literary critic, wrote in 1943 a respectful article for *Harper's* indicating something of the sense in which King could be said to have partly lived among the dead. King, Brown said, "lives much in the past...what he says and does must satisfy the ghost of Sir Wilfrid...." Even Brown may not have realized how literally Laurier continued to populate King's thinking. According to Brown King was "a great conciliator" who possessed "an intuitive mind." King had, in Brown's view, grown "into the most astute politician of his day and country." Yet King's thoughts were "much with those of his friends who are dead...." Brown noted how in King's writings "the harsh concrete word never comes; the world is wrapt in a musical dream. The style suits a man for whom spirit is real and matter unreal, for whom emotions are dangerous things to be touched lightly and with infinite caution." Brown noted how harshly Canadians could judge King, in that "multitudes of his countrymen" saw his actions "as timid shilly-shallying. His careful unobtrusiveness is sneered at as weakness of fiber."

King took great offense at the appearance of Brown's *Harper's* piece, but not because it might have been taken to have hinted at his spiritualist tendencies. King instead objected to his being

6

characterized as friendless: "one of the loneliest beings alive."[15]* It was typical of King to have been attracted by such talented young intellectuals as Brown. And King might well have been justified in his resentment since such staff members could only know him in his later years, and not in his youth when he took great pride in his capacity for friendship. According to Hutchison, King was "a man so conceived and so completely self-dedicated" that he "could not expect or wish to have many friends...Still, it was typical of King's perversity that he liked to think he had troops of friends."[16]

Those of King's personal assistants who worked with him in public life had to be aware of some of his notable peculiarities. He could find significance in tea leaves, or in the meaningfulness of cloud formations. The hands on the clock were known to be important to him; 2:45 was a time of the day which King thought specially propitious for decision-making, and the pace of events in his office speeded-up then. He could not go to visit a medium without at least some of his staff knowing what was going on. And it was said by one of my informants that by pointing out coincidences (such as a book being opened to a certain page) one could get King's special attention. As one of his former secretaries wrote in 1962, "to him there was no such thing as chance: in this ordered universe every person, every happening, a falling leaf, the position of the hands of the clock in his study, had secret meaning for the discerning eye and ear and mind."[17]

Psychologists tell us that in so-called "schizoid" people, "the emotions of these persons generally appear to be inadequate...They may be surrounded by many people and indulge in many activities; but they have no real friends." And to full-blown schizophrenics, "everything perceived has another meaning, sometimes a hidden, sometimes a clear one, but nearly always a prophetic and symbolic one. The patients may become subject to revelations of all kinds."[18] For someone as religiously devout as King the conviction of hidden purposes may have a special meaning, beyond the ken of atheistic psychoanalysts; but the congruence between King's propensities, and what textbooks say should be expected to go together, ought not to be entirely dismissed.

Whatever some in King's office may have been privy to, one of King's former Cabinet members, Paul Martin, Sr., told me that he did not know anything about the spiritualism until he was informed about it by *The New York Times* correspondent in Ottawa the day after King's funeral.[19] (Martin seemed to anticipate, which was not at all the case,

7

* One of King's private secretaries reported that King sent an unflattering letter about Brown to the University of Virginia, where Brown was looking for an appointment.

that my mind might be searching for possible latent homosexual traits in King.) To make the whole story of King's spiritualism even more bizarre, a few years later this same *Times* reporter, when retired, claimed to have had a conversation with King's ghost while sitting on a park-bench at King's summer home.[20] My own trips to King's graveside had the conventionally mundane purposes of trying to learn as much as I could about my subject matter, as well as paying my respects to the dead.

In retrospect King had been running a serious political risk because of the way he entertained his curious beliefs. It must say something about the state of Canadian journalism in King's time that none of this scandal-making material got out until after his death. (Yet John F. Kennedy could while in the White House sleep with at least one gangster's call-girl, despite the notorious inquisitiveness of the American media. It remains to be seen what the political effects of Bill Clintion's apparent sexual recklessness are going to be.) One might even have thought that knowledge of King's peculiarities would have left him open to implicit private blackmail by those he worked with intimately. As far as one can tell King, who did cancel at least one scheduled visit to a medium because he wrongly thought the news of it had publicly leaked out, always managed to dominate those he worked with. He successfully intimidated his cabinets and mastered the House of Commons itself. His governments were ones in which public servants, no matter how high up, could never be sure he would not be calling up at odd hours to find out if they were doing their jobs effectively.

King's administrations were securely under his thumb; yet he picked strong and able associates, in the firm belief that one should choose good people for office and then leave them alone. King's managerial talents were helped by his keeping people at a distance. It is inappropriate, I think, to suppose that King's tactical achievements "were not the skills of a man with a warped or inadequate personality."[21] Hutchison was closer the mark when he quoted a "celebrated" saying of King's to the effect that "he could deal with men best when he saw the least of them...."[22] King's detachment from run-of-the-mill emotional reactions was a positive source of his political strength. At the end of his career, when he ran into trouble in connection with what sort of attitude Canada should take in foreign policy over Korea, King encountered an issue on which his own isolationist principles meant a conflict with those around him; after these differences were resolved King wisely decided that it was time for him to retire.

King's own published words, if paid close attention to, should have given away at least some of his own superstitiousness; someone as sensitive to style as E.K. Brown realized that King's writings could be the tip of the iceberg. In King's first book, *The Secret of Heroism* (1906), King had written a memoir in behalf of his deceased friend Henry Albert Harper who had died trying to save a young woman from drowning. King openly said he thought a magical coincidence had occurred in connection with the statue of Sir Galahad which King arranged to be erected on Parliament Hill to honor Harper. As King put it, "subsequent to the making of the award" commissioning the statue it was learned that the sculptor "had been born on the same day of the same year on which Harper was born."[23] No one for years seems to have noticed how odd a conjunction of dates King had made notice of.

Such a finding of hidden meaning, in the light of what we now know about King, is a special signal to a side of him which has received so much publicity since King's death. It makes sense in general that different periods should perceive contrasting elements in the past, and that shifting perspectives bring to light fresh insights; an era of television coverage, for example, highlights traits of apparent individual personality in public leaders. (In 1988 Donald Brittain produced a television program called *The King Chronicle.*) No statesman should have a static reputation, and as events unfold we ought to be able to reconsider past judgments. It has become commonly acknowledged that each generation is entitled to reinterpret history in its own terms. This should not mean that we have abandoned the ideal of objectivity, or that we are authorized to invoke our own prejudices in making sweeping evaluations of the performances of others. Although we conscientiously should try to see things as they actually happened, as best we can overcoming our own second-guessing, it is not surprising that with the passage of time new eras concern themselves with aspects of history that were neglected before. Even so, something unusually striking would appear to have been the case in the rise and fall of King's reputation.

In his lifetime King was renowned for his caution and moderation, and often blamed for his inability to make up his mind. One of the difficulties of working immediately under him was that he could give his staff inconsistent instructions. On the whole, however, King was remarkable for being acutely aware of the costs of decisiveness. One of his most careful judgments was the notoriously discreet 1942 promise of "not necessarily conscription, but conscription if necessary." King was determined not to allow his government to tear Canada apart as had happened during World War I. King might privately have thought that Hitler would turn out to be "one of the saviors of the world," but still King attended the funeral of the wife of a Jewish member of Parliament. King's "political artistry" was oriented in behalf of keeping Canada intact, and he was "astute" enough to know that in immigration policy "there were no votes to be gained in admitting Jews," but "there were ... many to be lost" by any such policy.[24]

Yet this sagacious pragmatist was so imprudent as to have repeatedly risked engaging in seances that could have destroyed his political future. Hutchison wrote of King that "the breach of his secret probably would have ruined his political career. The few who knew it had long been bound in a conspiracy of silence never to be broken until his death, and then only by his spiritualist counselors."[25] A number of different people might have blown the whistle on him, since no country, especially one as conservative-minded as Canada in King's day, likes the idea of its political fortunes being in any way dependent on the whims of clairvoyants, or those who consult with them. Only after President Reagan left office did it become known that his wife had consulted an astrologer. It turned out that King himself also had a special attachment to the number "7", which led him to be concerned about keeping a special license plate for his car. As we shall see, King held some even odder beliefs which have remained unknown until now.

Journalistic standards of propriety have broadened in the last half century or so, and what once would not have been reported is now more likely to appear in the press. American standards of investigative journalism are still different than those in Canada, and reporters in the U.S. have been all along characteristically freer in disclosing the private lives of politicians. But there have been world-wide changes in this direction. In France, for example, Presidents of the 5th Republic have been able to have wives completely sheltered from public scrutiny, yet in François Mitterand's last months in office he went out of his way to acknowledge publicly the existence of an illegitimate daughter. It is striking to contrast the recent British press's coverage of the royal family to what had once been considered appropriate concerning Edward VIII and Mrs. Simpson in the 1930s. Only toward the end of King's political career, and while away in London, England, did he – already in poor health – run the risk of allowing two mediums to visit him at his hotel.

Canada has had far more publicly florid Prime Ministers than King, which is perhaps why the 1951 revelations about him, and the subsequent elaboration of the complexities of his inner world, created such a stir. Sir John A. Macdonald was known as someone who could publicly drink to excess; and John Diefenbaker gained a reputation in the 1950s as both cranky and crusty, "a suspicious, irascible old codger"[26] who sometimes seemed paranoid. Canada would seem to have had more than its share of strange political leaders; but then modern psychology teaches us that the closer one inspects anyone the more psychopathology is apt to be found. The problem is always, especially with talented and creative people, to understand how such apparent flaws can mysteriously lead to stirring fresh feats of originality. To outside observers King had always seemed a model of conventional deportment; so his unusual private emotional life, starting with the revelations in the *Maclean's* article, had to be enduringly news.

And then King's literary executors (Norman Robertson, Fred McGregor, J.W. Pickersgill, and Dr. Kaye Lamb) compounded the problem of King's reputation by the way they chose first to preserve the diary that King had kept for some fifty-seven years, and then to destroy accounts of some seances once the public's imagination – and indignation – had been aroused. Some of the occult material about King is still closed to inspection.[27] King had throughout his adulthood been communing with the diary as a way of dealing with his isolation and objective solitariness; how often he experienced the emotion of loneliness is another matter. King had been made Deputy Minister of Labor in 1900, when he was not yet twenty-six years old; and public life did restrict the kinds of associates and friends he could make. King kept working at the diary, and later wanted to save it with the idea that a written record would prove useful for the sake of his ultimate retirement and memoir-writing. Richard Nixon, as a President in an era of tape-recordings, was similarly inclined to gather documentation for purposes of self-justification.

King's diary is unique in its being almost unreadably extensive and convoluted. It subsequently got typed up (and later put on microfiche) for the sake of the official political biography of King that first started coming out in 1958. King was well served by these authoritative volumes, and his diary has proved to be a fundamental scholarly resource. Yet when the diaries for the Second World War were published in a multi-volume edition, "private" matters were to be kept out of the limelight. So that as scholars eventually got unrestricted access to the full original documents, precisely those controversial issues which had been deliberately left out of the public record inevitably got highlighted by the previous suppression.

Remarkably enough King had in his last will left instructions that only those passages in his diary were to be preserved that he had explicitly marked beforehand. King had always taken great pains to safeguard his privacy.[28] But his health was not good even in his final days as Prime Minister, and after his retirement in November 1948 he did not get far with his proposed literary projects. Book-writing, as we shall see, had been a special source of stress to King in 1916. Once out of office he had evidently planned a three-volume autobiography, with ten volumes of documents, and he did get around to hiring some assistants. (The Rockefeller Foundation was willing to subsidize his autobiographical efforts.) King remained undecided about either burning or publishing his diary. Like others who are physically ill King tended to deny how badly off he was.

After he died those he had trusted as his literary executors made an odd if understandable decision. King had made no indications about which parts of his diary were to be saved. The extensiveness of his private musings, which have now become a central source for our understanding of twentieth century politics, seemed too important to destroy. Even the edited-down version of the World War II years, which started to come out in 1960, made up two huge volumes; a couple of more large books carried the story down to 1948. This helps explain why, after King's literary executors got legal advice sanctioning how they could proceed, they chose to save the diary in its entirety.

The whole diary is so immense and complex that to my knowledge no one has ever read it from beginning to end. King's executors, when they made the decision to preserve it, had simply not looked at some of the most potentially compromising passages, for example having to do with what sound like King's youthful frequenting of prostitutes. At least that is the excuse that one of the key executors gave to an irate former private secretary, who felt that anyone who had served King was somehow besmirched by the full contents of the diary. All King's high-sounding moralism had, in the light of such apparent hanky-panky, to make him look hypocritical.

If the diary were thoroughly studied, which would require an extraordinary degree of patience, I do not think it would be straightforwardly rewarding since King's reflections were, as one might anticipate of such an on-going informal autobiography, so self-serving as to be seriously misleading about what actually went on in his day-to-day life. As we shall see, some of King's personal letters, and other documents also, provide an essential historiographical corrective to the diary itself.

Such a diary, involuted and extraordinarily subtle to follow, should provide exactly the sort of psychological material that students of psychology and politics have craved. Too often psychologizing about leaders has been based on generalizations which amount to abstract speculations about the inner motives of major political actors. Elaborate theories about human development can be mistakenly assumed to be scientifically proven. It is too easy to use psychology in a cookie-cutter way, reducing complex motives to fit preconceived conceptions which change in fashion every little while. No textbook summaries of so-called normal development will appeal to sophisticated specialists, no matter how eager for simplicities the outside public may remain. Nor can any set of theories be more authoritative than the rich individuality of unique life stories; yet, as we shall see repeatedly, that which is considered "normal" does depend on certain conceptual commitments. And therefore psychological concepts require scrutiny by all practicing social scientists. King's own uncertainties about preserving the diary at least indicate that it had to do with intimate matters that touched on his most private self. Therefore the existence of King's diary has to be a rare source of documentation about an unusual public figure's private thoughts.

But the extensiveness of the diary implies special problems all its own. So often King's record of what happened is the only one available, since few of the people he dealt with kept anything with which his own account can be compared. And therefore it has been tempting for some, especially strictly political historians, to think that King's diaries can be used as conclusive. In fact, however, I think that the diary King constructed has to be treated as a kind of imaginative sort of literature, subject to the inevitable distortions of King's own special set of idiosyncratic perceptions. With someone like King in mind, who left such a voluminous account of his inner life and its bearing on politics, it is not so much a matter of whether we should or should not make use of modern psychology, but exactly how psychological insights are going to get used with an adequate degree of experienced knowledgeability.

It is surely not enough to use King's diaries for debunking purposes. Everyone in politics has to make enemies since that is inherent in the nature of partisan strife. Getting ahead means, because of the conflicts in democratic politics, triumphing at the expense of others. King was such a phenomena of endurance and conquest that it should not be surprising that he also inspired hatred among opponents, and even with some members of his own Liberal party. But I found that King, however many allies he made in politics, somehow did not induce, as I have already indicated, personal affection from his own staff. A contemporary of King's, far less adept politically, was the Conservative R.B. Bennett, and it would seem that he, although also a bachelor, had some warmer human relations with those he worked with. Hutchison went so far as to maintain that King "rode his secretaries to nervous breakdowns....,"[29] and while doubtless that was a journalistic excess on Hutchison's part, it communicates at least part of the flavor of King's ties to his immediate underlings.

I was told by one of King's assistants, who had great distaste for him, that I had to remember that during the Great Depression of the 1930s any alternative jobs were hard to come by; so much as he did not like working for King, the pay was excellent, and King was providing the best opportunity that this young man could hope to land. Yet even this source, who was full of unflattering stories about King, insisted that when in the mid-1930s King was about to travel to Europe, he left explicit instructions that if he were to die while away the whole stack of his diaries were to be destroyed. (When he asked King where his will could be found, King reacted as if he were struck in the face – because none then existed.) This particular private secretary, not at all well disposed toward King personally, was the one who could not fathom how King's literary executors could have allowed material to survive which was bound to make all of them, who had ever worked for King, look foolish by association.

In the late 1930s King was often in the habit of dictating his diary entries to a former court reporter he had on his staff, who seemed unfazed by anything King might recount. But in earlier years King had kept up the diary by himself in hand-writing. At his death he had become a national institution, and his will left his surprisingly considerable estate of almost a million dollars to the nation; some who knew the exact details of King's years of restricted public salary, and how frugal and careful he was about spending money, were shocked at the news of his considerable wealth. (A neighbor at Kingsmere, who loaned King a gardner thinking he was impecunious, was startled.) The exact records of how he amassed his fortune remain sealed by King's executors. King had left no personal heirs with a genuine human need to protect his reputation. One might have expected that at least King's political associates would have been more determined in wanting to secure his public standing; as a result of what came out about King's private life he became a standing national joke. And this mockery has continued in spite of the fact that absolutely excellent political biographies of King have been written by such experts as R. MacGregor Dawson and H. Blair Neatby.[30]

C.P. Stacey is in large part responsible for this current state of affairs, and the year 1976, when he published *A Very Double Life: The Private World of Mackenzie King*,[31] has to be considered a watershed in the saga of King's standing. Stacey had become a university professor in Toronto but before that was an army historian. King always thought of himself as a peace-maker. "What this country needs," he insisted in 1935, "is not the fist of the pugilist but the hand of the physician."[32] This attitude led to what Hutchison thought was the "fatal blunder" of isolationism: "King's error from 1923 onward, the cardinal error of his life, was his refusal to admit the possibility of war."[33]

In the late 1930s King participated in what amounted to the appeasement of Hitler. This policy was to be a central blemish on King's record, although it has to be remembered how much he was reflecting prevalent Canadian as well as world public opinion. In the mid-1930s King had been less than bold in failing to encourage the League of Nations to impose sanctions against Mussolini's invasion of Abyssinia. Stacey was well aware of all these short-comings, and may even have had a set of political scores to settle against King, who for a variety of reasons had been no great friend of the military even during the Second World War.

Stacey's version of King, which continued in another 1976 book, *Mackenzie King and the Atlantic Alliance*,[34] was unremitting. The existence of Stacey's work seemed so damnable among old Liberals that it made them receptive to being interviewed by me. Stacey thought that King's "chronic insecurity" (surely a psychological construct) accounted for his feeling "the need of support from the spirit world."[35]

Stacey's latent hostility to King shines through the dry-seeming recital of all King's inner problems. In 1897, while a graduate student at the University of Chicago, King had, at the age of twenty-three, become enamored of a nurse (Mathilde Grossert) he met while hospitalized for typhoid fever. His family however disapproved of her, and instead of Stacey extending compassion to King for how "increasingly distracted" he became, Stacey savored King's having quoted a letter from her in his diary for 1898 when there was no longer any hope for the romance succeeding. "My worst fears are confirmed," King quoted her as having written: "neither your letter nor your actions are those of a sane man."[36] His emotions may well have appeared to her to be inadequate and/or excessive, which might in itself lead to certain retrospective diagnostic conclusions. Yet how rational is anybody in dealing with frustrated love? Whatever King's failure in this particular intimate human relationship, the two people stayed in touch; and King was able to become about the smartest handler of men in Canadian history.

Stacey saw himself as trying to describe what he called "a very peculiar personality." As he speculated about another woman in King's life, with whom he became infatuated in 1918, "it is conceivable that...[she] felt that she was dealing with an individual who was the next thing to a madman." In reflecting on King's painful struggles over sexuality, Stacey unkindly maintained a studied distance: "I am content to let the psychologists and psychiatrists resolve these riddles, if they can." Stacey was bent on making King ludicrous, and as much as anyone established King as a figure of fun. For example, Fraser's *Maclean's* piece had not been based on an exploration of King's diaries. Stacey proceeded to document numerous examples of King's reliance on spiritualism, and added King's use of table-rapping which meant he could do without the help of mediums, or perhaps act as one himself. Although King's turning to these odd practices might have been a way of his relaxing with a few intimate friends, Stacey constructed his narrative so as to highlight how amusing table-rapping could be. For example, after a trip to Europe in 1934 King returned to Canada: "Back home in Ottawa, King rushed for the little table. The broadening of travel is reflected in the guest list: Leonardo da Vinci and Lorenzi de' Medici appear, as does Louis Pasteur, at whose tomb

King had prayed in Paris."[37]

Stacey proposed that "King's meticulous records of his sessions with the little tables are a revelation of his inner mind." Stacey even adopted the terminology of psychoanalytic thinking: "conversations with the other world...came straight out of King's subconscious mind."[38] But Freud's outlook should be used for extending our understanding, not for encouraging polemics. Psychoanalysis ideally promotes compassion, tolerance, and caution. Still, it is hard to underestimate the degree of crudeness that persists about what Freud added to intellectual history. One political scientist in 1976 found abundant "Oedipal evidence" in King's diaries from the 1930s, but instead of seeing psychoanalysis as an attempt to comprehend our most intimate loves and hates, he commented: "If I thought there was anything worthwhile in Freud, it would not be much of a task to push such an analysis."[39] The old Leninist dismissal of Freud still survives, and would be shared by many on the Right as well, although for different reasons. It sometimes seems as if the Catholic Church has been blaming Freud's influence for the way some of its own clergy has been encouraged into misbehavior.

A recent historian (1989), less partisan than Stacey, has conscientiously tried to follow up on the material connected with some of King's involvement with spiritualism, continuing in Neatby's judicious footsteps in evaluating King's occultism in order to try to understand King's most curious thought-processes. Reflecting on how King could juggle his interest in the number seven, for example, this scholar has freshly asked: "Was he mad?" Surely it is only a provisional way out for a serious student of history to conclude: "historians are not psychiatrists: who are we to pronounce who is sane and who is mad?"

The most we can say is that in practical terms, madness involves failure to build a wall between reality and fantasy. There is only one other figure in Canadian history whose inner world is as well documented as that of Mackenzie King, and that is Louis Riel. Riel lost the ability to distinguish between the two worlds of the mind. Mackenzie King did not.[40]

Riel was executed (despite intense opposition from within Quebec) for helping to promote insurrection, but because of his part in trying to protect the minority rights of Métis he has at least for some been a symbol of heroism in behalf of the defense of French and Catholic cultural rights.

It has not been hard to develop how King's place within Canadian popular mythology has seriously deteriorated since his death. He is not generally remembered as the extraordinarily able political craftsman that he was for so many years. His seances, religious pieties, and a series of relationships with women that he maintained by means of his constant letter-writing, have obliterated for most people, if not among impartial scholars, the record of his genuine political accomplishments. It became impossible for me to mention King's name in large Canadian college classrooms for students not to snigger at the memory of his various recorded bizarre-seeming doings.

Both political scientists and historians have been wary of using modern psychology, partly because in the past these sorts of hard-to-handle categories have been used for purposes of demeaning (and occasionally white-washing) the reputations of historical figures. Excessive expectations have led to a series of magical hopes about how much such psychologizing should be able to accomplish. On the other hand it is difficult to over-estimate the degree of know-nothingness about psychology which persists, despite how much Freud succeeded in transforming our everyday conception of human motives. The abundant material in existence about King means that he is one political leader who appears to demand psychological interpretation, no matter how tricky such concepts may be to use well. As one historian put it, "if ever a historic figure cried out for close psychological investigation and provided many of the means in an extraordinary set of diaries, King is such a one."[41]

In 1980 a political scientist systematically sought to explore the avenue of depth psychology in order to understand King sympathetically. Joy E. Esberey's *Knight of the Holy Spirit* aimed to cope with the nature of what she thought of as King's "neurosis." Esberey rightly was dubious about "the tendency to separate Mackenzie King's private life from his public career, an approach which makes much of his behavior inexplicable except in the crude terms of hypocrisy or political expediency." She thought it worth challenging as "misleading" the "double vision" view of King, as she sought "to demonstrate that the separation of the private and public King is invalid." Esberey's thesis seems to me as self-evident as it is unfortunately impossible to prove to the satisfaction of certain skeptical historians. Whether King can be said to have been neurotic, however, becomes a complicated question of a theoretical nature. But it would be in agreement with the general consensus of the students of King's career that Esberey considered King "one of the best known and least understood of all Canadian prime ministers."[42]

Like others Esberey remained unaware that King had in fact consulted a world-famous psychiatrist at Johns Hopkin's Phipps Clinic in Baltimore, Maryland. Heather Robertson in her 1983 novel *Willie: A Romance*[43] quoted from a portion of the hospital records. But a shortened version of the fascinating clinical document, appearing almost three-quarters through the book, remained unexamined or even commented upon, and must have seemed to most readers an aspect of Robertson's artistic inventiveness.

That 1916 psychiatric file on King can be explored in order to cast special light on his occult beliefs, his failure ever to marry, yet also, I think, on some of the sources of his political strengths. The ups-and-downs of King's standing are in themselves a striking aspect of Canada's past. But it only adds to the strangeness of this unusual man that all the details connected with his psychiatric consultation, despite a widespread preoccupation with the state of his sanity, should have remained undiscussed until now. It should go without saying that before theorizing about the nature of King's character all the available psychiatric data should be brought to light and critically examined. But before giving a narrative account of how King came to see the physicians at Johns Hopkins, a short detour is necessary to explain Meyer's special place in intellectual history.

Chapter 2
Dr. Adolf Meyer: "A splendid character!"

The extensive collection of the papers of Adolf Meyer (1866-1950) is now housed at Johns Hopkins in a large room which has been specifically humidified for the sake of preserving historical documents. An immense amount of scholarly work would be involved in going through Meyer's mass of materials with scrupulous care; more than one scholarly life would be consumed by trying to tackle the legacy that he left behind. Someone like Zelda Fitzgerald, Scott Fitzgerald's wife, had once been a patient of Meyer's. It was widely known within the psychiatric profession how uniquely trusted Meyer was as a therapist. At least one famous psychoanalyst, trained earlier by Freud, had turned to Meyer when suffering from an acutely serious mental breakdown.[1]

If Meyer had preserved all kinds of documents that he had accumulated throughout his long life, King had been even more of a saver. It was a striking aspect of King's egoism that he preserved so many scraps of paper, including copies of what he wrote as well as material addressed to him. As a result the Mackenzie King papers account for some two million pages of archival documents. King kept such a conscientious record of all his own medical consultations that in the Public Archives in Ottawa today can be found, completely open to scholarly inspection, a typed account of the 1916 hospital summary of King's stay at Johns Hopkins Hospital. Even more striking was the fact that King had written at great length in his diary about his decision to consult with physicians in Baltimore. Yet nobody in Canada has recognized the significance of Meyer's name, or even that he was a psychiatrist.

Meyer forms an intriguing sort of opposite to King. Meyer's whole life was spent in the pursuit of scientific understanding, and he lived, as we shall see, largely within the confines of a university world. King had as a young man also entertained the possibility of pursuing an academic career, and had even been offered teaching posts in the Economics Department of Harvard University as well as later at the newly founded Harvard Business School. King claimed that his interest in para-psychological phenomena, which is the way academics talk about spiritualism, was part of the quest for knowledge on his part, an aspect of his search for truth. King went on to become as we know an important figure on the world political stage, while Meyer remained influential within the psychiatric profession. But Meyer, although in a different way than King, has had his once formidable reputation more or less lost to the general reading public.

Rockefeller money, originally made by John D. Rockefeller, Sr. in oil, was of key significance not just to the building of the Johns Hopkins School of Medicine, but afterwards – through King's direct personal influence – on medical education in Canada. The Rockefeller Foundation in New York was set up in 1913 thanks to more than fifty million dollars in Standard Oil shares. Key figures at the Foundation, being headed by John D. Rockefeller, Jr., were also involved with the making of Johns Hopkin's medical school. In 1916, just to take an example of the complex interconnections that existed by then, Meyer was first suggesting to the Rockefeller's China Medical Board what sort of direction psychiatry should take in China.[2]

In 1919, by which time King had already become well acquainted not only with the Rockefellers but with Johns Hopkins itself, King made a special approach to John D. Rockefeller, Jr. in behalf of Canadian educational institutions. King's efforts succeeded in helping to encourage John D. Rockefeller, Sr. to give further securities to the Rockefeller Foundation, calling special attention to the special needs of Canadian medical schools. Those universities were soon notified that they would be receiving five million dollars from the Rockefeller Foundation.[3]

At the time of the initial rise of Johns Hopkins as an institution, medical schools in America were not much more than diploma mills. In law, too, apprenticeship training had preceded the legitimization of academic accreditization. Yet as early as 1904 John D. Rockefeller, Jr.

was allowed by his father to give Johns Hopkins a gift of five hundred thousand dollars. (It would require a financial specialist to explain just how to multiply any such sums to arrive at what would be involved in terms of today's dollars.) In hindsight it does look like it was at a relatively late aspect of the medical pioneering at Johns Hopkins that the field of psychiatry came to be prominent. Thanks to the money of the philanthropist Henry Phipps, who had become involved with the problem of caring for the insane, in 1908 funds were made available for the opening of a new psychiatric clinic and the endowment of a professorship of psychiatry.

Adolf Meyer took up his duties as the first director of the Phipps Clinic in 1910, although the Clinic itself did not open until April 1913. The official inauguration of the Clinic was "a grand occasion."[4] A speech was made by William H. Welch, who had done an immense amount as the head of Johns Hopkins to facilitate medical reform there.[5] A leading American surgeon, Dr. Harvey Cushing, also spoke. Sir William Osler, by birth and undergraduate work a Canadian, had left Johns Hopkins in 1905 to accept the Regius Professorship of Medicine at Oxford, but returned from England for the ceremonies in behalf of the new Phipps Clinic. (One of Osler's most memorable dictum's was that "the good physician treats the disease but the great physician treats the patient who has the disease.") The famous Swiss psychiatrist Eugen Bleuler also travelled to Baltimore and, along with Osler, spoke. That both Osler and Bleuler had opinions and views which can today help understand King's own psychiatric file is a tribute to the breadth of their interests and outlooks.

Looking in perspective at what was happening it would seem that late nineteenth century American psychiatry was relatively backward compared to what was going on at the great centers of European learning. Hospital facilities, it is true, had long been founded in the New World to help take care of those whose families could not manage to put up with these unfortunates. But although such institutions already existed for the custodial guardianship of people in dire straits, relatively little had been achieved in the way of efforts at modern scientific understanding. Starting in the late nineteenth century European doctors were coming to the States and taking the lead away from the old-fashioned asylum superintendants.[6] To be fair to what was developing on this side of the Atlantic, in Europe psychiatry as we know it as an academic discipline was just starting to get going.

General paresis at a late stage of syphilis was, for instance, "commonly thought to have psychological causes,"[7] and it was only in 1927 that Julius Wagner von Jauregg, a psychiatrist and contemporary of Freud's in Vienna, became the first and only member of his profession ever to win a Nobel Prize. Wagner-Jauregg's central innovation had been the malarial treatment for general paresis, reducing by the physical means of fever one of mankind's great scourges. Wagner-Jauregg earned genuine claims to fame. He studied in three fields where his reputation deserves to be lasting: the problem of cretinism and goitre prophylaxis, the reform of laws concerning the insane, and malaria therapy.[8] Wagner-Jauregg's work preceded the development of other means of somatic therapy for psychiatric syndromes, even if the later discovery of penicillin made malaria therapy unnecessary. Wagner-Jauregg had not succeeded in eliminating general paresis by introducing malarial treatment; it remained a common late manifestation of syphilis. But it was notable how, in contrast to other Viennese psychiatrists, Wagner-Jauregg was not content to try to relate diseases to hypothetical brain lesions. (To Wagner-Jauregg Freud seemed too abstract and ambitious, a generalizer.[9])

Adolf Meyer was himself another thoroughly unusual, although now generally forgotten, leader in the history of modern psychotherapy. At the turn of the century, though, he was in spite of his youth already "a famous person."[10] He went on to become "the most influential American psychiatrist of his generation,"[11] and he had a major impact on the international level; both in Great Britain as well as Japan his concepts have played an important role. When John Hopkins first decided to build its psychiatric unit, Meyer seemed the obvious person to hold the new professorship.

By the time of Meyer's retirement in 1941, at the age of seventy-four, it was possible for a distinguished medical historian to write: "the best tradition of European psychiatry was introduced in the United States by Adolf Meyer, who for almost fifty years has been and is at the time of this writing the dominant figure in American psychiatry."[12] Similar tributes can be assembled about Meyer's genuine historical standing. One scholar has agreed that Meyer "was the instrument through which major psychiatric innovations were introduced into American medicine from Europe."[13] Another authority has observed: "Precise, exacting, and stubborn, Meyer became the dominating figure in American psychiatry between 1920 and 1940."[14] However easily

24

medical pioneers can be ignored, and no matter how Canadian historians failed to understand the significance of King having gone to Meyer, he was widely seen as "probably the most prestigious figure in American psychiatry before World War II."[15]   Still a further professional view is that Meyer was "one of the most influential figures in American psychiatry from the 1890s through the 1940s."[16]

Certainly no one who had been practicing in the New World exerted more influence, for example, than Meyer did in England.   Sir Aubrey Lewis, the most powerful figure in British psychiatry during the 1940s, 1950s, and 1960s, studied with Meyer and was an enthusiastic follower of his.   Lewis founded the Institute of Psychiatry at the Maudsley Hospital in London, and Lewis was the first professor of psychiatry at London University.   If only because of how deeply Meyer was admired by Lewis, Meyer's broad and inclusive categories were to affect the whole development of British psychiatry.

The past gets constructed arbitrarily, and just as King's current status is now in relative eclipse, so Meyer has also suffered in his own way among students of modern psychiatry as well as within the general reading public.   Meyer was rarely a clear writer, and the complications of his prose could almost be as mushy as King's own writing;   Meyer's unfortunately indirect style has helped mean that his works have largely become dusty relics in medical libraries.   One central source of his fading reputation was that he did not produce rabid disciples, but rather sought to enlighten students to become independent workers in their own right.   Freud's thinking, if only because of the clarity of his own theories, lent itself better to creating avid followers.

Fanaticism pays off in intellectual history, as it can in politics generally.   For those who are true believers, and capable of advancing their cause with fierce passions, are bound to have a disproportionate impact, at least for a time, on the history of ideas.   Meyer was however a pluralist who believed in a "common sense" approach to psychiatry; he wanted to take a wide variety of factors into account, environmental as well as biological, in explaining the sources of mental illness.   As Meyer wrote in a 1929 letter, he had a scholar's approach which left him as skeptical about psychoanalysis as he was about advances being made in understanding conditioned reflexes: "I am afraid I am a little with regard to Pavlov and Bechterew as I am with Freud;   interested and appreciative and yet bristling with question marks."[17]   Meyer's broad-mindedness was a source of his being considered the top psychiatrist, even if it has also meant that he is apt now to be scarcely remembered. Great system-builders like Freud do not suffer from a comparable dilution of their impact. It should not therefore be surprising that historians reading King's diaries did not stop to notice the significance of King's having consulted Meyer in 1916.

Meyer had been born near Zurich in Switzerland in 1866; he was the son of a pastor. Carl Jung's father was also a minister. Freud's own hostility toward organized religion should be a sign of how much his new profession was designed to replace the traditional care-taking of the soul. Part of the reason that Freud had picked Jung to be his own "crown prince" was that Jung was a product of Swiss psychiatry, which at the turn of the century, as well as now, is among the best anywhere in the world.

Meyer had enjoyed an excellent medical education at the University of Zurich. He became familiar not only with psychiatry, and its concern with the mentally ill, but also he was intrigued by the latest developments within modern neurological science. Yet psychiatry did not then seem attractive as a career, and Meyer preferred to pursue the study of neurology. He was a qualified physician by 1890. Psychiatry was so lacking in medical status then that over a decade later in Switzerland someone as promising as Jung was warned that he was ruining his career by specializing in that field. Medical schools are once again today, long after the hey-day of psychiatry's reputation in mid-century, experiencing a similar fall-off in the profession's prestige and number of applicants.

Although on this side of the Atlantic the boundary lines between psychiatry and neurology, like all other academic distinctions, have tended to be more fluid than in Europe, in the Switzerland of Meyer's training, as in the Vienna of Freud's own lifetime, psychiatry and neurology were considered widely separate medical specialties. (Wagner-Jauregg was the leader of official Viennese psychiatry, whereas Freud, a neurologist, attracted his own following in the new field of psychoanalysis from students coming to him from outside Austria.) Meyer travelled to Paris, Edinburgh, and then also London in order to continue his professional education in neuropathology. He did a research project connected with the brains of reptiles, still steering clear of clinical psychiatry.

When Meyer emigrated from Switzerland to the United States in 1893, his official position was supposed to be that of a pathologist.

(The brilliant psychoanalytic psychiatrist Sandor Rado admired Meyer immensely, but Rado thought that Meyer suffered from the after-effects of being primarily an "anatomist."[18]) First Meyer worked at the Illinois Eastern Hospital for the Insane at Kankakee; then from 1895 on he was at the Massachusetts Insane Hospital in Worcester, and later at the New York State Psychiatric Institute where he was a professor of psychiatry at Cornell University Medical College.

One immediate complication associated with Meyer's coming to America was that his mother developed the fixed delusion that he had died. At the time she was already a widow, and although eminent psychiatric authorities decided her condition was hopeless, Meyer does seem to have intuitively understood the underlying human meaning of her condition: she missed him terribly. In the end she recovered, which was said to have fed Meyer's own skepticism about the search for psychiatric disease entities. (She had another depression when his brother became engaged.) Meyer wanted to talk about reaction types, not illnesses. Any one-word diagnosis has to miss out on "the processual, reactive, life-long coping complexity (and constitution) of the daily performance of personhood...." Meyer maintained that it was "the story" that counts in understanding a person.[19] The particular terms Meyer coined were tongue-twisters, "found rebarbarative and never caught on."[20] In stressing the significance of reaction-types, Meyer meant that particular clinical entities are flexible, and can be reversed or prevented. Meyer was "teaching an instrumental, pragmatic psychiatry"; his students were encouraged to do whatever they could to make the patient better.[21] As "biological psychiatry" has flourished over the years, and especially during the last generation, Meyer's repudiation of the disease model has had to damage his contemporary influence.

Meyer was optimistically convinced that even schizophrenic patients could be helped. In general he thought that the mind and the body had to be seen as a functioning unit, and he talked about "psychobiology"; for him the mental and the physical form an integrated whole which is held together by significant interchanges. And so Meyer was responsive to the native American school of philosophical thinking he encountered after emigrating from Europe; for American pragmatism resisted artificial distinctions and was holistic. Meyer read philosophers like Charles S. Pierce and William James; also, Meyer entered into personal friendships with John Dewey, George Herbert Mead, and Charles Cooley. In an effort to combat the construction of abstract conceptions in connection with how we think about mind-body problems, Meyer developed an approach which he called psychobiological integration. He sought to collect material about the life history of each patient, and to understand everyone in terms of their unique biographical capacities and experiences.

Meyer was notable in encouraging the art of good case-history writing. Pre-Freudian psychiatry has often been under-rated in this regard. In 1965, for example, R.D. Laing took one of Emil Kraepelin's textbook illustrations to show how the patient could be understood as making subtle fun of even the greatest of old-fashioned psychiatrists.[22] But it is easy to overlook the achievement of classical psychiatry in encouraging case histories which are ample enough to allow for such later self-correction. By now the pendulum has swung so far that throughout the literature the lives of individual patients tend to get lost.

By the time that Freud in 1909, along with his then leading disciple Carl Jung, came to Worcester, Mass. to accept honorary degrees from the relatively new Clark University, Meyer too was being honored with an academic award. He may have been the most famous psychiatrically of the three, although Meyer's failure successfully to create a school of his own has helped both Freud and Jung to pull far ahead of him long before now. Freud far surpassed the others as a great writer. (Although a dispute exists about just how many thousands of Freud's letters have managed to survive, the collections of his various correspondences will eventually dwarf in size his formal publications.)

Just because Meyer lacked the immortality that goes with being a remarkable stylist, it is worth recalling that in Meyer's prime he was widely admired for the breadth and flexibility of his vision. And his down-to-earthness meant that he was considered someone who could be humanly relied upon. Psychiatry has always attracted more than its share of odd-balls, but Meyer was notable for clinically having had both feet on the ground. It is perhaps indicative of Meyer's standing at the time that when the honorary degrees at Clark were being handed out, he went ahead of both Freud and Jung, even though they had had to travel across the Atlantic to receive their awards.

At Clark Meyer chose to speak about the psychological interpretation of what was then known as "dementia praecox" and now as schizophrenia. Meyer was rejecting the idea that mental illness could be attributable to some unknown brain "toxin." It is striking how much the same problems confronted him then as we face now. Meyer sought to work as a pragmatic matter with the strengths that patients brought to their treatment. He urged that a patient's resources be mobilized in therapy, as he melioristically sought to counter the inevitable personal deficiencies in those he sought to assist. Although by 1909 Meyer was still welcoming toward what Freud could contribute, Meyer never thought that psychoanalysis's ideal of rational insight could succeed in being curative. And Meyer was not, like Freud, recommending that patients should be encouraged to regress to childhood. Meyer was one of those rare souls who objected to therapists who encourage infantilism, no matter how much power he thereby had self-denyingly to resist. Meyer, I think, deserves to be honored for how early on he had stressed the legitimacy of a therapist being thoroughly supportive toward patients. And he kept up with advances in organic medicine.

Although at first Meyer had been appointed in the States as a pathologist, he would make his mark within psychiatry. The history of that discipline is taught at least as haphazardly as any other aspect of our past. Medical schools are primarily concerned with the training of contemporary practitioners, as well as with the advancement of science, so that the study of history has almost necessarily taken a back seat. But if psychiatry's past does not get taught at medical schools, where else can it be properly studied? A few academic units exist which are devoted to the history of science, but then psychiatry is itself only a small part of a much larger field within medical traditions.

It is only within the past few years that the history of psychiatry has started to become established on secure academic grounds. For many years medical history in general was more or less consigned to the concerns and hobbies of retired physicians; but lately it has become possible to conceive of people pursuing an interest in the history of psychiatry not only at the outset of their academic careers, but as means of normal professional advancement.

So many competing ideological schools of thought have been bitterly at odds with one another that it takes effort to make sure that the history of psychiatric medicine does not fall into any one partisan camp. Thinking back on how exceptional a figure Meyer was, we should be reminded of the need to avoid the dangers of what has been designated as "Whig" history-writing. The category of Whiggery is designed to awaken us to the fact that the past ought not to be looked upon solely through the telescope of our own moral preferences; it is of course impossible to disengage ourselves entirely from our most cherished beliefs, but the job of the historian ought to be distinct from propagandizing in behalf of our pet preconceptions, since every generation is apt to consider itself as uniquely enlightened. "Whig" history would be an account of the past which is unduly oriented to the standards of what has up to now been a success. Any teleological thinking in historical studies is likely to be misleading, and we can be confident that the next generation will conclude that our times have also been sorely lacking in insight.

I am contending that for a series of different reasons Meyer has received almost as bad a shake from history books as Mackenzie King himself. There is simply no way of ensuring that merit gets adequately rewarded. Meyer went on to live until 1950, the same year King died, although Meyer was born eight years earlier. Meyer's immense clinical reputation, which continued throughout all the years during which he led the Phipps Clinic, proved impossible to sustain. His work fell between the two stools of biological psychiatry and psychoanalysis; he had rejected both the illness model, which looked for "toxins," as well as the Freudian confidence in what could be achieved therapeutically by means of a reconstruction of early childhood in an analytic situation. In its own time Meyer's special viewpoint meant a breath of fresh air in American psychiatry, but Meyer was so tolerant and wide-ranging as to have his work dissipated as an enduring psychiatric force. Meyer was eclectic enough as to exclude from his school of thinking the dogmatism characteristic of true believers.

Yet almost from the beginning of Meyer's career in the States he had been a reforming influence. He stood against therapeutic pessimism, in its many guises, connected with the treatment of those who were most seriously ill. In the context of those times it meant that he was attacking "the prevailing assumptions that insanity resulted from a brain lesion in those with an inherited predisposition."[23] We like to think there have been many psychiatric advances over this past century; without in any way minimizing the gains that have been made, I think psychiatry today is as beset with the threat of excessive diagnostic labelling as in Meyer's own early professional career. And some of our own most advanced psychiatrists are still too single-mindedly in search of the solution to the puzzle of the brain chemistry of the great mental illnesses. In his Clark lectures, at the time he met Freud, Meyer "argued that the psychoanalysts' clever interpretations of complexes and symbolism had gone far toward explaining the apparently senseless symptoms of dementia praecox, the earlier term for schizophrenia, a variety of insanity then regarded as organic and largely incurable."[24] Meyer's position held out a friendly hand to psychoanalysis to the extent that Freudianism was more outgoing and hopeful than a strictly classificatory approach.

At Johns Hopkins Meyer was establishing the first psychiatric teaching hospital that was built up on a European pattern.[25] So the early support that he lent Freud's movement was, in the context of the time, momentous. In later years Meyer would grow highly critical of psychoanalysis, and in particular be dubious about the effects on students (as well as patients) of Freud's teachings. But in 1911, when the American Psychoanalytic Association, was first created at Baltimore, Meyer was among the eight founding members who were present. He also became an honorary member of the New York Psychoanalytic Society.

Because Meyer objected to the abstractness in the psychoanalytic outlook, he distanced himself from the mainstream of Freud's supporters and the cultishness Meyer abhorred. Meyer maintained his contacts instead through the study of scientific papers, letters, and by means of personal visits with the central figures of European psychiatry. In 1927 Meyer was elected the fifty-sixth president of the American Psychiatric Association, and "for years was considered the dean of American psychiatrists."[26] Meyer's wife also played a part in the story of his career, since she was to become "the first psychiatric social worker."[27] Meyer had himself been the one to introduce in 1914 "the first course on psychology for medical students" at Johns Hopkins; and Meyer's interest in post-graduate students led him to set up an early version of the current residency program.[28]

Nothing can be harder in the history of ideas than tracing influence; so the impact of a psychiatrist like Meyer has been hard to establish and make secure. Canadians might conceivably know of Meyer mainly because he was one of the teachers of Dr. D. Ewen Cameron of the Allan Memorial Institute of Psychiatry at McGill, which like the Phipps Clinic was a recipient of Rockefeller support. (Meyer and the Rockefellers had helped to establish the mental hygiene movements in both the U.S. and Canada.) Cameron today has a largely unsavory reputation, because of his experiments with mind control which were partly subsidized by the American C.I.A.[29] Yet Cameron, who had gone on to become the most powerful figure in

Canadian psychiatry until his death in 1967, also helped establish the World Psychiatric Association; whatever else Cameron may have done which has not withstood the test of time, he also called together "the first conference of psychopharmacology in North America."[30] For Cameron had picked up in the Australian literature the mention of the effects of lithium, a drug which subsequently transformed the treatment of manic-depressive illness. Within the professional literature there would be widespread agreement that Cameron's teacher Meyer had indeed been "the most eminent psychiatrist in post-1900 North America."[31]

When I was conducting my own interviews among Freud's patients and pupils, I remember one exceptionally intelligent female psychiatrist, who had been analyzed by both Jung as well as Freud, telling me with equal pride how she had once been a student of Meyer's at Johns Hopkins.[32] She was hardly the only one in the course of my research who made a point of having once studied with Meyer. He remained a courtly European who used to deliver his lectures in formal dress. Yet he was widely admired for his naive concern with everyday matters. According to one Hopkins legend the Queen of Roumania was once introduced to him with her correct title at the Phipps Clinic; Meyer proceeded mildly and patiently to inquire how long she had entertained that particular belief in her status. Jokes are notoriously difficult to interpret; but this tale got told because Meyer's commitment to psychiatry was such that everyone he saw professionally was subjected to scrutiny, which was of an exceptionally kindly nature. Meyer was without the sadistic need to investigate which has so marred the work of others in the field.

I have already described some of the steps by which King's reputation has fallen on bad times. But in Meyer's case what has to be historiographically striking is the extent to which people who were relative nobodies in their own time have nevertheless flourished subsequently, largely because they were members of movements which for a variety of flukey reasons have proved successful. Part of the imbalance in the history of modern psychotherapy has to do with the special impact of Freud's teachings. The creator of psychoanalysis was such a great organizer that his artistry has helped along the memory of all those who in any way had contact with him. And so although relatively minor psychoanalysts, loyal to Freud, have had their standing inflated by virtue of their having had their association with him, and certain of his enemies have been exaggerated in stature too, genuinely original and major figures like Meyer, who grew critical of psychoanalysis, have fallen by the wayside. Freud was aware of the power of great ideas, and how his movement flourished as the embodiment of his work.

One of the central defects to Freud's whole system of thought, which Jung had been early on presciently concerned with, was Freud's failure to differentiate clinically between neuroses and psychoses. Freud set out to understand and treat neurotic intrusions in people's lives: that means he took for granted that his patients had considerable psychological strengths, but were simply hampered in the pursuit of their goals by aspects of their character which were disruptive.

To be a patient of Freud's, or any of the early analysts, one had to be well-enough put together to be able to make one's way through a busy city to get to appointments at scheduled hours. Such people also had to have the ability to lie on a couch for purposes of free-associating, with the understanding that by exploring their past, with the help of analysis, rational insight would lead to a greater measure of self-control. Any analytic patient has to put up with the special frustration of a situation in which the analyst behaves as a relatively non-committal authority; the analysand is encouraged to develop a full-scale emotional reaction while the analyst is supposed to remain cool and detached.

But psychiatry centrally concerns itself with the great mental illnesses, when patients have become unable to deal with either their immediate families or the pressing exigencies of daily life. The therapist has to be extremely cautious in encouraging such people to uncover their emotional conflicts, lest they deteriorate under the pressure of an attempt at self-examination. Instead of seeing them as like neurotics suffering from self-deception, it is usually thought that they have to be assumed to have a special capacity for self-healing. On the assumption that nobody knows what precipitates a great mental collapse, reinforcing the strengths of the most seriously disturbed patients becomes the essence of a good therapeutic enterprise.

At first Freud had boldly proposed that there was a strict continuum between health and illness. He knew that his method of treatment could not straightforwardly extend to psychotics, too self-involved to be amenable to his own preferred form of technique. They were supposedly so stuck on themselves that they would be unable to transfer onto the analyst their emotional attachments from the past, and for that reason Freud ruled them out of bounds for the practicing psychoanalyst.

While Freud was in a way as standoffish toward the therapeutic possibilities of working with psychotics as the old-line psychiatrists with their incessant urge to classify, all through his career there were those in his circle who thought about the possibilities of treating psychotics. Freud sometimes unwittingly saw such people without his being able to make a proper psychiatric diagnosis, since that was not his field of medical expertise. Diagnoses in this area are especially difficult since even today psychiatry is not a hard science. As time has passed, and the early distinction between neurosis and psychosis has once again eroded, the category called "borderline" has expanded to cover an immense variety of clinical types. Freud had known something of his own special inadequacies, and one of the reasons he responded to Jung so warmly in the first place was that Jung was coming from an important Swiss center of psychiatric training. Freud eagerly sought to have his ideas successfully penetrate into academic psychiatry, and Jung was to be precisely such a vehicle.

At least once in the 1920s Freud treated analytically a patient he himself considered schizophrenic, even though his own theoretical reasoning would have declared such a patient beyond the bounds of psychoanalysis.[33] One increasingly suspects that Freud often violated his own formal rules about who was and who was not suitable for psychoanalytic treatment. In public, however, it was only in the early 1920s that he came to pronounce on the firm conceptual distinction between neurosis and psychosis, implicitly abandoning his earlier idea that psychotics could be considered "narcissistic" neurotics. Freud concluded that psychosis could not be handled with the rationalistic means that his own form of therapy had at its disposal, but he still looked on with mild encouragement as others in the large following he led sought to make changes in psychoanalytic technique in order better to understand and handle psychotic difficulties.

At the time of Freud's 1909 trip to America Meyer viewed psychoanalysis as a positive contribution in that it represented an additional burst of hopefulness about what could be therapeutically accomplished. By the 1920s Meyer had grown relatively sour on Freud's field, since it then seemed to him narrow, dogmatic, and sectarian. But at the outset Meyer was open-minded about any system like psychoanalysis which might prove useful.

William James too had been willing to give Freud the benefit of the doubt, and had read some of his earliest papers from the 1890s. James came to Clark University for the 1909 degree-awarding ceremonies in order to get to see Freud, but came away with a rather dim view of Freud as a person. Describing his visit to a Swiss colleague, James wrote:

> I went there for one day in order to see what Freud was like, and met also Jung of Zurich, who...made a very pleasant impression. I hope that Freud and his pupils will push their ideas to their utmost limits, so that we may learn what they are. They can't fail to throw light on human nature; but I confess that he [Freud] made on me personally the impression of a man obsessed with fixed ideas. I can make nothing in my own case with his dream theories, and obviously "symbolism" is a most dangerous method. A newspaper report of the congress said that Freud had condemned the American religious therapy (which has such extensive results) as very "dangerous" because so "unscientific." Bah! [34]

James was bridling at Freud's criticism of the native American branch of psychotherapy, which was by no means hostile to traditional religion; but James had also not warmed to Freud as a whole. James wrote to another colleague:" "I strongly suspect Freud, with his dream theory, of being a regular *hallucine* [deluded individual]. But I hope that he and his disciples will push it to its limits, as undoubtedly it covers some facts, and will add to our understanding of 'functional psychology.'"[35] Freud, on his part, remained impressed by having met James; but at the age of thirty Freud had prophetically written to his fiance:

> I consider it a great misfortune that Nature has not granted me that indefinite something which attracts people... It has taken me so long to win my friends....[E]ach time I meet someone I realize that an impulse, which defies analysis, leads that person to underestimate me.[36]

Around the time that James was commenting so negatively about Freud (in contrast to James's appraisal of Jung), James was writing in a letter about Meyer: "That man has the levelest mind on psychological matters that I know! A splendid character!"[37] James had taken students of his to Meyer's psychiatric demonstrations at the

Worcester State Hospital, "and the two men discussed psychiatry and scientific method."[38]   James was admiring of Meyer based on his personal acquaintance with him, just as James had been put off by Freud's tunnel-vision.   But within psychiatry as a whole, to which James had a significant relationship if only because he had himself gone through medical training, James's judgment about Meyer was to be echoed by many others as well.   For example, in 1919 E. E. Southard, then the president of the American Psychiatric Association, paid the following tribute to Meyer:

> No greater power to change our minds about the problems of psychiatry has been at work in the interior of the psychiatric profession in America than the personality of Adolf Meyer... I shall designate him as a ferment, an enzyme, a catalyzer, I don't know that we could abide two of him. But in our present status we must be glad there was one of him.[39]

Meyer was repelled by close-mindedness, and like James would be put off by anyone in psychiatry "obsessed with fixed ideas." Meyer has been credited with an unusual degree of tolerance, which as we shall see he was able to extend to Mackenzie King. Meyer went on to develop modern staff conferences, and he invented the "life chart" as a way of describing patients. According to Meyer "the psychiatrist had to understand his patients as individuals by studying their biographies – it was not enough to assign them to diagnostic categories."[40] Although Meyer welcomed, like James, what Freud was bringing in the way of new knowledge, "as early as 1915 ... Meyer challenged Freud's stress on 'infantile sexuality.'"[41] As we shall see, his differences with Freud did not mean, when it came to examining Mackenzie King, that Meyer failed to appreciate the possible sexual significance of King's troubles.

Curiously enough, although Meyer and King came from such different backgrounds and pursued entirely separate kinds of careers, both men had come in contact with Jane Addams and her co-workers at Hull House in Chicago. Meyer was to pioneer in promoting the mental hygiene movement in America, and apparently Jane Addam's was "a formative influence on Meyer."[42] King first heard Jane Addams speak in Toronto, and she stimulated his interest in settlement work. In 1896, when he was a student at the University of Chicago, Jane Addams showed him around Hull House, and he wrote home to his family about it. He worked there for a time, although eventually he felt disappointed with what could be accomplished in the context of her approach.

Meyer easily assimilated to his American surroundings, and so did King; even as Meyer always remained distinctly European, King retained his character as a Canadian. (While his most intimate friends called him "Rex", only Franklin Roosevelt and Winston Churchill got away with calling him "Mackenzie.") Meyer was, one of Freud's pupils once wrote, "a shy, reserved little man, grave and serious, always slightly apart from his environment...." Although Meyer "never used psychoanalysis as a therapeutic technique," early on he was demanding of his staff that they "become familiar with the dynamic approach as an aid in interpretation and diagnosis." By the "dynamic approach" this analyst was referring to the motivational interest that Freud's kind of psychology encouraged an interest in. All previous psychiatric categories were, in Meyer's view, insufficient to cover the rich clinical realities. And Meyer "reiterated that a full collection, if not an investigation, of 'all the facts' in a life history of a patient should always be assembled." To this particular analyst, however, Meyer was held to be deficient in contrast to Freud, on the grounds that however tolerant Meyer might have been "facts without theory, just as theory without facts, are not enough."[43] Yet within psychiatry itself, where a succession of rival theories have come and gone without settling much, Meyer remains outstanding for his resistance to passing fashions.

In an effort to redress the imbalance of how unkind history has been to both King and Meyer, I am going to be exploring the specifics of the relationship between the two men, from different parts of the world, who for a brief period were in contact with one another. Lytton Strachey (whose younger brother James was Freud's translator and editor) is remembered as a great writer and biographer, the author most notably of *Eminent Victorians*; he realized that a full-scale history of the Victorian age could never be written: "we know too much about it." Strachey went on to say that "ignorance is the first requisite of the historian – ignorance, which simplifies and clarifies, which selects and omits, with a placid perfection unattainable by the highest art." Strachey was writing in the midst of World War I: "concerning the age which has just passed, our fathers and our grandfathers have poured forth and accumulated so vast a quantity of information that the industry of a Ranke would be submerged by it, and the perspicacity of a Gibbon would quail before it." The papers of Meyer and King are dauntingly abundant, which makes Strachey's recommended approach helpfully relevant:

> It is not by the direct method of a scrupulous narration that the explorer of the past can hope to depict that singular epoch. If he is wise, he will adopt a subtler strategy. He will attack his subject in unexpected places; he will fall upon the flank, or the rear; he will shoot a sudden, revealing searchlight into obscure recesses, hitherto undivined. He will row out over that great ocean of material, and lower down into it, here and there, a little bucket, which will bring up to the light of day some characteristic specimen, from those far depths, to be examined with a careful curiosity.[44]

So I will be adopting here Strachey's recommended tactic. I propose to drop down, into the great ocean of what might be said about the primary documents of both Meyer and King, "a little bucket" in order to bring to light a unique episode which has until now gone unnoticed among historians. I will not though be treating what comes up as a "specimen," since that sort of approach implies, at least in Strachey's own use of his technique, too much distance which easily shades into ridicule. Stacey has done quite enough debunking on King as it is.

King's personality and character deserve to attract a lot of attention, and he would seem tailor-made for the whole subject of psychology and politics. Part of the interest in political psychology has turned out to be as an instrument of high public policy-making. Once Saddam Hussein posed a military and political threat in 1992, then the American government commissioned psychiatric profiles of him in order better to understand under what circumstances he could best be brought to reason. The reliance on psychiatrists by high public officials is no new phenomena; during World War II the administration of Franklin Roosevelt authorized a psychoanalyst to undertake interviews with those who had once known Hitler, in order to help predict how he could be expected to behave as Germany lost the war. Subsequently that study appeared as a book.[45] (No such project was allowed, even though it was proposed, to be undertaken about Stalin on the grounds that he was an ally. Psychological probing was deemed appropriate for political enemies, not friends.)

It is known that during World War II the famous Washington psychiatrist, Harry Stack Sullivan,[46] had a special White House pass; it has never been entirely clear for what purpose he went to the White House, although there has been speculation that he was treating one of the President's top aides. Freud himself, as I have mentioned, collaborated with one of his own patients, Ambassador William C. Bullitt, in writing their controversial study of President Woodrow Wilson. Characteristically we are apt to think of psychological explanations for political leaders who find themselves in political trouble. Once Richard Nixon was forced to resign from the presidency, there has been a flood of conjecturing about how he was himself in part responsible for his own undoing in the crisis known as Watergate.

As I am a political scientist with a special interest in the various uses of psychology, the fact that a psychiatric file existed on King was bound to be strikingly interesting. Meyer was a meticulous note-taker; and King too, as I have said, saved the record of his hospital stay amidst the mass of his other medical documents now in the Public Archives. I am therefore presenting this story now because of its inherent interest. I want to explore the exact steps by which King took the unusual course, at least in that era, of turning to a psychiatrist for help. The symptoms that the records describe can be, I think, enlightening about King's character as a whole. Although the treatment he received was extremely short-term, and not exclusively psychological, the doctors at least did King no harm. Within a few years he had become the elected leader of his party, and then he went on in 1921 to become for the first time prime minister of Canada.

I think that this small tale, not only about King but in connection with the fields of psychology and politics, can be singularly instructive. This "little bucket" of history, as Strachey put it, can bring forth material which is unique about the sources of political strength in an immensely successful political actor. For although King was as of 1916 in a special sort of predicament, his career as a whole remains an outstanding story of triumphs over adversity. By examining the details connected with his 1916 hospitalization at Johns Hopkins, we can gain not only special insight into his own career but also get some understanding of the special sources of political talent.

If now Meyer is relatively forgotten, then it can be easy to help establish his standing as of 1916 because of King's having gone to him in the first place. Both men have, in different ways, suffered from a series of historical slights. Psychiatry still today has its dogmatists, even though they are scarcely the kinds of people to recommend to others who are in need of therapeutic help. The good treatment that King got, and the ease with which he recuperated, should be a reminder that when dealing with creative people all therapists should be obliged to proceed with due humility and caution.

Chapter 3
A Political Career in Suspension

In the fall of 1916 Mackenzie King felt in a sufficient degree of emotional difficulty that he agreed to seek medical help at Johns Hopkins, which is how he came to have his contact with Meyer. In his going to Baltimore, King was acting on the advice of John D. Rockefeller, Jr., as well as other officials at the Rockefeller Foundation in New York, for whom King had been working. But before turning to the specific circumstances of how troubled King was then, and what the precipitating event of his presenting symptoms were, more about King's general human and political situation at that time needs to be appreciated.

People do differ in their approach to doctors. Some are highly suspicious of physicians, and even well-educated and sophisticated professionals can be overly reluctant to put themselves in medical hands. Doctors themselves are frequently the worst offenders in failing to get regular check-ups, or in medicating themselves. King, however, was over at the other end of the spectrum of the variety of attitudes toward medicine. He seemingly was unusually overly concerned about his health and readily sought out the advice of doctors, even if he could be self-willed in cavalierly putting aside what he was told. The multiplicity of physicians King saw left him with a wide range of options about which course to choose to adopt. As a result of the surviving evidence we now have probably more material about the background to his crisis of 1916 than concerning any other psychological problem in King's life.

King was born on December 17, 1874, so by 1916 he was over forty-one years old. Life expectancy has been extended considerably since back then, so we have to assume that at the time of his hospitalization King's age seemed further advanced than it would be apt to appear today. By then King had had his share of emotional turmoil. The 1958 official biography of King, which covered the years 1874-1923, was written by Dawson, an expert in constitutional history, and he subtitled his book "A Political Biography."[1] Dawson's work, assisted by Rockefeller grant money, stands as an excellently well-rounded piece of scholarship. But Dawson was temperamentally and by conviction prone to underplay some of the more psychologically puzzling features to King's personality, and it is no surprise that Dawson entirely missed the key significance of King's 1916 troubles.

The picture Dawson portrayed of King was so humanly detached as to leave the door wide open to Stacey's subsequent debunking. Curiously enough King's private secretary from those years of World War I, Fred A. McGregor, was reported in a 1955 interview to have "known nothing" of King's interest in spiritualism, and he said that it had come "as a surprise and a shock to him."[2] It would seem that although King was privately troubled, and this McGregor knew about, in 1916 King was not yet actually a practicing spiritualist; until now nobody has sought to link King's emotional difficulties with the motives behind his interest in seances and the spiritual world. McGregor was in later years to be in close enough touch with King to have become one of his four literary executors; but he, like the other executors, were professional acquaintances of King's, not personal friends, and all of them knew relatively little about King's inner life. McGregor was also named by King to be a trustee of his estate, and in 1962 McGregor published an important book called *The Fall and Rise of Mackenzie King: 1911-1919*.[3]

While McGregor knew that King had stayed at Johns Hopkins in 1916, and as we shall see even published a paragraph about it, McGregor did not appreciate what was psychologically and medically going on, or been informed enough to relate it in any way to King's subsequent spiritualism. Dawson, however, who was authorized to publish about King's early years, did in that same 1955 interview interject, at odds with McGregor, a knowledge of King's spiritualism. According to a document in the files of the Rockefeller Archive Center, Dawson said that he had known about the spiritualism "all along," so had one of King's political opponents, and "a great many people knew it."[4] Dawson did not, however, go on to explain why none of this inside-dope got used to damage King politically. Nor was Dawson able to investigate the psychological implications of King's peculiarities. Until we get a more rounded view of how to integrate King's spiritualism with the rest of his accomplishments, an unsatisfactory situation will remain in which King appears simply as an enigma, without any effort going into trying better to fit the pieces of this curious puzzle together.

By the time Dawson was working on his own lengthy volume King's political critics had at their disposal one key book, co-authored by H.S. Ferns and Bernard Ostry, which was rough about what King's World War I work for the Rockefellers added up to.[5] Dawson was not, I think, so much answering Ferns and Ostry as he was trying to present a more impartial account, based on primary sources, of the whole first phase of King's political life, carrying King into his first administration as Prime Minister. The indictment of Ferns and Ostry, which saw King functioning as a hired gun for the Rockefellers, could be undermined by simply exposing the degree to which their partisan account had relied only on secondary documentary literature.

Even though Dawson had had little interest in undertaking an exploration of King's idiosyncracies, he did at least allude to some of those eccentricities. He mentioned, for example, how King had liked to "try to sign public documents on anniversaries or family birthdays...."[6] Dawson also noted in King's diary from 1918 a reference to the significance of the position of hands on the clock at the completion of King's *Industry and Humanity*. According to Dawson it was "some quaint fancy"

> on King's part that moved him to "exclaim" when the hands of the clock came into certain positions (together, opposite, or at right angles) at the moment certain "facts" of importance made their appearance...In later diaries, particularly in the thirties and forties, the frequency of these references suggests that the idiosyncracy was becoming something in the nature of a fixed obsession.[7]

But Dawson did not choose to explore this side of King's character, even though he thought it touched on "a fixed obsession." Dawson did suggest that the "coincidences" that King perceived between clock-time and political events may have been taken by King "as confirmation of the rightness of the decision reached or the action taken at the particular time." Further, Dawson thought that King "may have taken them, for reasons which only he could understand and never explained, as a grand indication that he was in tune with the infinite. They comforted him." Dawson shrewdly noted that King never saw hands on the clock as a disapproving sign, or any kind of warning, in connection with his own possible conduct. And Dawson concluded that King's approach to time always had "religious overtones,"[8] without spelling out how King's religiosity differed from that of most believers.

Dawson, like most other political historians of that time, took the approach, even with the enigmatic King, that psychologizing was by and large an irrelevancy. What that amounts to however is that such anti-psychological work has simply proceeded by taking for granted an implicitly assumed set of psychological notions. For example, Dawson in describing how King was chosen as the federal leader of the Liberal party in 1919 noted that King had "political suitability as a young man with a promising record and a somewhat engaging personality."[9] One wishes to know what Dawson's criteria for King's being "engaging" amounted to, and I wonder what we are expected to make of the qualification "somewhat." And in connection with King's work as a conciliator, shortly after becoming Deputy Minister in 1900, Dawson tells us that King was successful because of "his friendly manner and exceptional charm." According to Dawson's version of King at the time "most people found difficulty in resisting his courtesy, his patience, and his genuine interest in their problems."[10] Such a characterization of King would not fit what I was told by those who later worked for King, but I am ready to believe that King could make use of such talents when they were needed. Still, we are given no real feel, for example, about the nature of that "exceptional charm," or the circumstances in which it manifested itself.

Dawson may have dodged explicit psychology, but at moments he could dip into territory which is bound to be tantalizing. For instance, he noted how King as late as 1919 was thinking about the issue of marriage, and whether he would have enough money to be able to afford it. When Laurier (who, like the John D. Rockefellers, Jr., had taken steps with his wife to try and arrange a suitable match for King) finally died in 1919, Dawson remarked that this loss meant that King's "own sense of loneliness and isolation, never long absent, was rendered all the more acute...."[11] (McGregor took a somewhat different view: King "has often been pitied for the loneliness of his life, and he was lonely, but at the same time he found rest and contentment in solitude. He needed to be alone to build up reserves of physical, nervous, and spiritual strength."[12]) McGregor, like Dawson, could not adequately account for King's times of trouble. Dawson did also note of King that earlier, while he was a graduate student at the University of Chicago, King had become "nervous and worried. Fearing a breakdown he consulted a doctor, but was reassured to find that physically he was in good shape."[13]

To be fair to Dawson, and to others who have written about King with the aim of approximating the ideal of historical impartiality, whatever disturbing blips in King's life could be detected he did seem to possess the capacity to transcend successfully the difficulties he encountered. So for Dawson King's numerous oddities were a minor matter. By now there has grown up a substantial and fair-minded body of literature connected with King's occult practices and beliefs. Neatby excellently dealt with such matters under the headings of "The Distortions of Reality" and "Beyond Politics."[14] King was of course a man of his times, and others besides himself were attracted to the possible significance of spiritualism.[15] Still there has been the nagging suspicion that more needs to be understood about King's psychology, even if no one has yet made use of King's actually having consulted with Meyer, or understood how King's various 1916 symptoms might bear on his later involvement with the world of seances, mediums, table-rapping, and so on.

It has been easy to slip over the evidence of King's 1916 psychiatric consultation partly because by all outward standards his life had by then been a series of mounting achievements. His childhood was spent happily enough in Kitchener, then known as Berlin, Ontario. His maternal grandfather, for whom King was named, had been so much the leader in the 1837 rebellion that he had had to flee with his family to the United States, where he served almost a year in prison; King's mother, the last of thirteen children, was born abroad, but came back to Canada with her parents after an amnesty was finally declared in 1849. King spoke to many about the harsh conditions of his mother's childhood, and hypotheses have been advanced that his political career was designed to redeem the life of his mother and her own unconventional father.

Although William Lyon Mackenzie had suffered a life of hardship because of his fanaticism, King's own parents were reasonably integrated within Canadian culture. King's father was a lawyer, and if not any great financial success he was an expert in the arcane matter of libel law and a lecturer at Osgoode Hall in Toronto for twenty-two years, eerily the same amount of time his son was later Prime Minister. John King also served on various university committees. Although the family did not move to Toronto until 1893, King had already entered the University of Toronto in 1891. He was a steady letter-writer home, and until his graduation in 1895 he was notable for his abilities as a public speaker and a leader among his fellow students. He had been chosen by his classmates to be their president in his second year. And before graduating he was prominently involved in a controversy over the dismissal of a professor; King played a leading part in a student boycott.

While King was hoping for a graduate fellowship from the University of Toronto, where he had studied political economy, he also undertook to be a newspaper reporter. King worked at covering police court matters. Although he had decided not to follow through with an initial commitment to become a lawyer, nonetheless in addition to pursuing journalism he studied for law on the side, and received his L.L.B. in 1896. After King tried to get a scholarship at several universities, both at Toronto and in the States, he succeeded at the recently established University of Chicago where he enrolled in the next autumn. Chicago may have been his first contact with Rockefeller philanthropy, since the family had played such a large part in endowing this new university.

First at Chicago, and the next year when he went on to Harvard, King seemed to be more recognized abroad for his academic abilities then in his native land. It is a tribute to King's extraordinary intellectual abilities that he should have been impressed by the remarkable creativity of the great social theorist Thorstein Veblen, who was then teaching at the University of Chicago. Veblen was notoriously unconventional and eccentric, believed in giving all students only C plusses, and went on to have one of the most wretched academic careers imaginable; but he may be today the most prominent North American social thinker whose systematic approach is now widely recognized throughout the world. Veblen's journal published some of King's research. (Although Veblen's thinking was obviously influential on King, Veblen's name somehow does not get cited in King's *Industry and Humanity*.) King was still concentrating on studying politics and economics, although Veblen's influence had

46

pointed in an idiosyncratic direction; while King was drawn by the possibility of becoming a Presbyterian minister he also was inclined toward the attractions of following a strictly academic life.

On returning to Toronto for the summer of 1897, King pursued investigations for some newspaper articles on current social problems like bad housing conditions, the way new immigrant groups had to live, and the sweat-shop system of labor. Not only were piece-workers dreadfully under-paid, but the sanitary conditions in which they lived were terrible; the government was directly responsible in that its agencies gave out contracts which got fulfilled under these appalling circumstances. Before leaving to attend Harvard King was commissioned to do a study about labor conditions by his father's friend the Postmaster General, and later that fall King prepared further reports which were to be implemented by the government; this work was applauded by reform-minded circles.

At Harvard King arrived with a letter of introduction written by Toronto's eminent intellectual Goldwin Smith, who had once taught at both Oxford and Cornell. Although King's father has often been under-rated, it was he who had had the stature to see that Smith wrote about Mackenzie King to Charles Eliot Norton, a figure of real literary importance in Cambridge, Mass. Through this contact with Norton, King gained admission to the most distinguished Harvard academic circles. King stayed for two years on fellowships, and also made some extra money tutoring the children of a rich industrialist.

King was ambitious about his career, and always had a keen eye out for possible advancement. He performed well enough and made a sufficiently good impression to be awarded a Harvard travelling grant for study abroad in 1899-1900; in England he met a number of prominent Fabian socialists at the London School of Economics, and King also went to Germany, Switzerland, and Italy. For someone from his background he had achieved a remarkably cosmopolitan perspective. By the summer of 1900 he could have accepted an instructorship back at Harvard; he was so highly thought of in Cambridge that later on King would be offered a chance to become Dean of the Harvard Business School. But instead of King's teaching at Harvard, here again his father played a key role in advising his son; at the suggestion of his father King agreed to the well-paying job of becoming in Ottawa the new editor, under the Postmaster General, of a journal to be called *Labour Gazette*. Although it might look like he had vacillated professionally King was well launched as a high

Canadian civil servant.

King was only twenty-six years old, and by September 1900 he became Deputy Minister of Labor under Sir Wilfrid Laurier's Liberal government. King had a small staff, and soon made his mark as a labor conciliator. Such mediation work required not only detailed knowledge of industrial work conditions but also considerable tact and patience on King's part. He must have had the ability to put himself in the shoes of others, without becoming humanly over-involved, as he pioneering in labor mediation.

The Industrial Disputes Investigation Act of 1907 can be credited to King. As Dawson summarized what the Act established, it "provided that no strike or lockout could be legally declared in a public utility or mine until the differences which had arisen had first been referred to a three-man board of conciliation representing the employer, the men, and the public."[16] Strikes would be forbidden in federally controlled industries unless such an investigation had first taken place. King stood for principles of conciliation at a time when industrialization was in a phase when neither management or workers felt inclined to be idealistic in their approach to the sharp tensions between them. King sought to pacify labor, putting an end to the class struggle anticipated by Karl Marx; as Meyer sought to be a mediator between rival theoretical expectations, King did too. Aside from King's civil service duties, he also filed reports on matters connected with child labor, immigration, and the opium trade. And King was entrusted with various diplomatic missions abroad.

Prime Minister Laurier was pleased with King's work, and the Lauriers took a personal interest in him. King welcomed Laurier's paternal concern for him, and relied on the older man's advice about forwarding King's political career. King wanted to become a Cabinet member, but was unsure which constituency would be best for him in order to get into the House of Commons. North Waterloo, two thirds of whose constituents were of German descent, was finally chosen. Although the seat had been held by a Conservative since 1896, the margin of victory had been small at the last election; after a strenuous campaign in the General Election of 1908 King was narrowly elected along with a Liberal majority in the rest of the country.

After the post of Minister of Labor was created King was appointed to it, and he was sworn in as a member of the Privy Council on June 2nd. As Minister of Labor he helped establish a Royal Commission on Industrial Training and Technical Education, and also steered through the House of Commons the Combines Investigation Bill, an effort to curb business mergers. In addition King was responsible for a law which prevented "the importation, sale, or use of opium other than for scientific and medical purposes."[17] King sponsored other government bills as well, but despite how productive his first two years in Parliament had been, he was about to be swept up in a broad political defeat which he shared with Laurier's government.

For in 1911 Laurier's administration had concluded the negotiations on a "reciprocity" treaty with the United States, which meant that Canada and America would both reduce tariffs on a wide range of farm produce, fish, lumber, and even some manufacturing goods. Although King was concerned about how this agreement would play in his own riding, as a junior minister in the government he went along with his seniors. Then it turned out that the manufacturing forces were worried that this treaty would bode ill for Canada's future; bankers, railway executives, and industrialists joined together to oppose the treaty, in contrast to their later support for free trade in the 1988 general election. Although the Government had been optimistic about how its policy would be received electorally, by the September general election it was apparent that a swing to the Opposition was at work.

Laurier's Government was unpopular even in Quebec, partly because of Laurier's naval policies; the Naval Service Act, providing for a Canadian navy, had been passed in 1910. Canada had not built any ships for the Royal Navy. Although Laurier's approach had been designed to get Canada out of British naval matters, it was interpreted by many in Quebec to have the opposite effect. And in war-time the Canadian navy would be integrated with the Royal Navy. Laurier, seventy years old, was attacked for being disloyal to his French-Canadian roots.

Within his own constituency King not only had to deal with anti-reciprocity sentiment but the Government's naval policy was deeply unpopular since it seemed part of an attempt to help Britain cope with the power of the new German navy. Given the ethnic make-up of his riding King had special electoral problems of his own; many of his voters were Mennonites with pacifist convictions. When the Conservatives won the election King was not able to hold onto his seat. Dawson thought that King's defeat in North Waterloo could "probably be explained by the reckless way in which he spent his energies in addressing public meetings in constituencies other than his own."[18]

Although King had been offered full professorships back at Harvard, teaching economic history and labor matters in 1906 and at the new Graduate School of Business Administration in 1908, he had been successful enough in politics that he had turned aside such offers. He had submitted to Harvard various government reports that he had written, and one of them had been accepted as a thesis entitling him to be awarded a Ph.D. in 1909. King remains the only Canadian prime minister to have earned such a degree.

Following the general election King's political career was temporarily suspended. His position within the Liberal party had not been senior enough for him to bear any of the responsibility for the Government's 1911 defeat; and he had been unsparing of himself during the electoral campaign itself. Six other Liberal ministers had also lost their seats. The taste of political life had been immensely gratifying, and King was determined to resume his career as soon as possible. There was no way of his anticipating just how long it would take him to return to the House of Commons. But it would not be until October 1919 that he again sat in Parliament; by that time he had just been elected as Liberal leader, Laurier's successor.

Although within a few weeks of his 1911 electoral loss King was writing in his diary to the effect that he was convinced that God had selected him to be a future Prime Minister, his realistic expectations were discouraging. His diary entries for the next few years were unusually sparse, but his private correspondence is revealing. As he wrote in 1913 to a British woman, Violet Markham, who had been helping him financially and as a friend, "I try to be strong and brave and not shew to others the depression I often feel, and I try to carry the load that is upon me, but I sometimes wonder if I should give up further thought of public life."[19]

By the "load" he was carrying King was evidently also referring to his special family responsibilities. King was his parents' elder son, and his father's health was declining. John King finally died only on Aug. 30, 1916, but his last years were marred by illness, including glaucoma, and a variety of financial worries. King's sister Bell, a year older than he, died on April 4, 1915. King's brother Max was four years younger and a physician, but he contracted tuberculosis and moved to Colorado for the air; King's mother, who died on Dec. 18, 1917, was also ailing. King would be left only with his one married sister, Jennie, who in the end outlived him. King's family problems came at a hard time for him politically. As unsympathetic to King as Stacey was, still he noted: "When his sister Bell, his father, and his mother all died within three years in 1915-17 the effect upon him was traumatic. This, it seems clear, is the origin of the spiritualism that came to play such an important part in his later years."[20] Whether or not Stacey was correct, the concept of trauma is one of those ideas we owe, whatever its merits, to the impact of the popularization of Freudian theory. Stacey had skipped over King's 1916 psychiatric troubles without considering what role they played in his later spiritualism.

After the 1911 Liberal debacle Laurier had put his mind to figuring out how to get his defeated former allies back in the House of Commons. According to McGregor, Laurier's outlook on King was always burdened by King's "very sensitive nature," which "could also magnify out of all proportion any sign of indifference." It did not help King, in contrast to the "joviality" of one of his Liberal rivals, that McGregor and others could detect "a certain aloofness on the part of King; there was a feeling among the members of Parliament that King considered himself in some sense superior to them." Perhaps this attitude of King's had been fostered by the way his family had treated him. But "such disparagement of others, though never expressed in public, was only too likely to filter through to the consciousness of those criticized."[21]

Eventually in March of 1913 King was able to secure the nomination for North York, which was connected to his grandfather's career. But the outbreak of the First World War in the summer of 1914 meant that the Canadian Parliament was later able to extend its own life; King therefore had no opportunity to contest the North York seat until the general election of 1917, and even then, because of the way the conscription issue had managed to tear the Liberal party apart, King was unsuccessful.

Throughout the period after 1911 King had to feel insecure on several counts about his future. Other of Laurier's former Ministers also had a claim on his help in getting back into the House of Commons. King had a small income from his savings, which he augmented through speaking and writing articles. He turned aside the idea of becoming leader of the province of Ontario's Liberal party, although he helped in the provincial election of December 1911; the Liberals, though, were beaten. In late 1912 King did succeed in being put in charge of the Liberal Information Office in Ottawa, and he edited for a year, starting in 1913, the *Canadian Liberal Monthly*.

By June 1914 King was invited by the Secretary of the newly established Rockefeller Foundation to go to New York City for a consultation. The contact with the Rockefellers had come through King's Harvard connections; former President Charles W. Eliot was a trustee of the Rockefeller Foundation, which wanted King's help in regard to a terrible strike that had started in September of 1913 against the Rockefeller coal mines in southern Colorado. Miners had first left the company camps for tents that the United Mine Workers provided. In a bitter and violent confrontation in April 1914 the tents had been set on fire by kerosene; in addition to some strikers who were killed, eleven children and two women had suffocated to death in a place where they had sought safety. President Wilson had had to order in federal troops to restore order. Angry parades took place in New York, and the Rockefellers — already in trouble because of the impact of muckraking journalism — found they had a new public relations disaster on their hands. So the Rockefeller Foundation wanted King's assistance as an expert in labor relations and industrial problems.

King was hesitant about what associating himself with the Rockefellers might mean for his future in Canadian politics. He reasoned that working for the Foundation itself, rather than one of the Rockefeller corporations, would ensure that his commitment be more likely seen as a humanitarian one. King was given the mandate to conduct his own research as head of a new Department of Industrial Relations; and the salary of $12,000. a year, a huge amount of money then, was obviously attractive. Over and beyond what he earned immediately, contact with the Rockefellers proved to be lucrative; the Foundation later not only assisted King in retirement as he tried to write his memoirs, medicine in Canada benefited, and even Dawson also got support.

For the sake of his new position King had no need to give up his residence in Ottawa, but this new job complicated his future role within Canada. The more time he spent away the greater the risk he ran with the voters. King originally arranged to accept the position with the Rockefeller Foundation for one year; he gave up the Liberal Information Office, the editing of the *Liberal Monthly*, and also resigned as president of the Ontario Reform Association. The outbreak of World War I in August 1914 was to complicate things further for King, since he was serving the Rockefellers instead of participating in the Canadian war effort.

King established a particularly strong friendship with John D. Rockefeller, Jr. They were almost exactly the same ages. Rockefeller had left a terrible public impression as an absentee capitalist because of the Colorado strike and how it was handled. He had testified before a congressional committee in early 1914 and seemed too adamantly opposed to labor unionization; and he had wanted to shift the responsibility for what had happened in Colorado away from the family's head offices. He had given "the appearance of believing that by delegating authority to the operating officials in Denver he had discharged his full responsibilities as director and stockholder."[22]

Only a couple of weeks later the bloody "Ludlow Massacre" took place in Colorado on April 20th. Afterwards Rockefeller had felt the need of help not only in rectifying the specific problem in Colorado but in transforming the public's perception of the Rockefeller image. At the time the Rockefeller Foundation alone had over one hundred million dollars in assets, so King had certainly landed on his feet. His enemies would later criticize King for his involvement with the Rockefellers at the time of a Canadian national emergency; and as we shall see King anticipated the specific lines of attack that this future criticism would take. In the meantime King developed a real person relationship with Rockefeller. The degree of King's personal self-confidence seems hard to exaggerate, and King must have owed some of his self-possession to the way his parents reared him. King had begun to give Rockefeller advice

on many things that had nothing to do with industrial relations; his excessive seriousness, his method of living, his failure to see enough of his family, his aloofness, his inability to relax, and the need for him to get away from detail and to deal with major issues. "The truth is," King admitted to his diary, "I see in Mr. R. precisely the same mistakes which I have heard others complain of in myself."[23]

When Rockefeller had to give testimony to the United States Commission on Industrial Relations in January 1915, King coached him so that he would make a better public impression. Rockefeller had become a walking symbol of the worst excesses of American capitalism, and King could not single-handedly reverse that reality; but Rockefeller was later immensely grateful for what King had been able to teach him. Even though the mining company had not been eager to have King come out to Colorado, King headed there in March to see for himself what had gone wrong. King, though of course working for Rockefeller, thought that both parties to the strike had to be held accountable for the tragedy that had taken place. King's solution, once he had familiarized himself with the details of the situation, was a plan for labor representation and cooperation with management that would amount to an industrial "constitution."

There would be, for example, a series of grievance procedures set up, and for every one hundred and fifty workers one employee representative would be elected. King's "plan" was essentially one which sanctioned a company union. Although King cannot have seemed a partisan of labor, and someone as conservative as the American labor leader Samuel Gompers was critical of King's proposal, King insisted that for a worker to join a union ought not to be a reason for dismissal, and he held that union organizers should not be excluded from the work site. Nor would workers have to make purchases at company stores. King persuaded Rockefeller himself to go to Colorado in September 1915, so that he would learn for himself the bases for the various proposals King was making. According to what Rockefeller thought later, King "had an intuitive sense of the right thing to do – whether it was a man who ought to be talked with or a situation that ought to be met."[24] King was recommending a form of industrial paternalism, and one with which friends of the labor movement, who insisted on their militancy and self-respect, were not happy with. But King thought that the objective of union recognition ought not to acquire a life of its own, as long as the company could be made to ameliorate the conditions of the workers. Only when the 1935 Wagner Act prohibited company unions did King's plan become out-dated. So there were genuine grounds for Rockefeller's being grateful for what King had accomplished in Colorado for him.

No one factor in itself can be held responsible for the dilemma King found himself in by 1916, but at the time everything in his life seemed to be going badly. His father was virtually blind, and his mother and brother seriously ill. King, who thought of himself as a writer, was having trouble putting together *Industry and Humanity*, and the first reaction to it from the Rockefeller Foundation had not been enthusiastic. He was not getting the response he had hoped for from the trustees, and "the questioning attitude of some was discouraging."[25] (The elaborate charts at the end of the book, which were supposed somehow to be illustrative, seem to me an example of the presence in King of a mystical streak.) The war in Europe was dragging on, and 1916 was a bloody year for Canadian troops in Europe. "At the end of 1916 total casualties numbered 67,890, with 16,466 dead and a further 2,970 missing."[26]

Although a general election would normally have been held by the fall of 1916, the Government and Opposition agreed to extend the life of Parliament for another year. King kept in touch with his constituency in North York, but he had to be keenly aware that his political future, along with the troubles of his immediate family, did not leave him much in the way of promising prospects. The urgency of the call from the Rockefellers was over now; Colorado was quiet and the mines were becoming profitable again. Ferns and Ostry were harshly unsympathetic to King, but they saw 1916 as a turning point. "By 1916, Mackenzie King seemed lost as a Canadian politician. He was out of office, out of Parliament, and out of the country. He was engaged in an unpopular and fundamentally unsavory business." But these highly critical authors thought that Mackenzie King's "behavior in the Colorado affair poses a number of psychological problems...Was he willing to do anything for the sake of power? Had the desire for power so completely corrupted him that the sympathies of his youth were dead in his heart?" To these observers King's policy seemed "to have been based on self-deception, purposeful forgetting of the facts, an undemocratic theory of politics, a powerful ambition and the need for a job."[27]

Exactly what had transpired medically for King over the summer of 1916 is still obscure. McGregor knew that an Ottawa physician had found King "nervously over-wrought."[28] King had not been paying much attention to his diary, and except for the most perfunctory entries he would seem to have discontinued it. Then King started his diary up again in a substantial way (perhaps a sign of his personal distress) from June 22 to July 2nd. On the other hand, McGregor, who was King's secretary at the time, seemed to think that when King neglected his diary that was "an indication in itself of a troubled mind."[29] King resumed the diary on October 13th, after which the record for the rest of the year is pretty complete. He had been keeping the diary assiduously over so many years that I think his working at it now was also an important affirmation of his continuity and identity.

In June King had had to move both of his ailing parents out of the family home in Toronto into a different residence, and he surely was concerned about their limited life expectancies. On June 22nd, when he started up on his diary-keeping again, after having "discontinued" it for "many years," the first item of his daily life he recounted was his having spent a week in moving his parents within Toronto. It was characteristic of King's private thinking that he also on this occasion noted of his brother's medical practice: "It was a beautiful coincidence that on the night father and mother slept in their new home – which represents freedom from former cares in large measure and new life as well – Max should have earned his first professional fee in Denver." In those days information through the mail was almost unbelievably prompt.

King was writing at Kingsmere, his country house where he had been going for summer holidays since 1901. King was clearly unhappy this year. He still felt dissatisfied with the way the manuscript for *Industry and Humanity* was coming along. According to McGregor, "to avoid interruption in his work he had his telephone taken out and for a while he lived like a hermit."[30] King was hoping that country life would be restorative. "I have literally fled here, to get back to the quiet of deep thought and peaceful living – fled with the city's unrest and burning in my veins to seek God and live again with my own soul."

King felt restless about the reaction to a presentation he had made to the trustees of the Rockefeller Foundation. McGregor thought that King was nevertheless "not utterly cast down. He still had faith in himself and in his book. The next year and a half was, however, to be a period of painful attempts to concentrate on his writing in the face of many long and frustrating interruptions."[31] King thought that the invitation to meet with the trustees had "interrupted the course of my work and thought, instead of accepting the invitation gracefully I rebelled in thought against it." This had been around Easter, when he had gone to see his parents; King's mother was sick, and the prospect of his parents having to move "added to my unsettled state and caused me to fret and worry, acting impulsively, yet not wholly so." He had decided to take his mother and Jennie along to New York with him, giving his mother "in this way the change she needed," but he felt out of sorts both about how his presentation had gone as well as troubled about the state of his family.

King was partly worried that "a serious misunderstanding with President Eliot" had come about "in correspondence," which it is impossible now to reconstruct, other than that it was somehow connected with Rockefeller work. Whatever the matter was King wrote it had "worried me beyond all else, so for a couple of months past my work has not been what it should have been."

> At times I have been depressed and disheartened and unequal to the task. My thoughts have turned away from the ideals I have cherished, and I have found myself in an encounter with my own nature such as I have never known before. It has been at times as though a fire would devour me, and I have been unable to get rest by night or day.

> Out of this sort of chaos I have come to this little home, come deliberately and prayerfully to win the peace my soul craves, the quiet my mind needs, the force that my will requires.

When King wrote about his painful yearning for a "home" of his own, he was probably also thinking of his never having married. He had had an addition built on to his cottage for the sake of having a "guest." He reproached himself that he had made too many sacrifices to building up his savings, but he thought the enhanced size of his cottage would amount to a good investment. He planned on his place being large enough so that he could still work while his parents joined him that August.

Working outside on the grounds seemed to King "just what I needed to get my mind off other things." He was struggling to get down to work on his book manuscript. He read and swam, while arranging to incorporate at Kingsmere some of his family's Toronto furnishings. McGregor came out to bring him some books and groceries. King's entry for June 23-26 includes:

> Finished reading Arnold Bennett's Mental Efficiency tonight. I like his view that the body is servant of the mind, and the mind itself the instrument of a higher something which is the real spiritual self. This I believe. Experiences I have had have shewn me where one's self may pass almost completely as it were from the body, and that the invisible and intangible is more real than the visible.

King's convictions about the significance of the spiritual dimension were shared by others of his time and religious background. But these beliefs, still alive today, could sometimes be used to sanction conduct which otherwise might be interpreted as ruthlessness. If one's "self" could "pass almost completely from the body," then what takes place in this world is of no lasting consequence.

King deliberately chose to isolate himself from social engagements, and continued to try and write his book. He reported having been "bothered" by "calls to answer the telephone across the lake," but he refused to go. And he turned down an invitation to go elsewhere for a visit. "I am cutting out all I can," he wrote in the diary, "in correspondence and seeing people, and pray it may lead somewhere." Meyer would later deem these efforts of King a mistake, an exaggeration of King's usually successful attempts to restore his equilibrium by being alone. King reported that his plan had been "to feel more rested for the quiet days." But he found that he felt "discouraged because of returning unrest and agitation."

McGregor came out to Kingsmere again, and they went swimming; King was regularly writing in the mornings, and reserved "rough outside work," and then a swim, for the afternoons. On June 27-29 King indicated that his scheduled routine was not working:

> I continue to worry over the nervous condition I find myself suffering from at times. I fear that there may be some injury to my spine, that the pressure on the nerves of it is the cause. I shall consult a physician if the rest and change does not eliminate the feelings I sometimes have, for it holds me back in my work and besides makes me most uncomfortable both alone and in the presence of others. The tendency to worry is something I must guard against. I incline towards it too much and become unduly suspicious that things are against me, when there is no reason for it.

Ferns thought that Mackenzie King's

> fantasy life was full of enemies; imperialist, patronising British aristocrats, Canadian Tories who were either fat cats in St. James Street or lackeys of British imperialism, hard hearted capitalists who sweated labour and hated trade unions; and there were heroes, too, in this fantasy world, notably his grandfather who, he believed against all the evidence, had established responsible government and democracy in Canada and, of course, the ultimate heroine, his mother.[32]

Stacey had noted of King, without dwelling on this passage about how he felt "uncomfortable both alone and in the presence of others," or any other aspect of King's diary that bears on his 1916 psychiatric consultation, that "we must take note of a distinct paranoid streak."[33] Hutchison, when writing about the conscription crisis of 1944, could find no basis for the nightmare of plots that King conjured up.[34] Perhaps it was an asset to King's political survival that his "nervous condition" made him "unduly suspicious," so that he could see so many more political ghosts than anyone else around him.

King wrote that he "felt greatly discouraged at not having made more headway with my book." On the one hand it seemed to King that he had put in a lot of time on it, yet also allowed too many interferences with his writing to take place. King thought that some fundamental conflicts in his life were bothering him. "I sometimes fear that seeking to keep 2 avenues open I may fail to get very far on either and lose both." King had in mind that he might foul-up with the Rockefeller Foundation and his writing, at the same time that he failed to get back within the swing of things in Canadian politics. "It is difficult to keep ones'[sic] hand in politics. I feel the neglect of the riding, to which I should devote some attention, on the other hand I feel the neglect of the Trustees of the Foundation and the work I should be doing in the United States."

King's not taking part in the First World War was a clear source of distress, unlike how Trudeau seems to have reacted about having stayed out of World War II. King recorded that:

> More than all I feel the neglect of work in connection with this war. I should like to be taking some active part, and yet save raising money by speaking there is little I can with advantage turn to. Recruiting I do not like, I cannot ask other men to go to fight when I don't expect to go myself, & to go myself, with the obligations to father, mother & Max and his family, & the opportunities of larger service to the same cause – freedom – which I have, would seem to evidence a lack of perspective.

As of March 1916, England had Conscription for single men under forty. And in Canada that summer Tories were accusing Laurier of doing nothing in behalf of the war, even though that was an unfair allegation. Laurier in fact had made numerous speeches in behalf of recruiting. "If I were young enough myself," he declared in 1915, "I, too, would be in the firing line."[35] Non-combatants who failed to enlist ran the risk of being pinned with white feathers symbolizing cowardice. By August 1916 the Canadian government was responding to public pressures, and introduced "major changes in recruiting procedures in an effort to end the unsystematic raising of men."[36]

Many of Laurier's colleagues were working hard in behalf of the recruitment effort. The Liberal party thought conscription was fair, and King evidently believed in it too; his apologies about himself reflect his own guilt feelings. It was not so much King's age, which he failed to mention, as all the other considerations he listed that kept him out of World War I. One suspects the force of a personal myth he had of the need to redeem his mother. He felt consciously torn between his Canadian and American careers. "The only thing," King concluded, "is to endeavor to continue to try to do my obvious duties faithfully and let the unknown Future take care of itself." King then touched on an intimate subject that would recur throughout his life: "What I would like most of all to settle is the settlement of life with one I could love." However King's work for the Rockefellers might have been rationalized, to unfriendly critics by 1916 the "job was done, and he had the leisure afforded him as an officer of the Rockefeller Foundation to look over the irons he had in the Canadian political fire."[37] But King's private demons would not give him such perspective, and "leisure" at Kingsmere only exaccerbated his torments.

Chapter 4
Electrical Influences

During the summer of 1916 something emotionally troubling was bothering King that he did not know quite how to cope with. On June 30th he reported having had a bad night's sleep, "lying awake in fact from about 4 to 7." Then he fell asleep the next afternoon when he should have been working. He went out for some exercise, but found he then had an even worse night's sleep; he was awake this time from three until almost seven. King made up his mind to consult medical assistance: "I decided I would go and see Dr. Chevrier again, and have him examine me thoroughly." In later years those who knew King would be astonished to hear of any bouts of insomnia, and presumably they were unexpected for King too. According to one biography he slept an unusually long amount of time. Paul Martin, Sr. told me King was "always sleeping," and a private secretary reported that King could "sleep on a dime." Only at the end of King's life, in late December 1949 and when he was once again out of office, do we find Rockefeller writing King with advice about a recurrence of sleeping problems.[1]

McGregor knew of at least some of King's problems, and he went with King from Kingsmere back to Ottawa. McGregor later wrote of King that this "was a period of abnormal introspection."[2] On July 1st King had his consultation with Chevrier, who made

an examination of my spine, etc. He said I was in perfect physical health and condition. That I was simply nervously overwrought, and needed something to get my nerves quieted. He gave me a few tablets for after meals and some sleeping tablets, and said to knock off work and get my mind occupied with other things. As my worry comes mostly from not making headway with my work, I cannot do this, but I shall try and cut out worry as far as I can.

King, as well as apparently Chevrier, remained wedded to a pre-Freudian concept of "worry." In 1918 an exasperated-sounding psychoanalyst Horace W. Frink, tried to combat this sort of old-fashioned reasoning:

Worry is often spoken of as a cause of insomnia, of depression, and in fact of almost any sort of psychoneurotic state, particularly among those all too numerous non-medical writers who flood the popular magazines with shallow articles on medical subjects. "Don't worry," they glibly advise, "and then you won't have insomnia, or depression or nervousness or whatever it is you may be suffering from." They might just as well say: "Don't have insomnia, and then you'll sleep," or "Don't have depression and then you'll be cheerful." For, generally speaking, "worry" is not a *cause* of the neurotic state, but a *symptom* of it. The worry which these writers would regard as a cause of insomnia, nervousness, and so on, is really a morbid anxiety which, in common with the insomnia, depression and other symptoms in the case, results primarily from conflicts, resistances, and a damming up of the libido.[3]

As we shall see, King's libido may well have been "dammed up," or at least his doctors thought so, but he continued to think his problems arose from conflicts connected with his work. And he persisted in isolating "worry" as an independent variable despite any possible reasoning to the contrary.

King's own brother Max in his posthumously published book pointed out that "worry simply is fear that we shall fail to get what we want...Obviously if one could give up the wish, or become indifferent to the outcome worry would vanish." Max knew intimately about his brother's 1916 troubles, and in his book sought to account for "worry" in terms of morbid disappointments, or "denial of wishes." Max's reasoning was more in accord with psychoanalytic thinking than

King's own invocation of "worry" as a so-called separate entity. Max pointed out that "some people more than others find it very hard to be denied their wishes; every want assumes an exaggerated importance; consequently every disappointment is passionately acute. Such persons are chronic worriers...."[4] One can only guess whether Max might have had his older brother in mind here, although the argument he developed would certainly logically be applicable; as we shall find, Max sought an explanation for such worrying in how some mothers treat their sons.

In 1916 Mackenzie King had not been minimizing the extent of his distress. As he wrote about his seeing Dr. Chevrier, "I can well see wherein I have become almost morbid. I felt all right after this talk just as I did after the one I had three weeks ago, but better satisfied this time. I can see where very little excites me, and I must keep quiet and be regular in habits and work." (Hutchison later wrote that throughout the worst years of World War II King had "lived as regularly as a grandfather clock."[5])

We do not know what medication Chevrier prescribed, nor is it possible to find out about the consultation with Chevrier three weeks earlier; but King's immediate reaction after seeing the physician on July 1st was to be reassured. He had a good night's sleep

and felt much better today. Have made up my mind to be indifferent to things I have been worrying about, and to relax as much as possible. Spent the day, hanging pictures, putting new ones into old frames, and putting away the several articles brought from home. I found my emotions getting a little the better of me as I looked at some of these old home pictures and thought of the changes the years have brought.

King was brooding about his sister's death and his brother's illness. The diary once again stops, until July 29th King noted simply: "Father and mother arrived at Kingsmere today."

King's papers at the Public Archives contain the following statement of Chevrier's, dated July 29th; perhaps King had seen him again in Ottawa, just prior to his parents' coming to Kingsmere.

I hereby certify that I have presently under my care Hon Mackenzie King who is suffering from the incipient symptoms of a severe form of neurasthenia which have been brought on by overwork. Therefore I strongly insist that he should take a good rest for two or three months before resuming his mental activity and usual duties.

King saved this curious sort of testimonial, along, characteristically, with the bill he paid Chevrier, although it is not clear who the audience was for whom Chevrier was writing. Presumably he had in mind officers of the Rockefeller Foundation, and he probably can be assumed to have been excusing King from his responsibilities there. Chevrier was also letting King know in writing what he thought he should do with himself.

In that era the diagnosis of "neurasthenia," which the seventeenth century considered "scholar's melancholy," was an over-used category for a wide variety of upper middle-class maladies. According to one late nineteenth century authority, neurasthenic symptoms included: "General malaise, debility of all the functions, poor appetite, abiding weakness in the back and spine, fugitive neuralgic pains, hysteria, insomnia, hypochondriases, disinclination for consecutive mental labor, severe and weakening attacks of sick headache...." The precipitating events were thought to include a hereditary predisposition as well as certain immediate causes, including "the pressure of bereavement, business and family cares, parturition and abortion, sexual excesses, the abuse of stimulants and narcotics, and civilized starvation such as is sometimes observed even among the wealthy order of society, and sudden retirement from business."[6]

Neurasthenia was supposedly a consequence of tired nerves, "exhaustion of the nervous system."[7] According to its chief advocates as a diagnosis, it could also be acquired independently of any hereditary taint. Feeling anything too sensitively was supposedly a sign of neurasthenia. Lack of "nerve force"[8] was another way of accounting for this syndrome. The concept of neurasthenia was first coined by the American neurologist George Beard in 1869. This combination of "exhaustion, weakness, and diffuse bodily complaints believed to be caused by inadequate physical energy in the central nervous system" is oddly enough today "an official diagnosis in China...."[9] But neurasthenia was "expunged" from the "American psychiatric association's" system of nosology in 1980, and "it had ceased to be an acceptable professional term several decades before."[10] But the diagnostic system of the World Health Organization continued to include neurasthenia as an officially designated term.[11] (During the last generation we have had episodes of fashionability for hypoglycemia, Epstein-Barr syndrome, and chronic fatigue syndrome, each of which bears resemblances to neurasthenia.)

Freud would emphasize the special role of neurasthenic sexual factors, connected with masturbation for example, which Beard had also singled out. But Freud was "among the first to draw attention to the fact that this whole syndrome was being invoked too widely."

> He felt that the category of neurasthenia should be broken down and part of its extension be taken over by other nosographical denominations. He nonetheless held neurasthenia to be a neurosis in its own right, characterized by feelings of physical tiredness, intracranial pressure, dyspepsia, constipation, spinal paraesthesias and the impoverishment of sexual activity.[12]

Freud put neurasthenia under the heading of being an "actual neurosis," like anxiety neurosis, and sought its source in sexual discharge which was incapable of being adequately satisfied. Here is where masturbation was supposed to come into the picture. For what it is worth, around the time Freud was most intensely discussing this whole subject he privately considered himself to be neurasthenic.

As Frink, who was a leading psychiatrist and a follower of Freud, complained in 1918:

> Not very long ago practically all neurotic disturbances which on the one hand were not manifest cases of hysteria nor on the other of major psychoses, were as a rule grouped indiscriminately under the designation of Neurasthenia. Though this easy if slipshod diagnostic practice is not yet entirely done away with, even among neurologists, nevertheless most neurologists and psychiatrists now clearly recognize that what was formerly called neurasthenia really comprises several distinct disease entities differing from one another in clinical characteristics and pathological structure, and that, as applied to most, if not all of them, the term neurasthenia is a decided misnomer.[13]

Today the term "depression," or the category called "borderline," are being similarly stretched. The Freudian use of "neurosis" has been so over-extended that it has professionally been replaced by the concept "disorder." The notion of "worry" itself has long since yielded to the concept of anxiety, but in King's time those engaged in "brainwork" were viewed as particularly vulnerable to neurasthenia, a problem that was then thought to afflict both the body and the spirit.

King had been hoping to stay at Kingsmere for most of August 1916, although his diary records that he felt "obliged" to go to New York on August 4th for Foundation business, and then on the 7th he left New York for Rockefeller's summer home at Seal Harbor. King did not return back to Kingsmere until August 15th, which meant his parents had had to be there without him; he came in with them to Ottawa on the 21st, and then they left him for Toronto on the 22nd.[a] No diary entries cover the death of King's father on the 30th, although when they resume in October King is obviously preoccupied with the loss.

King did write a long, but rather impersonal, letter to his brother describing his father's death. Although the diary remains silent about King's travelling, since he did not go back to working on it until Oct. 13th, in September he had taken his widowed mother to Colorado "for a short visit" with his brother. King wrote about this trip in the course of a letter to Lieutenant Colonel William Hendrie at Camp Borden.[b] McGregor noted that when King returned to his diary-keeping in mid-October, references to the book he was trying to write are scarce. "He was occupying himself with other things, not because his doctor had so advised, but because his highly nervous state made concentration all but impossible. It was for him a dark and difficult time. A new sense of loneliness overwhelmed him...."[15] Hutchison agreed that these "years were comfortable enough but heartbreaking. The death of King's sister Isabel was followed in 1916 by that of his father. In his Ottawa apartment his mother was nearing her end. His brother was dying in Denver. The decree of lifelong loneliness had been issued."[16] One study, obviously unaware of the full nature of what was troubling King, refers to "the onset on psychosomatic illness which King experienced at this time."[17] Such loose use of terminology does little except sow further confusion.

King was clearly beset by the complicated emotions connected with his father's passing away. Freud once went so far as to say that that was "the most important event, the most poignant loss, of a man's life."[18] From Freud's point of view the child nurses hatred toward the

[a] Somehow McGregor mistakenly says that King "had yielded to local pressure...by spending the month of August 1916 with his mother and father...at a farm house near Aurora...."[14]

66

[b] Cf. Ch. 6, p.3.

parent of the same sex, which continues unconsciously; and any realistic loss necessarily reawakens fantasied guilt feelings, as the bereaved is suddenly confronted with the fulfillment of what is a necessary turning point in growing up.

King now felt for sure that "for the first time in life I had no home to go to." He felt intimately identified with his father: "Dear Father, to be like him in spirit and heart is my ambition now. To be a Christian gentlemen that was my thought as I stood beside him at the end, to be that must be my supreme endeavor from now till the close of my life." King felt reassured by how close they had been able to be at the end. Among other chores King had to clear up parts of his father's estate. King must have been worried about who would now take care of his mother, and how the means would be secured. King concluded his Oct. 14th entry with some renewed concerns about himself: "I have been troubled a good deal today with the nervous irritation from which I have been suffering, but am determined to conquer it if I can. But for the nervousness I should be better than I have been for many years. I am striving hard to make every hour count and to [be] noble in all things."

The next day King tried to go about his business; he was interested in who was going to win the American presidential election in November, and also explored with a friend the prospects for the European war and the Canadian government. King noted, however, that during the day he had become "very restless with the nervousness I suffer from and had to lie down for a while...." He concluded that day's entry with concerns about himself: "This nervousness is a terrible affliction and I hardly know how to conquer it, but shall persist."

On Oct. 16th he reported that an Italian sculptor had "written suggesting a bust of mother in marble. I fear I cannot resist it. After all she and father are more to me than all else, why should I not preserve as far as I may be [able] all the inspiration of their lives." King would shortly be mentioning the matter of the bust in an interview with Meyer, and he wrote about it later to his mother.

King continued to process familiar items of business in his study, although a mysterious issue comes up in his Oct. 17th diary. King regularly courted a succession of more or less eligible lady friends, and he mentioned here a Miss Florence Lynch, "a very sweet, natural and beautiful girl, an Irish beauty – but delicate I fear." She was going to New York the next day, and he wanted to thank her for a letter he had received. He referred to her as having read him "a little verse she had written on the bronze 'Visions' I have." From the context it would appear that he had a bronze statue called "Visions"; there seems to be no way of knowing more about it, except that it has to be tantalizing to what extent he revealed to acquaintances his mystical side. He thought he appeared "to be making a little headway in conquering my nervousness, out of this weakness must come strength." Religiously devout people still today look for hidden purposes behind the worst setbacks.

In going through his father's papers King was reminded exactly what kind of a financial struggle his father had had "and how he lived ever on the margin." John King had allowed his elder son to assist him, and his affairs brightened. But then the glaucoma made him slowly go blind. King's view of the relationship of the mind to the body was such that in commenting on how much his father "must have suffered from this long weary financial strain," he felt he could be "quite certain" in attributing the blindness to it. As late as 1925 a prominent Freudian would be looking for the psychological components in myopia,[19] and he was not so professionally in left field as to be laughed at for his conjecturing.

King's own problems were recurrently evident in his diary; on Oct. 19th he had written: "Re nervousness I maintain a sort of armed neutrality or running fire, trying to conquer or subdue." In straightening out his father's financial affairs, King was anticipating that it might not be long before he had to perform the same chore for his mother. He had started doing some exercises in the morning which he had "kept up most of last year but dropped this spring & summer." On the 22nd he included the diary comment: "My nervousness has troubled me a great deal today." Nevertheless King thought he was "better than I was when I reached here."

The next day King got a wire from Rockefeller asking him to come to New York for "a conference." Within hours King left on an overnight train. When he saw Rockefeller, it turned out that one of the trustees thought that King's report on industrial relations for the annual statement on behalf of the Foundation had been too concerned with problems in Colorado, and both King and Rockefeller agreed that it would be better under the circumstances not to risk stirring up unnecessarily that potential hornet's nest. It would not be surprising if King were more dissatisfied than ever with the state of his work.

When Rockefeller asked King how he was, he had "told him that

I had suffered a great deal from nervousness and was going to consult a specialist." King had in mind a physician in Cleveland who had written a book King had just finished reading. Rockefeller wondered why King did not go to a New York specialist; King said he feared the cost if it were known he came from the Foundation. Rockefeller though thought that that connection of King's would work just the opposite, and asked King's permission to speak with Dr. Simon Flexner. Flexner was then head of the Rockefeller Institute for Medical Research, first founded in 1901. Flexner promptly spoke to King, learned the nature of his troubles, and after speaking with Rockefeller advised King to consult Dr. Lewellys Franklin Barker at Johns Hopkins in Baltimore.

Flexner telegraphed Barker for the appointment, saying to King "it would not be expensive." King wrote that Rockefeller told him that

> Barker was the best man on the continent [and] not to be troubled about myself. He spoke of the strain Colorado had been and said he knew I felt the responsibility of it. He then spoke of his own examination for stomach trouble, & how it had been cured by expert examination. He could not have been kinder or more tender. He has just gone through the effects of strain himself and knows the nature of it.

King had hardly been secretive about his difficulties, but he overcame his natural hesitations.

> I feel I have done the wise thing in putting myself in the hands of this group here. They are the best men in America and true friends, and whilst I should prefer greater privacy I feel my work has suffered because of my physical condition, and it is well to have some one in whom the group has confidence. What the nature of the result of the Doctor's investigation may be I cannot say. I imagine it will resolve itself into need of rest & change. What will do me most good is to have an expert go over me from head to foot, and let me understand my own condition. This nervous trouble has lasted about a year now and has run along far too long. It will take time I am sure to cure.

King's general hypochondriacal predilections were observed by many, and seem to be consistent with his vanity and self-involvement.

There was no reason for King, or any other Canadian non-medical person, to know anything beforehand about Barker (1867-1943). But he was a known authority in neurology, heredity, and eugenics, who had been born and educated in Canada. He had first gone to Baltimore in 1891, and was to serve on William Osler's medical staff; Barker also held various positions at the medical school. After five years as an anatomy professor at the Rush Medical College in Chicago, Barker returned to Johns Hopkins to succeed Osler as Professor of Medicine and Physician-in-Chief at the hospital. Barker had retired from active academic life in 1913, on the grounds that it should be a full-time pursuit, and instead conducted his private practice. In 1916 Barker was President of the American Neurological Association. In 1910 Ernest Jones, later Freud's biographer, had reported that Barker was "very sympathetic."[20] King was to stay in touch with Barker for the rest of his life.

In 1909 Barker had written a text called *The Nervous System and Its Constituent Neurones*.[21] In a 1940 book *Psychotherapy* Barker wrote that he had himself "systematically made use of it in hospital and private practice for more than thirty years." He was still using the concept of neurasthenia, defined as "a functional neurosis characterized by irritable weakness, fatigability, and various mental and physical incapacities." But Barker was an outspoken follower of Meyer's, who Barker said "thinks of the individual as a whole, as a psychobiological unit, as a personality, recognizing that the physical body and its functions, including those called 'mental,' belong inseparably together."[22]

Although it was known among some of King's private secretaries who I saw that Barker was a medical authority King continued to turn to, no one in Ottawa ever seemed to realize that Barker was a neurologist. It would be Barker who in turn suggested that King contact Adolf Meyer. McGregor knew of King's going to Barker, and mentioned it in his book; but even though McGregor was writing in 1962, he does not seem to have grasped the nature of Barker's specialty. All McGregor said was that "within two days" of Flexner's recommendation King was "a patient under Dr. Barker's care. For two weeks the treatment continued, the most thoroughgoing examination imaginable, by as many as a dozen specialists. It was a satisfying experience, which gave needed rest and a chance for good counsel."[23]

King's appointment with Barker was set for the 26th, but Flexner had written Barker about King ahead of time on the 25th:

> He has apparently had 2 or 3 hard shocks of a private nature,
> such as sudden deaths, etc. in his family, and is pretty nervous
> and upset. He has himself on his mind a great deal more than
> is good for him and feels that he is thoroughly out of sorts. He
> has consulted already a number of Canadian doctors, I think
> one in Ottawa and one at Toronto, and what he now needs is
> to be set up by an authoritative person whom he will trust
> implicitly and whose directions he will carry out without
> feeling that he must still get other advice. In talking over his
> case with him, I was confident that you are the person to do the
> trick for him. Enough said.

King's father's death had certainly been sudden in that King had just
moved his parents into a new apartment. One might question whether
Flexner was communicating enough of the emotional conflicts that
were bothering King, but as a physician may have trusted Barker to
find out what he needed to know on his own. Yet those acquainted
with King in later years would emphatically agree with Flexner that
King continued to have "himself on his mind a great deal more than is
good for him...."

Even while King wrote up his diary before he arrived at Baltimore
on the 26th, he noted "experiencing at odd moments effects of
nervous trouble." King prepared himself for seeing Barker by putting
together a "series of notes to present to Dr. Barker, in outlining genesis
of my nervous trouble. The nervous strain of the past, symptoms, etc."
King also took himself for an hour's motor ride to see the sights of
Baltimore.

When King called at 3:00 at Barker's, King was immediately
impressed and as pleased as he could be. "He seemed to me as soon
as I saw him my ideal of a physician, a man of fine spiritual cast of
countenance, sympathetic, calm & confident manner, a specimen of
perfect manhood in appearance." Such an idealized reaction to a
therapist would later be taken to be a sign of "narcissism" in a political
leader.[24] Barker told King

> he was born in Canada, Oxford County, school at Whitby,
> University of Toronto, knew both father and grandfather by
> name and reputation. I gave him a full account of my case and

he took down everything minutely. Then he gave me a thorough physical examination, dictating to a stenographer on the other side of a screen all details.

In his 1940 text Barker had reported that in his practice "the patient is asked to undress completely, in order that a thorough general physical examination may be made. The physician then dictates to his secretary his findings."[25]

Barker, according to King, straight-forwardly addressed himself to King's "nervous" symptoms: "He told me the feelings I had and described, while they might be real as a sensation, were an absolute hallucination, so far as being caused by or having the effects I believed." According to the turn-of-the-century playwrite, Arthur Schnitzler, who was also a physician, Freud's teacher Theodor Meynert similarly "tried to convince patients with delusions that they could not possibly have them."[26] The term "hallucination" could be used by Barker in 1916 rather more loosely than would be the case today, but it would still refer to sensory experiences not based on any existing physical phenomena.

Instead of King's being alarmed at the term "hallucination" he felt reassured, and in terms of King's prognosis this was a good sign; he was able to distance himself from his problem. King had told Barker that even during the office examination he was having those "feelings." Barker "gave me the most positive assurance, and my mind has been much rested since. The examination must have taken 2 1/2 hours." Barker gave King letters to six Hopkins doctors, with the instructions to "speak frankly" to two of them. (Meyer was one; Jones had somehow written Freud that Meyer "bores me."[27]) King records Barker's concern over the nerve of a tooth, and that Barker thought King was twenty-five pounds over-weight.

King was "delighted" with Barker's whole method of examination. "It is something I have wanted for years, a physical examination in minute detail. Evidently Dr. Flexner, who wrote as well as wired, had said that Mr. R. wanted a thorough examinat'n made, and I have no doubt has intimated he will stand behind it financially, or partially so. This was the significance of Dr. Flexner's remark, that it wd. not be expensive."

King was to receive V. I. P. treatment throughout his encounter at Johns Hopkins. Other public figures have similarly benefited from their prior political service in their psychiatric encounters. King not only felt reassured about Barker's manner toward him, but obviously took special reassurance about what the costs were going to be, and as a result he had complete confidence in Barker.

> I came back from Barker's and knelt down and thanked God for the answer to my prayer, to find a means of freeing me from this nervous fear, and for Mr. Rockefeller as a friend. I also felt that father & Bell [his dead sister] were watching over and helping to protect me and to bring this about. My mind is greatly relieved tonight. It has been a sad torment for a long while past.

After Barker's initial examination on the 26th of October, 1916, he had written to Adolf Meyer about King. Both Barker and Meyer served together on the National Committee for Mental Health, and in 1943 Meyer, who outlived Barker, would publish an obituary.[28] In 1916 Barker had inquired about King: "Would you please give me your opinion on the mental state in Hon. Mackenzie King of the Rockefeller Foundation? It is a very interesting case. The principle subjective disturbance is that of being influenced electrically by others and of influencing others in this way." (Future historians will not have the advantage of such written evidence of letter-writing within the same North American city.)

One has to assume that Barker's idea of the "principle subjective disturbance" matches what King had been describing as his "feelings" which he said that Barker regarded as "an absolute hallucination." By the period of World War I the symptom of electrical influence was not that uncommon. In 1910 Jones, a neurologist, had reported to Freud an obsessive compulsive "case of a young man who *believes* unshakeably that he generates electricity, that he can transfer his thoughts to other people at any distance, etc."[29] Symptoms come and go over time, and for example nobody has satisfactorily explained why the cases of "hysteria" reported around the turn of the twentieth century have later become so rare. The philosopher Immanuel Kant (1724-1804), also a bachelor, had developed strange delusions about electricity, to which he attributed headaches. When Barker was writing to Meyer, he seems to have assumed that Meyer might know something about King's public activities: "He has been and is a man of great energy, as you know." Barker specifically told Meyer that "before presenting a bill in this case please consult with me."

It is not easy to be too confident about this electrical symptom of King's. On the one hand the earlier diagnosis of neurasthenia would indicate at least one physician's confidence that King was not off-his-rocker: "neurasthenia...was torn directly from the fabric of nervous illness and was not supposed to connote madness of any kind...Neurasthenia, with its emphasis on physical symptoms, became a favored diagnosis among the psychically distressed middle classes."[30] Involuntary sexual abstinence would be a common enough explanation.

When Barker called King "a very interesting case," Barker must have been unsure himself what to make of King. Electricity was the wonder phenomenon of the nineteenth century. In 1843 Emil Du Bois-Reymond had demonstrated that electricity and not some supernatural life force travels through the nervous system. Electrical massage had become a common therapeutic tool for treating hysteria. In someone who was inhibited, these feelings of electrical influence might have been a substitute for ordinary impulses and a sign of excitement.

On the other hand delusions of reference, including convictions about electricity as well as telepathy, were considered around World War I among the origins of schizophrenia.[31] The great psychiatrist Emil Kraepelin had written at the time about "ideas of reference" in what was then called paraphrenia, or alternatively dementia praecox. He observed in such cases "the idea, which occurs not infrequently, of hypnotic, magnetic, electrical influences" associated with the "transmission of currents." Kraepelin wrote about such patients who "feel themselves 'influenced by magic power,' 'governed by invisible power.'"[32]

In a paper Meyer read in 1921, "Constructive Formulation of Schizophrenia," he was cautious, although he did single out as a "schizophrenic reaction" both "delusions of reference and persecution." He was talking about "hallucinations" connected with "influence and passivity of feelings as expressed in automatism, mind-reading, electrical influence and similar phenomena." It was characteristic of Meyer that he maintained that "under no circumstances do we consider the mere formal material adequate for a prognostic forecast without a survey of all the dynamic or causal factors and a thorough trial of the responsiveness of the patient to a distributive, analytic and reconstructive study." For Meyer the "making of a prognosis depends upon the formulation of all the factors at work, the reactions present, and the response to one's effort at adjustment."[33] Barker would have anticipated that Meyer note carefully any schizophrenic-like symptoms accompanying a depressed state. For Meyer such symptoms might or might not have diagnostic and prognostic implications, depending on how they fit into the remainder of the clinical picture.

Sensations attributed to external influences and characterized as "electrical" were often connected in that period with patients who were called schizophrenic. Phyllis Greenacre, a psychiatrist working at Johns Hopkins during World War I and someone who later became a famous psychoanalyst, published a piece in 1918 on "The Content of the Schizophrenic Characteristics Occurring in Affective Disorders," which preceded Meyer in this area and he readily acknowledged her pioneering work. She thought that "the sensations of electrical influence...are almost uniformly poorly appreciated, erotic sensations and about equally frequent in elations and depressions. The ambivalence of power expressed in the patient's belief that he can exert as well as feel influence, send as well as receive messages, etc., occurs oftener in the excitements." For we who know of King's much later development into an active spiritualist, it is striking how Greenacre predicted that such "sensations of electrical currents" in depressive states can be "related frequently to the type of mystical cravings and credulity which moves people to consult spiritualists, and ouija boards, or seek outlets in theosophy and occultism."[34]

Barker himself did not draw such a daringly accurate conclusion about King himself. He noted after his physical examination that King had "a slight fine tremor, little more in left than right"; in later years King's occasional nervousness would express itself in his hands shaking so that he could not do things. Barker also observed that King's "left testis appears to be divided into two parts; had slight accident but this division always there." (Another physician commented on King's having a small testicular cyst.) Barker also also observed in King "ideas of reference (electrical influences) - sensitiveness, obesity, pathological emotivity, hallucinations of perineal sense."

The last symptom, even more than the first, is especially puzzling. Patients nowadays, unlike World War I cases, are apt to experience rays from outer space rather than electrical currents. But no medical historians I have consulted can be confident on the issue of what could have been meant by "hallucinations of perineal sense." The perineum is of course located between the scrotum and the anus. "Hallucinations of perineal sense" might imply that King thought he gave off a smell, and/or that he experienced tingling sensations at the anus. Hutchison later noted that at Kingsmere "on the wall of his bathroom he hung a disagreeable placard advising his guests how to keep their bowels in order."[35] Depressed people do overly worry about defecation. As when King saw Chevrier, King was more than a little concerned about the state of the base of his spine; and spinal "irritation" was associated with neurasthenia. Even though Barker was not eager for it King would have himself x-rayed there in order to rule out possible trouble.

There is going to be a certain repetitiousness in Barker's material about King, since he wrote more than one version of his patient for different purposes. It is well, however, to keep in mind all that Barker does put down, since it is an outside perspective which serves as an objective check on what we will come upon in King's diary. Barker commented about King:

> He is troubled with insomnia at times. Has always been emotional. Has seen several physicians. He is well oriented as to time and place. He says he is not sick and if it were not for this worry, he would be the healthiest man alive, could not be in better physical shape. Without this trouble, he would have the power of a giant and could tackle anything going. He is not sad to any extent but this thing makes him depressed. Recently, the death of father caused sadness. A brother about the same time contracted tuberculosis. Has no fears.

The reference to King being "well oriented as to time and place" must have been a way of being sure the reader did not get unduly alarmed as to the severity of King's psychological problems. (In keeping with the diagnostic profile that Greenacre's work outlined, in 1941 Gregory Zilboorg, a famous psychoanalytic psychiatrist, published a well-known article on "Ambulatory Schizophrenias" which maintained of such people that "while having a number of acquaintances, they have almost no intimate friends."[36]) It would appear from Barker's notes that "this thing" making King depressed was the "worry," presumably about electrical influences, which he could not seem to shake. "Has no fears" probably means that King was not inclined to think he himself was in danger of getting his brother's illness.

Although it means jumping ahead a few days in the narrative of the story, it is worth pointing out that King would be admitted to the hospital at Johns Hopkins on Oct. 30th, and was discharged on November 11th. (Harold Lasswell in his 1930 *Psychopathology and Politics* had predicted the future significance of hospital records on political leaders.[37]) The hospital diagnosis was given as "Psychoneurosis: Psychasthenia: Pyorrhoea alveolaris: Chronic sinusitis: Pityriasis rosea."

The first terms are distinctly psychological. "Psychoneurosis" was a Freudian term implying the existence of a sexual conflict. "Psychasthenia" was a concept that had been forwarded by the once prominent French neurologist Pierre Janet; he tried to distinguish between two principal categories of the psychoneuroses: hysteria and psychasthenia, which included phobias and obsessions.[38] "Psychasthenia" lost its terminological popularity by the 1920s, but under it Janet had "grouped symptoms such as phobias, depressions, and obsessions, fixed ideas and irrational fears, and impulsive and compulsive behaviors."[39] It was a concept so broad as to be short-lived in use, and neither "psychoneurosis" nor "psychasthenia" would still be employed today.

The abstract of the various comments by King's physicians is more humanly telling than any of the particular labels. Barker had observed:

> Pt. [patient] a member of a distinguished Canadian family. Has done construction [sic] work in the labor legislation in Canada and recently in this country. He is in good physical condition but has peculiar ideas in regard to his own person and other people. Has the idea that other people are influencing him by electric currents.

As we know from Barker's letter to Meyer, King thought he could influence others electrically as well.

> He is of a very sensitive nature; deeply religious and leads a strenuous political life. At present, is writing a book. Has fear that his present work may militate against political success in Canada. Has sensations referred to the perineal region. Has always been emotional and troubled with insomnia. Has seen

a number of physicians. Well oriented as to time and place. Does not feel sick. Is only disturbed by worry and feels if freed of this, he would have the power of a giant, and could undertake anything. Inclined to be a little depressed over this. Death of his father and illness of a brother who has tbc. have inc. [increased] this feeling. Has no fear.

By now this picture of King should sound like the man we have come to know.

According to King's diary, on Oct. 27th he had underwent a battery of medical tests,

> the kind of day I have wished for, for a long time, a day that I could have my system examined from the hair of my head to the soles of my feet; everything tested, everything sounded and tried, that if there be a weak spot anywhere it may be discovered and made right if possible.

Blood and urine samples were taken first, and proved fully normal. Then King's skin was studied; a rash was so minor that King and the dermatologist ended up talking about American presidential politics. An internist then checked King's "vital organs." King talked to him "about the depression I have felt at times and he said some of the things of which I spoke were simply an hallucination and impossible so far as physicians knew, they were due to morbid feelings which might be occasioned by strain." Presumably this "hallucination" had to do with the ideas about electrical influence which King had already discussed with Barker. King also talked about the world war with the internist. Next King saw a throat, eyes, and nose specialist, who recommended an x-ray of the head; King claimed that he could "feel the electric sparks on the back of my head as the rays were shot through the skull onto a plate beneath." King's tonsils were deemed "ragged." And the dentist thought King's gums needed treating.

King also reported having had on the 27th "a long interview with Dr. Adolph [sic] Meyer, Specialist in Mental Hygiene at Johns Hopins Univ."

> I outlined to him the strain I have had, the worries and morbid symptoms etc. I found him an exceedingly helpful man to talk with, understanding, sympathetic. I outlined the conflict in my

thoughts between spiritual aspirations and material struggles & conflicts, the fight with myself. This he explained was unnecessary and wrong, that all the phenomena I had described to him were natural enough, the circumstances mentioned being considered that what was health, I was mistaking for an evil passion.

It sounds as if Meyer might have been alluding to King's sexual side, possibly masturbation or nocturnal emissions.

In contrast to what King had been doing, Meyer "advised my enjoying more society and not withdrawing...." Meyer also recommended

> care as to the food for the mind as well as the body. He was particularly understanding and helpful with respect to my work and attitude toward the Rockefeller Foundat'n in it. Told me at all costs to maintain my independence of thought, and not to be concerned about the Foundation getting its full worth of my time etc. He told me to become calm as respects the internal conflict I had described, and then proceed "like a sun on its course" regardless of other men, or their views. To be myself. He was very strong on this, also on my preserving my idealism.

Evidently Meyer had tried to reassure King about the naturalness of his needs. A urologist who had examined King at the same time reported a condition "frequently found in continent males," and no treatment was advised.

King was clearly pleased with Meyer. Although Meyer did not specifically make the point to King, we now know that Meyer himself got very little sleep.[40] King commented:

> I felt this man had a soul which could understand mine. That he too was a man with ideals and could understand the ideal. He told me he had been having much the same problems with his work and the University, that he understood thoroughly. I told him my point of view on the Labour problem. He said that he was glad it was that. Before I came away I spoke of the saddness [sic] of the world in Europe, that he and I were helping each other as brothers in a common purpose of

uplifting mankind, both of us were moved a little, but said little. He, of course, is a German.

Meyer spoke with a strong Swiss-German accent, but was still Swiss, not German.

> As I left him he shook hands with me twice. Spoke of the pleasure it was to meet me, said he hoped we might meet again and that he could expect great things of me. This was one of the really important interviews of my life. A talk with a man of like ideals but with a profounder knowledge of life. It was easy to speak to him of the best that is in me.

King thought the 27th had been as a day "a truly remarkable one, but worth if needs be a month's, yes a year's salary." King must have surmised that he was not going to have to pay much if anything for this medical help, and that Rockefeller would take care of most if not all the expenses. Johns Hopkins people had helped set up the Rockefeller medical institute early in the century, and in 1916 Rockefeller money went toward establishing the school of public health at Hopkins. Philanthropic links between the Rockefellers and the medical school would continue. So King's musings about how much the medical assistance he got would be "worth" has to sound a bit hypocritical.

King could report "all day" having "been comparatively free of the feelings I had entertained before the talk with Dr. Barker." Once his mind had been set "right," it seemed logical that such feelings "vanish." By the end of the day King could conclude: "My mind is greatly relieved tonight, and I feel this visit to have been one of the providential events of my life. I had come to the point where I thought my work for the future would be undermined by this nervous dread. Now I believe it will be greater than ever before."

Meyer wrote Barker about King:

> My Dear Barker:
>
> The problem of our patient seems to be distributed about as follows: first, a perfectly obvious elimination of natural sex life from the intensely religious and spiritual trend of affection, which only once became focused away from his mother on a nurse, unfortunately without response on her part; second,

the strain from illness and deaths in the family, which, however, is now letting up; third, a most intense feeling of responsibility and also a feeling of jeopardizing his own position politically.

It sounds like Meyer had the story wrong about Mathilde Grossert's (the Chicago nurse) lack of "response" to King, but of course he had then only met King once, and may have been misled by what King told him.

Obviously, more needs to be understood about King's mother, and later* we will examine some letters between King and her during this period. Violet Markham, an English friend who never met King's mother, wrote in 1956 that "in the jargon of the psychiatrists, it is undeniable that the mother-complex was a misfortune" for King. Violet Markham felt that as the years passed King's natural reserve led him into becoming a recluse, and that he was "often open to the reproach of using words to conceal his thoughts." And she added: "I sometimes thought his personality might be likened to a set of those Chinese boxes which fit so surprisingly into each other, each box different in size and color and yet making a perfect whole."[41]

Once again we have come across a lay-person using Freudian categories to help account for King. I think Violet Markham's imagery of Chinese boxes more expressive than her appeal to the concept of a "mother-complex," but it is undeniable that one longs for more material about Isabel Grace King. On the one hand she seems to have been a powerful force within the family, and certain letters indicate she was the most telling in her opposition to his proposed involvement with Mathilde Grossert. A nurse would inevitably, to King's mother, come from the wrong side of the social tracks, and be a bitter disappointment to the plans and hopes King's family had placed in him. If King's mother was behaving selfishly, it would not be the first time a mother had sought to interfere with the romantic ambitions of her first-born son.

King's brother may have been alluding to Isabel when he wrote in his 1922 book: "familiar to everybody is the type of mother (and we all love her) whose maternal instinct produces feelings which quite outweigh reason." Although such mother-son relations might appear "very beautiful," King's brother thought the results of such maternal over-protection were "unnatural, unhealthy, and circumscribing...." The problem of "worry," Mackenzie King's complaint, was traced by

Macdougall King to the "fear that we shall fail to get what we want." If one could abandon such wishes, those worries would evaporate. But "some people more than others find it hard to be denied their wishes; every want assumes an exaggerated importance; consequently every disappointment is proportionately acute."[42]

Macdougall King's explanation for "chronic worriers", like his brother, rested on how mothers can evoke in sons a vulnerability to disappointment because too few of their childhood wishes had been turned aside. Macdougall King did not link such maternal excess to how women might, out of difficulties with their husbands, have unrealistic expectations of their sons as a form of compensation. At least one of Mackenzie King's private secretaries told me King had had to defend himself against a very real dominating influence of his mother. It is impossible to know whether Mackenzie King noticed any of these allusions to his own problems in his brother's posthumously published text. In his Introduction to the book Mackenzie King recurred to his own concern about not having served in World War I; Macdougall King, his older brother pointed out, had been in the South African War, but "because of his illness, my brother had been deprived of all possibility of active service in the Great War."[43] (Macdougall had been 35 years old when he contracted tuberculosis in 1913, but he also had a wife and twin sons.)

In 1916 Meyer had not done more than touch on King's "mother-complex."[44] He did not hesitate though to give King explicit advice, about the Rockefeller Foundation for example.

> I was very emphatic in reassuring him that he must take for granted that the organization cannot want anything but the best according to the agreement and that he must consider himself the only judge of fairness and justice of his position (naturally under the guidance of a consensus of opinion of the men in whom he has the greatest personal confidence.)

Meyer had started off by first itemizing the problem of King's sex life, then proceeded to the illnesses and losses in the family, and thirdly come to his professional and political troubles. A fourth set of issues surrounded King's "utterly unhygienic arrangement of life, partly due to his patholog. feelings and partly due to his excessive feeling of obligation and the suspicion that he had been asked to make a report to test his faithfulness to the work." King had made a good over-all impression on Meyer, who thought: "He is certainly an unusually fine man and I shall consider it a pleasure to waive all charges and feel sufficiently repaid for contact with one who is undoubtedly one of the greatest promoters of a greater harmonization of the classes of humanity."

Although Meyer was, as we have discussed, never a disciple of Freud's, Meyer did pick up immediately on the sexual theme in King's presenting clinical material. One has to assume that Meyer's letter to Barker was centrally addressed to what Barker had called "the principle subjective disturbance...of being influenced electrically by others and of influencing others in this way." It had been Freud who was then maintaining, as recently as his 1909 Clark lectures at Worcester, that "pathological symptoms constitute a portion of the subject's sexual life or even the whole of his sexual life...."[45] Even if few Freudian psychoanalysts would speak that way nowadays, and sexual conflicts be today put within a larger human context, Meyer's interest in early psychoanalysis helped lead him to conclude from King's interview that sexuality had to rank first in a list of the clinical problems he presented. Unlike so many Freudians then and now, however, Meyer had been respectful of King's idealism and religiosity.

Meyer's version of King got communicated in a variety of ways; for in addition to King's direct dealings with Meyer, as we shall see King himself got to read his own records at Johns Hopkins. The hospital extract of Meyer's views was consistent with the theme of toleration of King's instinctual needs which Meyer had tried to encourage: for Meyer like Flexner was recommending that King "needs to be for a time within reach of helpful arbiter before whom he can put his impressions and reactions. He needs a broader philosophy and an appreciation of what enters into his life and a more placid acceptance of himself, esp. of the parts he has been trying to eliminate."

Particularly interesting are some notes which Meyer kept for himself about King. (In 1912 Freud advised against such note-taking as a clinical distraction and interference.) The likelihood seems to be that Meyer jotted down these notes in King's presence, and Meyer was an advocate of the significance of old-fashioned good case-history taking. Unfortunately not all Meyer's remarks are decipherable, since he had a short-hand system for himself which has proven impossible completely to reconstruct now; even the best efforts have produced some abstruse passages. Although we cannot hope to be privy to the full range of the human emotions involved in the interaction between

King and Meyer, it is nonetheless highly unusual to have a therapist's outlook to double-check an account left to us by a patient. Meyer's notes consist of a series of paragraphs making up six short pages. I will do my best to comment on each of them in turn. Parentheses have been added to clarify Meyer's meaning; dots indicate where it has been impossible to make any sense whatever of Meyer's short-hand.

> Mr. Mackenzie King
> Travelling F(ellow)ship abroad
> 8 yrs at Ottawa - deputy minister.
> Contested a seat in Parliament - then
> Min. (ister) of labor at 33.
> Reciprocity campaign threw out his party 1911
> then months of phy(sical) exhaustion rather
> than a drep.(ession)....
> In the morning tired: rheum.(atism) and lumbago.
> Also a certain depr.(ession). Declined responsibilities.
> Another campaign; then depr.(ession)...ease up....

"Another campaign" presumably refers to the Ontario provincial election. So far Meyer's account will seem pretty consistent with what we have already come across, although he touches on the depressed moods more that one might have expected.

> As member...tells the good upper classes...1912...
> pressure due to financial obligation.
> Fa(ther) prof.(essor) of law, criminal and civil. His sight
> began to fail,
> glaucoma, last year and earlier. Writer.
> Emeritus and Addit.(ional) responsibilities.
> Older sister with her trouble died in spring 1915.
> And this summer his parents went with him. His father died
> suddenly
> in Montreal...Aug. 30, 1916.

Outside of Meyer having mixed up Montreal with Toronto, where John King died, Meyer seems to have understood the basic precipitating events of King's troubles.

> Distinctly relig.(ious) th(ough)t.

About Easter...To the Foundation like the
honor of confidence. Against writing the report; quite a strain.

Once again although Meyer's jottings are cryptic they sound
confirmatory of what we already know.

And then come some passages which, as far as I can tell, make little
sense other than to alert us to the existence in King of affective
symptomatology even more mysterious sounding about his feelings
than anything we have come across.

That time the following: that it was noticeable by others
that it was pleasing to others in the...phase of returning
vitality...
like the eyes as if it came from my body as I could go into
the room that...could teach this to some individual perhaps to
some...Thought it was meant to become more than a crashing
failure. This spells his...short...if not properly rested.
Later the future times the reached reaction nor any
hope...when
not more within next month...
Sometimes...twelve years ago...it was very strong...Happy
lately.
Little
to know...it happened and what followed from diary.

Obviously an essential problem here has to do with understanding
Meyer's elliptical short-hand; my hunch is that he was alluding in part
to King's own account of those feelings of electrical influence. The
mention of "returning vitality" might also imply in King the presence
of what we now know as cyclothemia, or mild manic depressive
illness, a problem considered then and today as predominantly
hereditary. Meyer's interest in biology was combined with his concern
for the environmental stresses King had encountered, which makes
Meyer's approach seem up-to-date. Even with contemporaries
mystery is inevitable, so in all historical inquiry it is essential to
acknowledge that there are aspects to the past which are bound to be
beyond our ken; but it is frustrating that Meyer's version of things
remains so tantalizingly incomplete. At least it sounds as if King had
mentioned his diary to Meyer as a possible source of evidence.

Even when Meyer's notes seem at their most incomprehensible

other passages show up which sound right on the mark.

> Mother, 74, never too strong. Always a matter of anxiety.

> 1914 industrial relations work.
> Oct. 15...R(ockefeller) very happy with me and was very nice.
>   It is in response
> November 15 at the exposition.
> Then in the crowd the following
> urgent in the body above his sex organ arrested coming back
> my vitality coming back again.
> 2 months later is not to give the book and no more making
> Sometimes for anybody...sometimes
> a play just the sort of tingling sensation.
> Sent book to...writing on industry the humanity
> Very strong following all R(ockefeller) F(oundation). It may...
>   someday.
> Very much keyed up (hands) from 1915 with sl.(ight) feeling
> of
>   tingling.
> Cut out telephone don't go out evenings;   spent time with
> Jane....

As I read through these hard-to-decipher jottings, I hypothesize that King may have been saying something to the effect that he was planning to give his manuscript for a book another couple of months, otherwise give up the project – but I am uncertain whether that would be an accurate way of rendering Meyer's meaning.

Thankfully Meyer went back to writing longhand, giving up his special way of telescoping King's interview. Perhaps it is significant that this change took place at the mention of sexuality. In accord with what we know about Meyer's operating principles at that point, I would guess that he tactfully asked King about his first sexual experiences. Thanks to the influence of the writings of Richard von Krafft-Ebing at the time "patients were being asked...to recall their first experiences"[46] with sex.

> First sex(ual) exp.(erience) very vivid. A girl touch(ed)
> him and spoke of her fa(ther) or some other adult to him
> when he was 4 or 5 y(ear)s old.

Then contact with the talk of servants.
At college 2 or 3 expeditions.
None during the last 6 y(ea)rs.

The word "expeditions" might refer to those presumed contacts with
prostitutes that Stacey, on the evidence of the diaries, made so much
of. Of course even if that had been King's intention to communicate
to Meyer, it still does not necessarily prove what actually happened;
King might conceivably have wanted to impress Meyer with such
manly-sounding tales. On the other hand King's diaries from the 1890s
do seem to imply his contact with street-walkers; for instance it is hard
to know what else he could have meant by his getting "into another
trap" which "cost him" a dollar at a time when he was describing "a
fierce war of flesh and spirit."[47] There would seem, however, to have
been an odd chronological gap in King's saying that there had been no
further "expeditions" during "the last six years," since King had
graduated from the University of Toronto in 1896, still leaving a period
of fourteen years unaccounted for.

King had brought up with Meyer the Chicago nurse, Mathilde
Grossert:

> Huge affection for a grandniece of Schiller's
> who was his nurse during typhoid and called
> him "Das Kind." He returned to Chicago
> to see her but she w(oul)d not see him and he
> learned she was engaged to a cousin and
> she is now settled in M(arylan)d.

(The rules of middle-class courtship were very different in 1916 from
now, just as it would be anachronistic to be too confident about
anyone's sexual practices then; conceptions of privacy keep changing
in different eras.) As we shall see, King would soon go to visit Mathilde
Grossert and her husband. Meyer's notes went on, as presumably
King had, from his nurse to his mother:

> Interesting attempt to get a silver bust,
> and desire to get a bust of his mother.
> Then "I know I have to get married
> if I find a suitable wife" – reassured
> against!

This exclamation point of Meyer's seems most telling, especially since King never alluded in his diary or elsewhere to having been given any such advice. Meyer sounds reasonably confident that King, despite his symptoms, was pretty O.K. But Meyer was cautious enough not to be entirely sure what he might have on his hands, and although with a young neurotic it might make sense to try and encourage marriage and the release of repressions, with someone of King's years such a leap might risk overthrowing the equilibrium of which he was capable. Bleuler had argued that "under all circumstances, if the disease [dementia praecox] is diagnosed or suspected, marriage must be discouraged with the greatest emphasis."[48] McGregor, as a layman, could allow himself to be more conventional: "What a different person he might have been, how much less egocentric, had he become a husband and father!"[49] McGregor's exclamation point makes an interesting contrast to that of Meyer, who was trying his best to rule out any further upheavals in King's life.

McGregor's approach also can be taken to imply that he did not think one could draw a firm line between the public and the private King. At the same time McGregor was continuing King's perpetual day-dream that matrimony could be a realistic prospect. King's idealized self-image was that of a married man with a family. This middle class norm seems so much a part of the literature about King that one might think there was no possibility of an unhappy marriage, or political success being founded on private unhappiness. Despite what McGregor, following King, had written, King was widely known for his "bachelor fussiness and uncertainty."[50]

The literature about King draws, in connection with his struggles over sexuality and the possible contact with prostitutes, a parallel with the British liberal William Gladstone, one of King's heroes, who it turns out also frequented street-walkers.[51] Perhaps Gladstone and King both shared in their minds the intention of reforming the whores. But King had to be psychologically different if only in that Gladstone had a wife and children.

In his notes to himself Meyer reported his own

Advice to adjust himself without deep
modifications such as immed.(iate) marriage etc.

Meyer was no therapeutic utopian; he was aware that even strange symptoms can come and go, especially in talented people. He was self-critical enough of his own profession of psychiatry to question how King might best be treated.

> Can such a case adjust <u>himself</u> or
> should he remain in contact to be helped
> with his relapses into the feelings?

In 1916, and even still today, mental health professionals have been notoriously apt to be keen on the advantages of therapy, whether if be words as in psychoanalysis or drugs with modern psychopharmacology, or some combination. Meyer was not so sure; King had of course come to him as part of his seeing other Johns Hopkins specialists, so it might have seemed to Meyer that King lacked the adequate motivation for extended therapeutic contact. But, at least the way I read Meyer's notes, he remained uncertain whether someone like King would not be better off left more or less to his own devices, which is I take it why Meyer underlined the word "himself." Even the most disturbed people, and King was hardly that, have been notoriously likely to be self-healing. Many schools of psychology, though, like to think that only those who get "treatment" can be counted upon to get better, and that aging only worsens pre-existing problems. Meyer was, I think, right to be skeptical.

Meyer's material then ends on a strictly political aspect of King's worries. (It has to be uncertain whether some of these pages of Meyer's notes have not been saved out of their original order.)

> Period of sexual exhaustion
> after let-down of the campaign.
> Mr. King was quite effusive in his
> admiration and attachment for the Germans
> near Berlin (now called Kitchener).
> He feels he is called a "pro-German."

I would presume that the issue of King's being "pro-German" might relate to his pronounced admiration for Meyer, whom King mistakenly took to be German. It will be recalled how King's old constituency in 1911 had been made up of so many people of German descent, and that in the election costing him his seat a large part of the voters had been opposed to the Liberal government's naval policy.

Meyer's notes, fragmentary as they are, and even though their partial indecipherability has to be frustrating, seem to me an extraordinarily interesting historical document. In the course of a short time Meyer came up with all this material, in King's presence, without losing track of his patient's attention. Another therapist might well have offended a patient by giving so much care to exact record-keeping. King could have thought that this aspect of Meyer's approach was a sign of Meyer's scientific seriousness. Meyer was, unlike so many in his field who have been prone to ascend to abstractions, determined to collect concrete accounts of his clinical encounters. To Meyer every individual was unique, amounting to an "experiment in nature," and fortunately for us Meyer went in for such detailed transcriptions of his interviews.

Chapter 5
The Hospitalization

The next day after he saw Meyer was Oct. 28th, a Saturday: King had only first seen Barker on Thursday the 26th. For a new set of medical rounds King got up bright and early, and started off with "a stomach specialist" who

> was to make an examination by x-ray process of my stomach, liver, kidney etc. The room was like a wireless one on board ship. I stood up for the first examination, which lasted a short time, the Dr. placing a large plate against my stomach, and reading from its surface in the dark room. As he read he said "You have not been troubled with any abdominal pains" organs are in fine condition, he pointed this out to Dr. who was also present then he made an examination of my chest and lungs, as I lay on my back on a table. He said "a great man" to the doctor at hand. When I asked him after what he thought of my chest he said "I have just been saying you are a great man" you are very strong and large in the chest. I could feel just a warm glow in my stomach and chest after the x-rays had passed through and I came away.

Given King's brother's illness it is understandable if he had special chest anxieties. But it is probable that King's fantasies about feeling the warmth of the x-rays, like his earlier claim as to experiencing sparks connected with the x-ray arranged for by the eyes, nose, and throat specialist, can be understood in connection with King's "hallucinations" of electrical influences. (Kraepelin touched on such emotions in a textbook on dementia praecox.[1])

The dentists thought that King's pyorrhoea needed treating, and a tooth extraction was recommended. All the medical treatment King got at Hopkins took place at a time when focal infections were being commonly related to mental illness; a kind of self-intoxication was thought to be the medical issue. The bacteriological theory of disease had recently triumphed in medicine, and in 1916 a student of Meyer's, Dr. Henry A. Cotton, was among those prominently implicating infected teeth in the causation of insanity. The tonsils too were sometimes indicted as a source of psychological trouble. (The gall-bladder, the appendix, and sinuses were also regions which were thought to need special attention[2]; Cotton for a time went on to recommend bowel surgery.) Cotton was in the forefront of those looking for systemic poisoning. Meyer was ambivalent about Cotton's findings, but when various scandals later broke out connected with Cotton's reports of the results he had achieved Meyer acted protectively toward Cotton's reputation.[3]

If Cotton's approach today sounds whacky, so does Ewen Cameron's much later "psychological driving"; he proposed to erase the adult mind, and then add things back through tape-recorded repetitions during induced sleep. Psychiatry has had its passing fashions which busy practitioners scarcely have time to remember. The practice of prefrontal labotomies had its own heyday; one has to remember, without endorsing any such mutilations, just how frantic psychiatrists have felt in the face of the great mental illnesses. Right now, even though a post-World War Two drug like lithium can have serious side-effects and no one seems to understand how it acts as a mood stabilizer, it is being widely prescribed often after only an hour's psychiatric consultation.[4] And the use of electro-convulsive treatment, another device whose effectiveness remains clouded in mystery, has staged a medical comeback.

King was fortunate to have come to Johns Hopkins, where the experts sound admirably cautious. He did have his own bee-in-the-bonnet about his spine, which Barker was willing to humor King about. King had suggested to Barker, who was overseeing all the medical treatment, "that I might have the base of the spine x-rayed. so that no question might arise concerning it. I have felt a little pain at times there." Presumably King's concern was also part of his perineal "hallucinations." According to King Barker agreed to the x-rays although he "did not think it wd. shew up anything. He thought it would be well to eliminate everything."

King had lunch, and afterwards felt vigorous enough to climb to the top of the Washington Monument, and also he visited an art gallery to enjoy "the sculpture and some of the paintings." In the later afternoon King saw Barker again. "He seated me to the left of his table, and had before him his own notes, and the reports from the several physicians, he began by speaking of the number of men I had seen, then said 'we have a system, I make my own examination and form my own opinions of all the others.'" For some reason Meyer's report to Barker had not yet come in, but Barker felt confident enough of his own diagnosis to proceed anyway. Barker

> apparently had arranged the reports in the order of their least significance as to future treatment. He began with the blood and urine tests, which indicated satisfactorily....blood pressure normal. The stomach, liver and kidneys etc...all excellent, in right place, shape, etc...nothing to report on particularly re urinal [sic] and utheral [sic] tract....

That tooth, however, was projecting into a sinus area, and Barker recommended an extraction. (This procedure would also be in keeping with Cotton's approach.) King claimed that a Hopkins dentist "seemed most interested in telling me of the x-ray plate. He had never seen anything like it." King sounds flattered by the idea of such an unusual, if harmless phenomenon. King agreed to have the tooth pulled at the Johns Hopkins Hospital, and Barker said he would himself be "on hand." Barker "made arrangements for a room at $7.30 a day in private ward."

> He also said to me "You have been under a great strain" and have suffered some nerve exhaustion. I told him of the effect of his talk the other day in causing the hallucination of which I spoke to him to pass away. He told me that he was quite right in what he had said, that if I had not believed him, he wd. have felt the matter serious, but he could assure me positively there was no such phenomena as I had described. I can see now wherein he is right, wherein my own vivid imagination has taken the actions of others as being significant in ways not at

all intended.

King's acknowledgement of the power of his "vivid imagination" seemed to check his paranoid-seeming tendencies about the significance of "the actions of others." King found Barker's reassurance meant "an immense load off my mind. I was struck by his quiet manner and few words, he read all the reports aloud, blue pencilling the important statements."

Barker's candor about the physicians' reports was reciprocated by King's; for he had brought his recent diaries along with him. "I read him part of this diary written in July to let him see my state of mind then. It seemed to me pathetic as I read it, he asked me if I wd. give him the extracts in addition to what he had. I thought from his manner that he seemed pleased with the shewing on the reports." Barker advocated that King be more open at the Rockefeller Foundation about the issue of King's belief in electrical influences.

> He seemed desirous of my telling Mr. R. about the phenomena of regarding people as near at times and of their exerting an influence upon me. Also that Dr. Flexner should know this. I take it that this is a bad sign if it becomes a fixed idea, and it may be a kind of case that these men of science wish to study more in detail. At first I hesitated about telling Mr. R. but agreed to. My only reason for hesitating was that I felt his vision is narrow in some directions & he might misunderstand.

King may only have partly been convinced of the unreality of his feelings; he was not allowing them to become "a fixed idea," and he fancied that the doctors might want to explore his case "more in detail." Barker asked King about the interview with Meyer in the absence of Meyer's report. "I spoke of him as 'noble' and 'helpful.' Indeed he seemed to me a man with wonderful spiritual insight, a very rare and beautiful nature, a man of ideals who lives by and in the light of them." King's diary accounts are full of such idealizations, and he could be equally bitter about political opponents whom he came to detest. King also said he thought "Dr. Barker's personality is one of the finest I have ever known."

King left that evening for New York, so he could spend the next day, Sunday, there, before going into the hospital in Baltimore on Monday. King awoke in New York "after the best night's sleep I have had in months, a really refreshing and helpful sleep." The contact with Johns Hopkins had been reasuring. King went to church, and thought he had

> heard nothing finer, nothing truer. I felt as I listened that helpful as had been the counsels of the eminent physicians I had met this week, this man's counsel as a healer was greater still. That it is at the feet of Christ individuals and the world are saved. This is my fundamental belief, is the back of all other beliefs.

In the afternoon King returned to hear the preacher again. "He developed the idea that no man can be isolated as to anything, that each lives influencing everything around him, as a child moving the air with a flag disturbs the universe, or a grain of sand altered in position affects the balance. Travel in the large orbit to be with God, was the idea he closed with – the need of the vast horizon of service."

Both sermons appealed to King "in terms of my duty to the life of Canada through the years that are ahead...." King's whole belief in electrical influences was intimately tied up with his religious convictions.

King telephoned Rockefeller in Tarrytown, explaining to a servant that King was going back to the hospital "for two weeks." King was "a little put out" at some of the difficulties he encountered in trying to reach Rockefeller, "knowing what I have done for him." But when Rockefeller called back

> he was as always very courteous & considerate, I felt he wd. be that. I apologized for ringing him up at all, but he agreed it was best to. I told him of the results at Baltimore, and he said to go back and take all the time needed without concern. That it wd. seem providential he had wired me to come down. Spoke of Mrs. Rockefeller having had troubled with her teeth, etc. which when readjusted improved her general health.

Popular opinion, following the views of medical experts, was prone to link psychological problems to infections, especially those connected to teeth. King had in talking with Rockefeller gone beyond his own difficulties in order to discuss Foundation business; but King thought Rockefeller "lacking the true Christian spirit" of charity in connection with an employee who seemed to be dying, and another who was resigning.

> After the talk with Mr. R. I felt a warm perspiration break out & felt as though I had again "interfered" to no advantage for others & to my own disadvantage. I am forever doing this, just as father, just as grandfather did, but am I not right? I did my duty as I saw it by two friends to help each and to help to save each. If nothing comes, I had done my part. Had I failed to do what was in my power for fear of self I would have been a coward.

King characteristically thought of himself as acting altruistically, but his egoism was so powerful that one has to worry about being misled by the possible silences in the diary.

King spent the evening with Simon Flexner, and "told him fully of my talks with Dr. Barker and of conditions." This was is accord with Barker's advice about speaking to Flexner openly. "Especially did I go into with him, my relations to the Foundat'n & the wisdom of being left to myself in my work." King reports that Flexner was fully supportive of King's views on Foundation matters. "As to my nervous trouble, he said I wd. be amazed how many men & women had just this experience, among those I know many that it would pass away, and that I never in life again wd. be similarly afflicted. He said to most men, this kind of strain comes once in their lives.-" Although there was not yet any such notion as a mid-life crisis, King obviously thought there was something special, within his own experience, to his 1916 troubles. King then wrote some "short letters home – to mother, also to Mrs. Hendrie & a note to Mr. Rockefeller thanking him." For King "home" meant not just his mother and a friend like Mrs. Hendrie but also Rockefeller. King then added: "I have been practically free from the dread I had since speaking with Dr. Barker of it, and almost free of the symptoms which produced it." Again, this would appear to be the issue of electrical influence, evidently a source of some continuing anxiety. But somehow King was able to separate "the dread" from the "symptoms" which he thought caused it.

The next day, Monday the 30th of October, King checked into the hospital. He said he wrote a letter to his brother Max "& others of a business nature." Barker spoke to King "about my staying on & working in the library over a period of time. But I told him I could work better in my own surroundings." The doctors were to "begin with the teeth, & then the nose." This was thoroughly in keeping with Cotton's latest recommendations. A dentist did a bit of work; the tooth itself was to be extracted on Wednesday. King shrewdly suspected that he had "a feeling that this treatment etc. is being strung along to give time for nervous system to be rested & watched."

King wrote that he "slept steadily from 8 until 4 when I woke after dreaming, then slept a little off & on till 7:30...." It sounds like King was back to being a steady sleeper. The Oct. 31st entry reveals:

> Yesterday the Dentist told me my teeth on left side were not in the good shape of those on the right – everything about me that seems relatively weak is on the left side. I feel pain in head left side first, eye on left side seems the weaker, the nostril and x-ray plate indicates trouble in sinus space on left side, bad tooth is on left side. – This recalls father's blindness began with left eye, & mother's paralysis came on left side. – I am glad to have all this inquired into.

King's hypochondria did not consume all his thoughts; he mentioned a talk with one of the doctors, "the X-ray specialist," about the effects of cancer on the "pioneers in x-ray work." He and a couple of other x-ray physicians "doubted if they wd. live long." King said he "could not but feel, that these are the men the Nation should honour & erect memorials to. Their lives have been given in the pursuit of scientific truth, which has benefited mankind.-" It was characteristic of King to be thinking in such broad terms, even if he himself were then only being treated for minor dental problems.

King recorded going on a walk with one of the physicians, and that they discussed "the advances he and others are making in detecting syphilis in its early stages, by its effect upon the eye. It has been funds granted by the R. Foundation that is aiding in this." In the past King had clearly worried about the dangers of venereal disease picked up on one of his "expeditions." This concern, and its link to eyesight, might have been fed by the knowledge of his father's own blindness, and perhaps King's masturbatory anxieties. It may not be coincidental that King also reported having heard from this same physician about the dreadful mortality rate of illegitimate children in Baltimore. The foundling homes seemed like death houses. "He got the only law in the world prohibiting separat'n of infant from mother for six mos.

passed in this state, but has been unable to awaken national sentiment. The problem of the illegitimate child he said, is a serious one, the way to meet it however is surely not by murder and death." These sentiments stand out in what otherwise was a pretty steady stream of King's personal medical preoccupations.

On Wednesday Nov. 1st King reported that he "slept most of the 10 hrs. last night, tho' wakeful part of the time...." In the late morning Barker "came in...and talked quietly for a little while. He said the x-ray plate of my spine shewed everything all right there." After the tooth extraction it could be decided if a further operation was necessary, but Barker wanted to avoid it; he though that the adenoids "might have to be removed, but that simple." By now Barker had certainly read Meyer's letter to him. Barker

> spoke to me of my view of sex problems, said he thought I over exaggerated significance of perfectly natural phenomena, that there was danger in so doing by a healthy man he advised reconciling in thought any conflict between the animal and spiritual nature. He had to do this himself, had been thro' the same conflict. He noticed I was inclined to be active in thought, to connect ideas quickly & to act quickly. He advised studying the habit of rest & repose, of not carrying too much, – that nothing matters save to be calm, and put one's best thought into the work of the moment.

Barker suggested a book on repose for King to read. "He told me he had had to learn all this, and had been able to, that in talking with me, he forgot about all else, the other patients he had to see, etc." Barker, as well as Meyer, managed to feed King's sense of being special without false artifice.

However frustrated and tortured by sex King may sound, it is still, I think, necessary to be careful in drawing conclusions about how King actually behaved, either in his earlier years or later on. In that era it would not have been unusual for some men to find themselves only potent under disreputable circumstances. By King's mother's standards any sex outside marriage was sinful. It is likely that King was trying to please, if not impress, his doctors; King might have thought Meyer wanted to hear about early childhood sexual experiences, and then that would by itself account for Meyer eliciting material about sexuality in his first interview with King. By the same token, in behalf of King's trying to look good to the physicians, it is possible he may have rather over-done the story of the absence of sex in his adult life. On the other hand King's symptomatology about electrical influences would itself argue in favor of his having lived an overly continent life; a set of ideas as strange as King entertained would be consistent with someone so out of touch with intimate human contact as to make unlikely satisfactory sexual relations.

King had for years been keen on Matthew Arnold's poetry, and King said he and Barker talked about it. They also discussed a book of essays King was interested in. A note had come from Rockefeller asking King to let him take care "of all the expense to which I may be put in this visit, including travelling, hotel, hospital physicians' fees etc. etc...." King claimed he felt "embarrassed to know what is best to do," but said he decided to "wait and see what the amount is. Certainly I have reason if any man has to be grateful to the Providence that has given me the friends I possess, and that has guided my feet into paths so secure."

Barker had also encouraged King "to 'follow my own bent,' in the matter of the method of work & kind of work. He said that a man can only do as other [sic] wished up to a certain point....He spoke of a slight 'kinetic' condition, which shewed by the eyes responding quickly...." The tooth extraction appointment "did not come off," King got "another hypodermic injection," and "went in to the city and bought" a self-help book entitled *Power Through Repose*. King read eighty pages of it that night, and "found it most suggestive and helpful – just what with my nervous tension I need most." He had also purchased a book called *Why Worry*.

On Thursday, November 2nd, King finally had the tooth out. "By the use of an anaesthetic the operation was almost painless, the results were as foreseen, by the x-ray...." And in the late afternoon King had an operation on his nose for sinus draining (Cotton had indicted sinus infections as a source of mental illness): "This too was painless through the use of anaesthetics, but an unpleasant operation and one inclined to be hard on the nerves." One of the doctors had used an anaesthetic from Germany: it "had been for sale before the war, he bought up all he could when the war came on." The box had "printed on it 'importation into Great Britain and Ireland the British Dominions and colonies prohibited.'" King thought that the exclusion of the drug "from a neighbourly and friendly nation in time of peace...certainly looks like a prophecy of war, and an act of hate."

On Friday King's gum was treated where the tooth had been extracted. King made a special point of going to secure "the x-ray of my spine", and despite Barker's assurances King proceeded to take the x-ray "later to a photographer's to get a blue print...." Barker stopped off and told King he could leave "early in the week." In fact King did not leave until late in the next week. Barker had given King advice about his diet, including "a list of things to eat & refrain from eating." Barker also suggested some exercises. "As to sitting he recommended sitting up straight in chair, with feet on floor but not crossed." Perhaps Barker was trying to help King minimize lower back pain. Barker had some books in mind for King, and King in turn suggested Barker read President Eliot's *Training for Manhood*. "I spoke to him about the sensations, I had been experiencing, he said they were all perfectly normal, and likely to be experienced where there had been nervous strain." Barker, like Meyer, was not of a bent to be too exploratory about King's problems, and seemed content to wait and see if King's natural recuperative forces would pull him out of his difficulties.

When King raised the issue of "the accounts," Barker said that "so far as Dr. Meyer and I are concerned I was thinking there would not be any charge. We both owe so much to the Rockefeller Institute and we are glad to have met you, and you are doing such good work in kindred fields, that we would rather not receive anything." King conscientiously pointed out that his own work was at the Rockefeller Foundation, not the Institute, but Barker thought they were "much the same." Barker proposed that "there will be lots to pay the other men, this hospital etc. so let me do this...." King was grateful: "I told him he had been like a little saviour to me, in helping me out of the torment of the sinner. He said he was glad, not to give that further thought. He hoped I would come down this way off and on."

In the evening King read more chapters in *Power Through Repose*, and also some speeches by Woodrow Wilson and his rival Charles Evans Hughes. The presidential election was being held the next Tuesday. "Personally I am inclined to think Wilson is going to win, though I should vote for Hughes if I were voting." Even if it might not seem, given how King reasoned back and forth, easy to decide King's preference, it would appear he was hoping the Republican challenger Hughes might topple the incumbent Democrat. King said he appreciated Wilson's having kept America out of the war, since "war is the last thing a nation should get into...." King was still insisting on this principle even though one might have expected he would be eager to have America firmly on the side of Canada and England.

King thought that Wilson had other options "short of war" that "would have been effective, non-intercourse is one of them. Hughes will not rush into war, but will stand straight." For King, Wilson was too "yielding" on union matters, perhaps thinking of his role in Colorado, and therefore to King Wilson was "double-faced." In King's mind Wilson was "too full of phrases to be sincere, his conduct shews he is not sincere, & his face shews it. His speech has a human ring about it, but it is maudlin." King may seem like a pot calling the kettle a name. "Roosevelt [Theodore] is just as human, but there is virility about it." King did not like the protectionist trade policies of Hughes, but doubted if protectionism would be tried if Hughes got elected. King sounded muddled about what he preferred to happen:

> Personally I don't like the Protection cry in Hughes' speech. I doubt it protection will be tried if he [is] returned, at any rate protect'n of principle is what is needed just now. If Hughes is elected it will be protect'n, the big interests, and indignation at Wilson on his labour & internal policies. I look nevertheless for Wilson's return.

On Saturday King had the tooth which had been bad "drained out," and wrote to Rockefeller to accept "his kind offer to meet the expenses of this illness. I have had some debate in my mind about this...." King never indicated in his diary any real hesitation in accepting Rockefeller's offer. King wrote that he felt "it would be mistaking his motive which is one of true friendliness not to do, and would be satisfying a mistaken love of independence for common-sense." Also, King said he felt "the personal service I have rendered Mr. R. is worthy of the acceptance of a personal service from him."

King was thinking more about the up-coming presidential elections; it would seem that on balance he preferred that Hughes win, but King expected Wilson to triumph.

> Both Hughes & Wilson have been moderate in their speaking. Wilson has been very general, very full of words and phrases, but will reach the masses better than Hughes on this account. Hughes seems a better executive, and I should think a man of saner judgment, more force of character. I do not like the protection issue. If it were not that Wilson's vacillation & lack

of back bone had been so great, I wd. feel disposed to support him, as democratic principles appeal more to me than Republican, but it is a man the nation needs at this time more than aught else, and Hughes is just I believe, humane & pro-progressive.

On Sunday King saw his dentist briefly, and then went to spend the day outside Annapolis on a farm "with Mr. and Mrs. Barchett, and their two little girls." Mrs. Barchett was the former Mathilde Grossert, the nurse who had helped him during his typhoid in Chicago. King was politically inquisitive about what the Barchetts were thinking in connection with the presidential election. "It interests me to see how many in these parts think Hughes will be elected. They were all of that opinion. The farmers do not like Wilson's truckling to Labour." King wrote that "both Mr. and Mrs. Barchett seemed better & stronger than when I saw them over a year ago, - a reflection of improved conditions on the farm." King did not allow himself many personal-sounding thoughts, memorable if only because of his continuing thoughts about the possibility of marriage: "Mrs. Barchett gave me a table cover she had worked for me, a beautiful cover. I debated after I came away if it [were] wise to have gone. She had such deep feelings & the friendship of 20 years ago remains strong. It has been a truly noble friendship." In the course of the passage of time King would come to seem isolated and friendless; but the lonely old man ought not to be mixed up with King at his prime.

On Monday, after a consultation with one of the doctors, King "spoke of having adnoids [sic] and 'Pollups' [sic] taken out. He thought it ought to be done, might avoid trouble later, so decided to take ether tomorrow and have this job completed." King managed to see his own medical records, once an orderly had given the papers to him for carrying.

I got hold of my chart & abstracts it contained from the difft. physicians...When I saw what it contained I read all over carefully. I had heard all from Dr. Barker, but there was a letter from Dr. Flexner I had not seen, which seemed to emphasize the need of my having a talk with someone in whom I had confidence. It was very kindly worded. Thought my trouble was due to worrying about myself, need to be told how to live. It referred to my being on salary and having had heavy personal drains.

Flexner's letter in fact says nothing whatever about King being "on salary," and by personal "drains" King was referring to Flexner having written about the losses in King's private life. King took no offence evidently at Flexner's having written: "He has himself on his mind a great deal more than is good for him...." (Presumably King also read the following passage in his medical file: "in an individual such as he is the direction of his attention to any small ailment would probably accentuate it and make him imagine that it was of a serious nature.")

King did see that Meyer's report "spoke in very appreciative terms of my character, said he wd. gladly forgo any charges because of my being 'a genuinely fine man' – and the work I was doing for humanity. He said I was over-conscientious, needed to be taught how to live in a hygienic way, and needed 'a broader philosophy.'" Barker saw King again, and told him "not to work too hard when I get back, to take it easy." King noted, apparently from Meyer's letter to Barker, that Meyer had "wondered if I could keep from reacting in the old way, if away from a strong character in whom I had faith to correct wrong impressions...." According to King is was Meyer who suggested King stay and work in the library at the Johns Hopkins Hospital. King said he had been getting a "hypodermic" which was "a strong nerve tonic."

On Monday night, because of the scheduled operation the next day, King reported he "did not sleep too well" and in the morning "felt restless, waiting to be sent for." He had to have nothing to eat on Tuesday, they also gave him an enema, so he "felt a little weak."

> At about one, they came for me to go to the operating room. I was undressed and waiting. Could imagine the terrible strain of condemned persons, awaiting the execution of a decree. Each stage seemed to be more terrifying. When we reached the operating floor, the place seemed "alive" with men and nurses in white coats, trousers, head bands, gloves, etc., like a fighting ground of death. I was put on a stretcher feet & legs strapped, then gauze put over my eyes.

There was a "preliminary sort of operation" on King's nose preparatory to the later procedure to remove the polyps.

> Then a nurse gave me the ether, gas first then ether – a rubber

socket was put over the mouth & gas turned on. The nurse said "it is not unpleasant," or words to this effect which I found comforting. I had made up my mind to recite a poem to myself, so began with "Abou Ben Adhem." I recognized that it was going to be difficult to conclude before under the influence of gas, so hurried rapidly reaching the last few lines in time to repeat "lead all the rest" with great emphasis.

The poem King recited was written in 1844 by Leigh Hunt (1784-1859), and concerned the night visit of an angel and the theme of humanitarianism:

Abou Ben Adhem

Abou Ben Adhem (may his tribe increase!)
Awoke one night from a deep dream of peace,
And saw, within the moonlight of his room,
Making it rich, and like a lily in bloom,
An angel writing in a book of gold;
Exceeding peace had made Ben Adhem bold,
And to the presence in the room he said,
"What writest thou?" – The Vision raised its head,
And with a look made of all sweet accord,
Answered, "The names of those who love the Lord."
"And is mine one?" said Abou. "Nay, not so,"
Replied the angel. Abou spoke more low,
But cheerily still; and said, "I pray thee then,
Write me as one that loves his fellow-men."
  The angel wrote, and vanished. The next night
It came again with a great wakening of light,
And showed the names whom love of God had blessed,
And lo! Ben Adhem's name led all the rest.[5]

One of the hard parts to follow about King was the ways in which his ambitiousness , spiritualism, and religiousness were all bound up together.

To King this particular poem seemed

a confirmation of a great truth, and triumphant in a way, the vindication of faith. After repeating the last line three or four times I was totally unconscious and remained so for nearly an hour, or possibly more. My mind was a total blank, there seemed only total darkness, oblivion & as I began to come to I thought I was being hurried along in an elevator, & unstrapped. This was right enough, then I gradually gained consciousness in bed in my own room. I recognized the light, & the walls, & spoke to the nurse....I remember thinking she was a noble woman, a sweet woman & a good woman, and I told her so and that God would give her happiness, and enable her to have a life of useful service. I remember saying that service to others was the only real sources of happiness, and feeling very strongly the truth of this, and indeed of all my spiritual beliefs.

In the midst of his medical problems, and the spiritual thoughts they engendered, the presidential race was strikingly on King's mind. The election was being held that day. We get an example of how King's spiritualism, at a time when it was being expressed partly through hallucinatory feelings of electrical influence, could spill over into the political realm. (It remains unclear to what extent King's religious beliefs can be seen as the tail wagging the dog, since his convictions about electrical influences were so powerful.) King had a vision about Charles Evans Hughes which was consistent with Leigh Hunt's poetic notion of angels.

I thought of the elections and the name "Hughes" by itself seem[ed] to stand out before my eyes, half visible, have [sic] heard, & I had the conviction it was an assurance as it were that seemed very real that Hughes would win because he was an honest man, that the people detected honesty. It seemed to me Wilson was not so honest, his trafficing [sic] for labor votes seemed wrong, something Hughes would never have done. This was at 2.30 this afternoon. Tonight it would seem Hughes is elected, though there is doubt. Different reports come in, I cling to Hughes as the winner because of this sort of revelation as it were from an invisible source.

It is not entirely easy to tell who King had been expecting to get elected president, since a few days earlier he seemed to imply that Wilson was better able to reach the masses. If, as I think, King preferred Hughes to win, King never indicated in any way that the gas or the ether from his operation might have played a special part in the vision he reported having had. The name "Hughes" had come to him "half visible, have [sic] heard," which would mean that it was a hallucination both auditory as well as visual. But King felt he had a "sort of revelation as it were from an invisible source." (So-called hypnagogic hallucinations, intense dream-like images, can take place in normal over-tired people while falling asleep.) King's experiencing the word "Hughes" would be an instance of his magical-sort of thinking having a momentarily direct impact on his political judgment.

King's mind moved immediately from politics to his family. "I thought of all at home, spoke to mother as if she were near by knowing what her sympathy would be...." King was as untroubled about his speaking to his mother as he was by his vision of the name Hughes. And King thought of Mrs. Hendrie and the wife of the head of the Rockefeller coal mine

> and thought they were different from one other [sic], then clearer consciousness came by degrees. I remembered everything distinctly to the moment of the last line of the poem, and was fully conscious of recovering consciousness could see how very alert and active my mind was, no confusion all quite clear – meanwhile the doctors had taken out the adenoids & the pollups [sic]. – It seemed as if I had been in some great workshop, but knew nothing of it. – I was a little nauseated very little, and had a bad pain in the head most of the afternoon & evening, could not sleep and slept very little all night.

In the evening King had read the headlines on the newspapers, and listened to the cries of newsboys to get information on the election returns: "first word Hughes elected, then Wilson, then Hughes all eastern reports strong for Hughes."

The next day, Wednesday November 8th, King read the papers in bed, still feeling the effects of the ether. According to the hospital medical records of that day: "Patient is getting along well after the operation. There have been no complications and he feels greatly pleased over the results. Feels that the def. source of infection has been removed and that this is going to react extremely favorably upon his nervous condition." King had suggestively accepted Cotton's then fashionable theory, which influenced Barker too, about the infectious origins of nervous difficulties. According to King's diary he had "thought much yesterday," in the midst of the problems associated with his operation, "of how men at the front were suffering and had suffered." No matter how he might rationalize his staying out of the war effort King does seem to have been deeply afflicted by guilt feelings.

Politically the election still seemed to have left uncertain results.

> Throughout the day there has been great uncertainty as to the ultimate victory of either candidate in the Presidential election. Though the Times the N. Y. Democratic paper conceded a Republican victory in its columns, both candidates have wisely refrained from giving out any interview both claimed victory. It looks by the States that are uncertain as if Wilson will carry. I hold to "my vision."

That afternoon King read a bit of William James, who was unusually tolerant about the existence of occult processes of thought; it was a piece of James's "On the Significance of Human Ideals," which King found

> a splendid essay on the need for the expression of an ideal in action, to make life significant, wherever found, whether in humble or in lofty circumstances, and the need of struggle to merit admiration in achievement. It is a great help to have one's own faith and belief confirmed by a man like James. Men of that type are alone entitled to be heard, for except a man "lives the life" he cannot know it. The doctrine of non-resistance...is splendidly brought out –...new light on the scriptural teaching of the non resistance of evil. All through my reading I cannot but regret that I did not come to a knowledge of all this sooner, that I might have helped father and little Bell. So much of their anxiety, & worry, which brought them in the end to their graves might have been avoided & spared. The art of living, how few know it.

King at least here really seemed to believe that "anxiety" and "worry" were responsible for the deaths of his father and sister. Such an approach would make his own problems life-threatening, justifying all his self-concern. Mainly King was still trying to come to terms with his father's death:

> I think much of the summer, and my impatience with father on one or two occasions. How deeply I regret it. All might have been saved had I known enough "not to resist." I would have known, had I not been overstrained for other reasons. Now I can see where for months I have taxed my mind & nervous system to the verge of bringing about a collapse. I have just been saved in time.

Even on Thursday, Nov. 9th, the outcome of the presidential election was still in doubt. Someone King considered a protege of his, Peter Gerry, had succeeded in being elected to the United States Senate from Rhode Island, and King sent him a congratulatory telegram. King thought that "in part" it had been his impact on Gerry at Harvard that had stimulated Gerry's interest in politics. King wrote: "How little we know of the influence of our lives on others!" King may have accepted that his feelings about electricity were hallucinatory, but the issue of being influential had to remain an essential constituent of King's public life.

On the 10th King saw Barker again "for a short time." Barker was leaving in the afternoon for an engagement in New York City, but the arrangements were for King to be discharged from the hospital on the next day. King reported that Barker had "said if I felt O.K. when in New York in December all right, but if troubled by any symptoms to come on and see him, to keep in touch with him." King told Barker of King's having written Rockefeller, and showed Barker the reply.

> He than told me how Dr. Flexner had written him etc. said he only wished the hospital fees could be cut out. I thanked him again, to which he replied "If I have helped you I am very glad." I told him I regarded this as an epoch, a new start, and could not be grateful enough. I asked to be allowed to secure one of his photos & for an autograph, he said he wd. give me one but I said no, to let me get it, he gave me the name of Mrs. Banoit & asked me to send him an autographed one of myself.

Once King had become later ensconced as Liberal leader in Laurier

House Barker's photo would remain in King's study throughout his career.

King spoke to Barker "of mother & her nerves & asked about the doctors in Toronto." Barker had a number of recommendations. King was, however, still concerned about himself: "As to legs crossed, he said to sit well back in chair & seek to overcome crossing as more restful,- wished part of diary I read him for his record." (Although Johns Hopkins has an extensive holding of Barker's papers, no trace of King's file would appear to be there.) Barker had detailed suggestions to make to King: "Oatmeal to eat very little of. Recommended 'Eat and Grow Thin' as book on diet. Spoke particularly of Dewey's and Paulson's books on my table." It is a bit hard to believe that Barker was dealing with someone who in five years would be Prime Minister of Canada.

King reported about Barker's opinion on a key subject in his life, the possibility of matrimony:

> Just before going he said, "Then if you can find the right girl, don't put off getting married. Psychologically it is better not to wait too long. A girl of good family, nice traditions, one who will [be] helpful socially." I said I wanted to devote my life to my work & my country & sought some one with like principles and aims. He said that is right. There are fine girls, you will be able to find one.

No passage demonstrates more clearly how the whole text of King's diary has to be considered a subject of interpretation. For he had a notoriously convenient memory. Technically King was not a liar, although he often appeared so to others; it does seem as if King could believe anything he wanted to. The issue of the choice of a wife was to be a recurring theme throughout all of his political career. As a talking point later on, King would go on about how he had been deprived of the comfort and satisfaction of a family. King rationalized his bachelorhood by emphasizing his own financial devotion to his family, and how his concern for others had entailed a personal sacrifice.

But in describing Barker's conversation with him on the issue of marriage King was, without actually lying directly, simply leaving out inconvenient or inconsistent suggestions. King never mentioned in the diary that Meyer's opinion had been decidedly against King's marrying. (The evidence about a seance written by one of King's mediums, at odds with his diary report, is also "a caution against taking the apparent immediacy of his diary accounts as absolute truth."[6]) King was to continue to write and talk about the need for a wife to share his life, although I think myself that not enough attention has been devoted to scrutinizing the implications of his desire and the meaning of its frustration.

Heather Robertson, who wrote a novel about King, once intuitively described him as "a passionate man unable to love."[7] But McGregor's view had been that marriage would have made King less egocentric and presumably a more human prime minister. For the rest of his life King continued to be involved with a series of married ladies, and he kept up his friendships through assiduous letter-writing. Later he settled on a bank-manager's wife, Mrs. Joan Patteson, as his official hostess; supposedly they often read poetry to each other at night. The "table-rapping" they engaged in was kept a secret, and without being unduly suspicious one does at least wonder what else might have been kept quiet.

King did not see Meyer after 1916, although there are a few brief letters between them. King sent Meyer a copy of his *The Secret of Heroism*. In contrast to King's dropping Meyer as a physician, King continued to consult Barker right up into World War II. King's aides considered him a difficult patient, who often did not do as his doctors told him. King was however implicitly following Meyer's advice in not marrying, even though what Barker had told him fit in better with King's ideal conception of himself.

It seems to me that the unreliability of King's diary, in leaving out Meyer's emphatic opposition to King's idea about possibly taking a wife, has considerable importance for our using King's diary as a whole. Since the diary has become such a key document in understanding twentieth century Canadian politics, and because King's version of things is often the only one available, historians have been too apt to accept King's accounts as unquestionably the truth.

In King's leave-taking from Johns Hopkins he was unambivalent about Barker's merits: "Dr. Barker's whole manner, appearance, spirit are so fine. It is the noble life that is there, a truly great physician because a truly great man, surely this has been the greatest blessing of the year." Presumably Barker was responsible for the November 10th comments in King's hospital report: "Pt. feels much improved and greatly encouraged. Feels that he can go back into his political work;

that he has a renewed grip upon himself and the problems that face him. Says he knows that he will now get rid of his nervous troubles." Before leaving the hospital King had to have his nose examined again, and submitted to having a periscope-like instrument projected into him. It would seem that King had his electrical convictions under some measure of control.

Politically, however, King's reasoning persisted in a surprisingly odd way. By Friday the 10th he had had to admit that Wilson succeeded in carrying California and therefore been re-elected. To King this meant not that he had erred about Hughes, but that King's "estimate at the outset was correct." King attributed Wilson's victory to the women's vote and the pacifist attitude, while labor had been divided. But what was King to do in explaining the "vision" he had had on the day of his operation? "Now as to my 'vision' of Hughes. The name was like a word flashed on a wireless. It was 'burning' so to speak in the air. What it may have been is that it was the word everywhere about at the time & being sensitive to impressions I caught it strongly, & was right for all this Eastern section." King, whatever he had been told by Barker and Meyer, still believed in his ability to be "sensitive" enough to absorb mysterious influences. California was simply too far away for the western Wilson electoral support to be able to manage to reach him in Baltimore.

If King had not been such a man of sound and careful judgment his way of handling the Hughes "vision" might be less striking. Even though Hughes had lost the election, King felt his assessment had been correct:

> As to conviction of his honesty I was right too. It appears that the "boss leaders" in California spoiled his chances there by not forgiving the breach with the Progressives. Privilege dies hard. As to fundamental policies my sympathies are more truly Democratic than Republican. In this way I am as glad Wilson has carried, but I wish he were a stronger man, less of a trimmer. Democracy needs honesty above all else in leadership.

By focusing on the reasons for Hughes's losing in California, citing the conflict over Theodore Roosevelt's Progressivism that had torn the Republican Party apart in 1912, King would wind up thoroughly pleased at an election result which might seem wholly at odds with his post-operative "vision."

On Saturday, Nov. 11th, the day of his hospital discharge, King saw Meyer again in the morning. They had "a pleasant talk." According to King, Meyer "spoke of my need of keeping in touch with friends, but going on 'unswerving' in my own career. Recommended Wm. James philosophy as most helpful, though he had been unable to follow him in all his religious views e.g. resources from invisible sources. (This is where I follow James & differ from Meyer.)" King was able to link his beliefs in "invisible sources" to religious convictions, whereas Meyer probably saw that side of King in strictly psychiatric terms. Meyer though continued to succeed in being supportive to King. King reported: "As novelist, light reading, corrective to over earnestness, suggested O. Henry's novels &...slang but healthy philosophy. Spoke of his brother's Study of Social Democracy in Switzerland & of my work in labor. Said it was a pleasure to do as a friend what he had done. Promised to write out a list of books to read."

King headed to a short holiday at the seashore in Atlantic City, and arrived back in New York City on November 14th. From then on he would resume his regular life, which included the writing of *Industry and Humanity* which appeared in 1918. Now that we have examined the most immediate evidence about his stay at Johns Hopkins, we should look at some other available sources that bear on this particular episode in King's life.

Chapter 6
Friends and Relatives: "Still a grand Pshah at heart!"

King recorded in his diary entry of Nov. 14th that thanks to what he learned at Johns Hopkins, now he had started "reading in bed as a new experience. Dr. Meyer having told me he did this every night, and Dr. Barker having told me the eyes do not suffer from use or electrical light, has given me confidence, and removed fears concerning eye strain." It has to be mind-boggling that King, a former Minister in Laurier's cabinet, was recording such apparent banalities, but Meyer evidently was obliged to discuss with King matters connected with his diet, and as we have seen Barker gave advice about how to sit in a chair. Meyer also had some specific books in mind to recommend for King's perusal, titles such as *The Efficient Life, Efficiency, The Human Machine, How to Live on Twenty-Four Hours A Day, Why Worry*, and *The Soul of Spain*. Meyer mentioned some of these books to King in a letter (Dec. 6, 1916) acknowledging his having received from King the memoir *The Secret of Heroism*. Meyer had had in mind that King dip into such self-help books on a regular basis, and King (Dec. 8, 1916) welcomed this assistance:

> Your suggestions as respects the books you have mentioned, that they should not be read more than a chapter at a time, interests me very much, for it is precisely the method I have adopted for some time past in the reading of books of that class. I am glad to know that this practice has a foundation in sound psychology.

According to King's diary, one of the key parting recommendations that Meyer had had for him was the suggestion that King keep in
touch with his friends. And although later in his career King was
relatively isolated, in 1916 he was able to be remarkably candid with
some people about his stay at Johns Hopkins. It is true that with
Charles Eliot, formerly President of Harvard, King was at best elliptical
and in substance misleading. King wrote him about other matters on
Nov. 21, 1916, and began by saying: "Since the morning I had the
pleasure of breakfasting with you at the Harvard Club, I have been
obliged to spend a fortnight in Johns Hopkins Hospital to undergo one
or two slight operations on my nose and throat." King mentioned his
medical problem as a way of excusing his delay in responding to
Eliot's inquiry about the Canadian Industrial Disputes Investigation
Act, for Eliot thought that Theodore Roosevelt had advocated a similar
measure. Eliot responded to King's news with an appropriate-
sounding reference to his own "slight" operations like that, although
they had not been enough to require hospitalization. But King had
not, in writing Eliot, made any reference to King's "nervous"
difficulties. As far as one can tell from King's other correspondence,
Laurier knew even less than Eliot. "In so far as Laurier's
correspondence is any guide to his activities he appears to have
dropped his connection with Laurier during the latter part of 1916."[1]

With Rockefeller himself the situation was obviously quite
different. On Dec. 18, 1916 King thought he should try to excuse to
Rockefeller the interruption in his work for the Foundation. "In ways
I have never expected," King wrote him, "time that should have been
given to concentrated thought upon my studies for the Foundation has
been lost, either through anxiety, or the meeting of domestic situations
of an imperative nature, to meet which I alone could be looked to."
King then proceeded to go through a list of his family troubles – his
father's blindness, the settlement of his estate, moving of his parents in
the spring, closing up of their new apartment, the illnesses of his
mother and brother. King concluded by his own immediate
difficulties:

> and then my own nervous condition over a part of the year, a
> condition which caused me considerable distress of mind and
> necessitated an absence from work for a definite period and
> much imperfect work and needless worry. I see the effect of

this worry on some of the work as I now revise it under the clear sky which is once again above my head.

King proposed to Rockefeller that because of this illness King forgo his next two months salary. On Dec. 22nd Rockefeller wrote back appreciatively about King's explanation for the "certain conditions" which had interrupted King's work for the Foundation "during the past year," but Rockefeller was not willing to accept King's offer to adjust his salary accordingly.[2] Rockefeller had been kept abreast of King's difficulties, proposed that he go to Johns Hopkins, and felt immensely indebted to him for all his previous help.

With others whom he had known longer than Rockefeller King had been also able to confide what he was going through. As we have seen, someone as close to him as McGregor, then his private secretary, did not seem fully familiar with what was happening. But King had, for example, written to Lieutenant Colonel William Hendrie at Camp Borden, Ontario when King took his mother, after John King's death, to visit his brother Max in Denver. King had become friends with both Hendrie and his wife for some years. As King wrote in the fall of 1916, he had been "more than busily engaged in closing up our Toronto home," which he had just set up. King also reported that his brother had "made considerable progress" and had resumed his medical practice "in a small way." We have to assume that Hendrie was intimately familiar with the King family problems, and Max's illness, otherwise this communication by letter from King would have made little sense.

Hendrie wrote back to King on Oct. 18th: "Mrs. Hendrie told me you did not look well. You should 'cultivate a change,' go back into nature somewhere where you can enjoy different surroundings, fresh air and exercise." Hendrie was also writing King about political matters, such as Hendrie's disappointment in Laurier's "pacifism." But King picked up on the theme of the concern his friends had for him: "Please tell Mrs. Hendrie," King wrote on Oct. 20th, "that I am not as sick as I look, but all I want now is a chance to get back at regular work again." Although it is not clear, since further letters on this matter do not survive, what else King wrote the Hendries, they certainly knew more than someone like President Eliot. William Hendrie, for example, wrote King again, evidently just before he went to Baltimore: "I do hope your sojourn at Hopkins will prove a benefit to your health. You worry over much – it's hard not to do so. I know because I have been 'it' but what's the use. One cannot do more than his best and when that's done leave *all the rest* to 'the one that knows.'" Hendrie and King obviously shared common religious convictions.

Mrs. Edward Hewitt was a New York City friend who found out a lot about King's 1916 difficulties, but her attempts to be helpful may have been more than King could stomach. They were in touch during the summer, and she wrote him playfully on July 12th about there being for her a "subconscious connection between mischief and you." Soon she realized that King was truly troubled. She wrote him on August 3rd: "I am sorry you are so tired. Of course you mistreat yourself beyond all sense, and must pay the penalty, but that doesn't make D.T. any pleasanter to a drunkard, does it? Nor nervous exhaustion to an ambitious man. But it isn't honest to treat yourself that way, not to get married, nor to distrust your friend." Mary Hewitt obviously knew King well enough both to chide him and to be intimately compassionate:

> Have I ever failed you? I don't write to you, because it seemed to me we had passed that point, that what you wanted from me was a refuge – at times when you needed it; a place to come and be yourself and in security of understanding and trust, talk out your hopes and difficulties. But letter-writing is a strain on your busy life,- and is barren if it is not spontaneous and incidental. You can't write that way; you make a duty of it, and I don't fancy myself as a duty. Isn't there something in algebra they call a spontaneous simultaneous equation? That is what a personal relation is when it is vital.

Mrs. Hewitt was not content simply to get formal letters from King, and she thought seeing him would have been better. Her spontaneity may well have been more than King wanted to handle. She reproached him, having heard from King evidently after an unwarranted lapse of time: "A long lost friendship! You need a spiritual valet if you misplace that sort of thing so easily."

Evidently King did not write her again until after he had left Johns Hopkins. She wrote him in December 1916:

> So it has been tooth, instead of heart ache, this long time has [it] greyed your outlook?...I'm very glad the end is promised. An experience in the gloomy paths seems to be essential to

human experience. I can't see myself without the dark years, but it does seem very...wholesome to emerge again! So here is to your debut into health and cheer!

Although we only have Mary Hewitt's side of the matter, since King's correspondence to her does not appear to have survived, she was articulate enough to provide insight into what he was like in those years, even though she seems to have felt that humanly he had let her down. As she wrote him on Jan. 2, 1917, in her "first letter of the year":

> I don't think too much sweetness and light has surrounded your pathway for now, many years. And yet – as you see it now, the struggle and the anxiety,...doesn't it make those happy days where your own ambition, whose fulfillment seemed so plain, was your guiding force, seem immature, a vision? I used to wonder how you would take trouble and what man would emerge from the "adorable boy."

Mary Hewitt seemed to think better of King for his having had his period of emotional turmoil. His "ambition" was to her ephemeral, a "vision."

> You have taken your great personal anxieties steadfastly; how glad I am that they are resolving themselves more than seemed possible, even a short time ago. And your constructive abilities are finding exercise in a different channel, but effectively. Your personal life runs on out of my intimate ken, but outwardly unchanged. Still a grand Pshah at heart!

It does sound like Mary Hewitt wanted rather more of King's friendship than he was able to reciprocate: she must have been referring to his self-importance, and his disguising some of his more important personal decisions; yet she was grateful for what he had been able to give her. One suspects that King was indeed, as she supposed, "still a grand Pshah at heart!"

> The mitigation being that your mind keeps you so busy that only the crumbs of your life fall to your personal relations. In the crumbs that have fallen to me, I frankly give thanks to heaven, as among the manna that sustains. Your friendship

has meant much to me...

> I am the happiest woman I know....Unknowingly, you lit the path that led my feet. So when you cast your debts and credits in heaven, what comes to many people, because I am serene, should balance against your naughty moments – It just so happened...but so did lightning just happen. That is what we say when we don't know the unseen causes. Perhaps those subtle personal influences, attractions and repulsions, stimulations and depressions, are as fundamental and inevitable as the mysterious rays of electricity.

Mary Hewitt seems to have known King well, and the imagery she used comes so close to the symptoms that Meyer and Barker were concerned about that it might be more than a coincidence that she wrote this way to King. But she was disappointed with him, and the difficulties which he sought to get treated at Johns Hopkins would seem to have been a turning point in their relationship. She felt she had derived a great deal from King. "All this of course does not make one any the less disapproving of some of your ways, and the essential feminine itch to set you right becomes very strong when I come to you, in my review of my own year."

Now she let loose on him: "Your fundamental fault, as a friend, is tyranny. You judge for both in relations when my instinct for friendship would demand equal voice in decision. The pleasantest companionship may be had, intermittently, on this basis, but friendship is too delicate, it must have equal strains on both sides." I suspect that King did not treat male friends, like Harper or certainly Rockefeller, the way Mary Hewitt complained of.

> It is a small matter, (perhaps) whether I see you or not, when you are in town but I should be allowed to judge, knowing my own sense of values; instead you decide that is not to be considered that for a problematical half hour, somewhat unlikely, that I give you a dull tea that you know nothing about. The emphasis I put on this is because it is the inherent unfairness of your mental habit, which will be most prolific of misunderstanding and hurt sensibilities to your wife, if ever you stop long enough to get one. Which leads me naturally to Ruth Fitch. Why did you ever give up that splendid girl? I

cannot comprehend that! A happy New Year!

Mary Hewitt may have known King too well for him to have been able to tolerate much more of this sort of give and take, which she expected of close friendship; although she may not have known of the medical details of his stay at Johns Hopkins, perhaps she understood the concern he had about the issue of electrical influence. Above all she appreciated his difficulties in being close to her, even if she could not absorb how that blockage might bear on why he had failed to find an appropriate marital partner. Like others Mary Hewitt tried to satisfy King's longing for marriage by introducing him to someone eligible. By Jan. 7, 1917 she wrote King that "Ruthie Fitch" was on her honeymoon. Despite Mary Hewitt's temporary dissatisfaction with King, she and he continued to stay on close terms.

A different side of King comes out in his correspondence with the Rev. George Duncan, who was then Minister of St. Andrews Church in Montreal, and at the time a candidate for the presidency of Queen's University. King had written him on July 29, 1916: "I have been at Kingsmere, Que., for the last six weeks, with the exception of a visit paid to North York and a short stay in Ottawa at the meetings of the National Liberal Advisory Committee." King said he had gone West to see his brother, "but also in the main to look into the workings of the industrial experiments commenced last year," which King thought "appear to have been working satisfactorily." King had dictated this letter, which McGregor then typed up for him. King wrote at the time of McGregor: "he is more secretive about my thoughts than I am myself."

As of October 5th King was back in Denver, this time with his mother, following the death of John King. George Duncan's own mother died while King was in Denver. The intimacy of the friendship between Mackenzie King and Duncan is attested to by the way Duncan addressed King as "Rex", a name only his closest acquaintances used. As far as one can tell from the existing correspondence, it was McGregor who let Duncan know about the impending stay at Hopkins. "Having been told by Mr. McGregor to keep your illness private," Duncan wrote on November 1st, he felt he could not discuss it even with his wife. "You have stood by me at big crises, physical, mental, spiritual. You have never failed me, and I feel, never will...." However little McGregor told Duncan, he was a good enough friend of King's to treat it as a matter of grave importance.

Outwardly, however, King was well-enough put together that Duncan was surprised at the news King had sent him.

Unlike with Mary Hewitt, whose generous outgoingness made King feel unable to unburden himself further, with the more reserved Duncan King felt he could allow himself to open up. As Duncan wrote King on Nov. 27th: "The best news you gave me was that advice of the Hopkins friends as to the dual condition. It is private. But my prayers – best wishes – are with you." Duncan was being tactful and discreet, calling King's physicians "Hopkins friends." King had obviously told him a good deal about what Barker and Meyer had been advising him; Duncan's reference to the "dual condition" might well refer to the sexual conflicts which King was coping with. (The physical or material as opposed to the spiritual would comprise the duality.)

It would seem that Duncan was rather more protective in writing King about the stay at Johns Hopkins than King himself. At least King was being extraordinarily trusting of Duncan, perhaps because they had both so recently suffered the loss of parents. On Dec. 7th King wrote Duncan as if they both were fellow recovering patients.

> Just a line to say that I hope you are keeping up the following:
> 1. Miller exercise before breakfast.
> 2. Half-hour walk in the open immediately after
> 3. At least one hour out-doors in the afternoon
> 4. "Eat and Grow Thin" diet at meals
> 5. A little reading on the list of works prescribed
> 6. Early to bed

Although it was King who had had to see the doctors, he felt Duncan could also make use of what King had himself learned:

I enclose a letter just received from Dr. Barker, which kindly return. My purpose in sending it is to quote what he says to me, and apply it to you. I have given you his prescription in full, and there is no charge for the service. I feel sure that you will be all right if you arrange your life according to the outline we arrived at in our conference.

Duncan replied to King immediately, and said he was following the advice Barker had given King; presumably King had been writing tongue-in-cheek (but perhaps not) about there being "no charge for the service." Duncan added one further point, the issue of marriage:

"I must see to your following out this Dr.'s prescription in one important aspect: Have you yet looked out for a wife? Let me know as to this costly item." King had obviously communicated to Duncan what Barker had had to say on how King should conduct himself about eligible women, but he failed to pass along Meyer's own different convictions on this subject.

Without even having heard back from Duncan, King was sending along further Johns Hopkins medical help for Duncan. On Dec. 8th he explicitly referred not just to Meyer by name, but to Meyer's professional title at Johns Hopkins.

> I enclose another letter from Johns Hopkins Hospital, in this instance from the Psychiatrist-in-Chief. This advice I pass on also without charge in the hope that it will, as nearly as possible, be followed to the letter, with the same kind of satisfactory results which I am experiencing from seeking to adhere faithfully to the new regimen.

While Duncan had considered King's earlier communication as "private," here King was making no attempt to disguise Meyer's profession as a psychiatrist. It may be hard for us to imagine what consulting a psychiatrist must have amounted to in 1916; in any event it was not a run-of-the-mill event, as it so often became later. In sending this advice on to Duncan, King was suggesting that he might benefit in his own grieving by turning to the assistance of friendship. "I wonder if the emphasis on 'a few friends' and 'the personal contact and conversation' which Dr. Meyer gives in his letter, are being met in as full measure in your case as they should be. Please return the enclosed when you have finished making a a memo of its contents." However isolated King might have become in his subsequent years, especially during his retirement, in 1916 he had real friends of his own that he could fall back on. For example, in thanking him for a cable Marjorie Herridge, wife of the minister of King's Presbyterian congregation, wrote him that year: "If anyone asked me for one characteristic of you – I should say – your constant remembering your friends...."

As helpful as King's friends could be to him during his 1916 difficulties, the two people we can be sure continued to support him most were his mother and his brother. It could be, of course, that King turned to other friends of his as well, but that the record of their assistance to King does not survive. King's mother and brother saved most of King's correspondence, and he theirs, so it is possible to fill out how King's family played a special role during the fall of 1916.

When King first had arrived in New York on Oct. 24th, he right away wrote a note to his mother; he had had McGregor tell her beforehand that he had received a wire on the 23rd calling him down. King mentioned to her having had dinner with Rockefeller, and that he planned "going on as far as Baltimore on Friday, just for the day." As yet King told his mother nothing about his intention to consult medically at Johns Hopkins. Before going there he again wrote to his mother, telling her of his breakfasting with President Eliot of Harvard. King told her that he had consulted with Eliot about the wording on the inscription to be put on John King's memorial stone at the family plot in Mt. Pleasant Cemetary in Toronto. King had also managed his relationship with Rockefeller in such a way that the line between family and professional life was a thin one; so that King could write to his mother: "Last night, Mrs. Rockefeller was asking particularly for you. She said she had been wanting and meaning to write to you, but did not know just where to address you. She asked me to give you her love, and to tell you I am...much in her thoughts. She also sent love to Jennie." (At that time Mrs. King was living with her daughter Jennie. She must have been immensely proud of her older sons' successes, and also reassured by his friendships.)

Once King had been to Johns Hopkins, and returned temporarily to New York City, he again wrote to his mother. On Oct. 28th he reported to her:

> You will be glad to know that we have located the cause of the nervous irritation I have been suffering. Apparently it is due to an old tooth which has had an abscess at its root – and may have been there for months. It will take an operation to overcome it, and drain the space properly so I am going back to Baltimore tonight to go into Johns Hopkins Hospital that the operation may be performed there. They have the necessary equipment at the university. Then I have to have my gums treated for pyrohoea so that I may have to stay at Baltimore for ten days or two weeks. It is a relief beyond words to have the source of this trouble known for it has driven me almost mad at times.

The extent to which King confided in his mother may be more striking than what he chose to disguise. King gave her a shortened version of his diagnosis at Baltimore:

> I had an x-ray made of my head, of my teeth, and of my spine, and it was in this way he found the trouble. The university specializing in all branches went over me very carefully, and there is not an organ or tissue that has not been subjected to analysis. Excepting evidence of nervous fatigue and this trouble I appear to be sound as a bell.

King wanted his mother to write to him at the hospital. He assured her: "There is nothing to be alarmed about in this affair, and I am only too grateful to be in the hands of the ablest specialists in America."

Isabel King replied to him immediately.

> My dear Billie,
>
> I cannot tell you how badly I feel that your nerves are giving you such trouble. I think you will have to leave the writing of your book until you pull yourself together again. Until these nerves master you [sic] it is almost impossible to get them in there [sic] place again. You have gone through a great deal – gradually one trial after has not let you...but I do hope with all my heart the doctor you are going to see will understand and crush out what you are suffering from.

Her maternal reaction was obviously colored by the death of one daughter and the serious illness of her other son; with King she implied that the stress of his book-writing might be at fault. But she also had to reply to her son's inquiry about the possibility of his having a bust made of her:

> About the marble bust – I do not know what to say – maybe when I am in Ottawa sometime I could have my picture taken unless time will improve my appearance. You know Billie you look at me with lover's eyes. May you always do so is the prayer of your mother.

Perhaps such a woman was none-too-eager to see her only surviving unmarried child liberated from her influence. It was only eight weeks since John King had been buried, and she noted this in writing to her elder son.

On Oct. 31st he wrote her keeping his mother up-to-date:

> I am sending this line just to let you know everything is going along in fine fashion. Don't imagine I am ill in bed. I am using the university's library to continue my studies while here, and going downtown when it suits me. I have to be on hand for treatment each day. Yesterday my teeth were all gone over to remove the tartar, today they are to be gone over to remove the puss formations. Tomorrow the troublesome tooth is to be extracted. Thursday they begin with my nose. I think my tonsils have to be cleaned up or taken out, but none of the operations are of a serious kind. All the facilities are at hand here, and everything most satisfactory. There is nothing therefore to cause concern. I hope you yourself are well, also Jennie – all her family – best love to you all.

In quiet contradiction to his mother's attitude toward his book-writing, King – at odds with what he reported in his diary – was emphasizing that he was continuing his studies even at the Johns Hopkins library.

On November 1st King wrote his mother:

> Just a line to let you know that everything is going along splendidly. I have had two treatments of my gums thus far, and this afternoon have the bad tooth extracted. After that we decide what it may be necessary to do with the nose. Dr. Barker hopes this operation may save the necessity of a further operation!

Once Rockefeller had formally written King with a commitment to cover the expenses of the physicians and the hospital stay in Baltimore, King wrote his mother about it:

> Could anyone have a truer or kinder friend! I imagine the bill may be considerable for I have seen the best doctors in America, but it will mean everything to me for the rest of life. No one but myself can know what I have suffered not for one

or two but for six or eight months back. I feel a different man
already.

Just before he was operated on November 2nd, King wrote his
mother a letter in handwriting that was much larger than usual; he was
clearly anxious about how things would go: "Best love to you and
Jennie, Max and all the children. This is just to let you know of my last
thoughts before this operation. May it mean much good for us all."
She answered at once: "I have received your two notes and been *so*
thankful the doctors have found the root of the evil. How more than
fortunate you are to have struck the right Hospital and Doctors. You
might have gone on for any length of time and not have found the real
cause." Like her son she idealized what Rockefeller's offer to
underwrite the medical expenses amounted to: "Mr. Rockefeller has
shown his true friendship. I am often of the idea that to work with a
man with such high ideals of right and wrong is beyond the wear and
strain of political life." (King would often echo exactly such
moralizing sentiments of Isabel King.) She obviously had heard some
of the background to King's problems with his nervousness. "I am so
thankful you will not have that nervous strain any longer. Nerves are
cruel and one hardly knows how and when they may attack one." (It
remains uncertain whether she realized how concerned about her
own nerves King had been.) She reminded him of Max's up-coming
birthday, and wondered what King himself might like for his own
birthday. This was, I think, a nice old-fashioned tight-knit family, one
which our own more anomic times ought to feel nostalgic for rather
than try to make fun of. "You are," his mother wrote King, "never out
of my thoughts."
There are a number of missing letters from King to his brother in
Denver. This is unfortunate, and perhaps not an accident, which is
presumably also true of missing pages from King's diary. Since King
had medically confided in his physician brother, it would be important
to get more of what he told his younger brother, and what Max himself
thought. Once the diagnosis had been made at Johns Hopkins, King
had evidently written his brother about the therapeutic program
which had been settled on. Max wrote him from Denver on Nov. 2nd:
"My dear Will. I was sorry to see by your communications from New
York that you have found it necessary to secure further medical advice
about that condition of which you spoke to me." It does sound like
King might have recently relied on his brother's medical knowledge

when he was visiting Colorado with their mother.

> I do hope that Dr. Barker may be able to help you. Let me be frank and lament, dear Will, that no doctor can help you unless you carry out his advice to the letter. Working at your book from morning until eleven o'clock at night, as you confided to May [Max's wife]...you have done since going home, is not only contrary to the advice you have received but is, even for a man in the best of shape, rank intemperance. You will have to map out your work with carefully restricted hours and stick absolutely within the limits. I am awaiting anxiously to hear the results of your consultation. Is it Dr. Lewellys T. Barker or what are the initials?

King had promised to speak to the Rockefeller people about promoting Max's own book dealing with the recovery from tuberculosis. Like his mother, Max thought that King's book-writing had been a source of his nervous trouble; a writer like Max could appreciate what genuine source of tension book-writing can be.

In the midst of Max composing his Nov. 2nd letter the postman brought another communication from King, this time from Baltimore:

> I have read with the greatest interest the findings of the various doctors. It is a wonderful relief...that nothing organically is wrong. Even if the results point to any one thing more than another it is the great necessity of placing careful limitations on your nervous activities and of being most regular in your way of living. From what you say in your letter I gather Dr. Barker is the man of whom I had been thinking....

Once the operation itself was over King wired the reassuring news to his mother and sister. Isabel King wrote him on Nov. 3rd: "It was very thoughtful of you to send the wire and we are delighted to know the operation is successfully over. What a blessing it is you discovered the cause of your nervousness and that it was something which could be remedied." She had adopted King's point of view, which attributed the nervous problems to his teeth; it was more optimistic to indict such infections rather than to fall back on biological or hereditary causes, and Cotton's theories went on to attract "considerable attention during the 1920s."[3] Max King, however, had concluded "that nothing organically is wrong."

King's sister, with whom their mother was now staying at Walkerton, Ontario, added a note of her own to Isabel's Nov. 3rd letter. She was reporting on their mother's weak health, as well as expressing a tender concern for King's own well-being. One of Jennie's letters to King (Nov. 5th) indicates how serious a reader Isabel King was; although an old lady and in a weak condition, still Jennie could report; "Mother has a book on the go at present so nothing else counts! She is reading Winston Churchill's *A Far Country* and I can't get a word out of her!" It is not surprising that a famous 1905 portrait of Isabel King showed her reading an open book in her lap, even though her letters to King displayed an inadequate command of grammer.

King continued to keep his mother informed about his medical treatment, rather minimizing his distress. He wrote her on November 4th:

> everything has progressed splendidly and...I hope to leave here on Tuesday or Wednesday of the approaching week. I have been able to go about all right most of the time except for the day that my tooth was extracted, and a hole bored through my nose so as to make a little canal through which the open space in the cheek called the *sinus* could be properly irrigated and drained. I did not take gas for either operation, preferring local anesthetics, so I was able to follow the whole proceedings with very little in the way of pain, though the nervous strain was important.

King thought his reading of *Power Through Repose* had given him a method for dealing with his nervous troubles, and he said he intended to speak with Barker about some of King's mother's own nervous problems. (The ether came for a later procedure, and King seems to have skipped bringing it to his mother's attention.)

On Nov. 8th Jennie gave birth to a girl, and King's mother was the one to let him know. The same day Max wrote to King, and he offered a relevant-seeming paragraph from a book on *Differential Diagnosis* since it seemed "to offer very clearly a point that we have discussed":

> the patient's focused and concentrated attention discovers sensations due probably to some of the physiological changes

occurring normally in the part to which attention has, unfortunately, been directed. These changes go on normally without producing any sensation noted in the brain. But when the brain is sensitized, especially in relation to the part attended to, even the heart-beat may be felt as painful.

Max may have been addressing whatever bothered King at the base of his spine.

It is not clear that King accepted his younger sibling's view of his problems. It is worth noting that in 1922, shortly before Max's death, King once again visited him in Denver. They had "a good talk" about Max's new book, *Nerves and Personal Power*, and King's own persisting "nervous condition." King was already Prime Minister by then. According to King, his brother thought the nervousness arose "from a psycho-neurotic condition, some complex due to suppressed emotions. He assured me some things I had believed to be real are not such but wholly due to effect of thought & will." While Max's thinking was consistent with that of Meyer, Meyer had recommended popular works of self-help whereas Max suggested some un-named psychoanalytic literature which King said he had found "helpful."[4]

Before King had departed from Baltimore in 1916, he had asked Barker about his mother's problems. Barker considered her "nervous troubles" to be, like King's own, susceptible to the method of treatment implied by an insistence on regularity of habits. By Nov. 15th Isabel King was resting up at the same hospital that her daughter had entered because of child-birth. By then King was able to write his mother: "I have not felt as well in years as I feel now. Partly getting rid of the infection and fears arising from it, partly from following advice concerning worry. Partly from dieting." On the 21st King was writing to his brother: "I seem to have gotten entirely over the nervousness I endured for so long, and have also taken off about ten pounds...."

King's worst fears about the fragility of his remaining family would soon be confirmed; for his mother died in 1917. King's relationship with Rockefeller, however, became closer than ever. One of Rockefeller's biographers thought that King had been not only "an indispensable guide" over the Colorado troubles "but probably the closest friend JDR Jr. would ever have." So that Rockefeller, when he sent word congratulating King after in August 1919 he had become chosen as the leader of the Liberal Party in Canada, must have appreciated the full significance of King's reply, which alluded to Rockefeller's help in connection with the stay at Johns Hopkins. King wrote: "I am conscious, as I write, that but for all that your great and generous nature has made possible within these difficult years, I should neither be in the position I am today, nor be in a condition of body and mind to bring to the tasks ahead the energies they demand."[5]

After King's death, some of his surviving friends wrote consoling each other. Julia Grant, the Countess Cantacuzene, was a grand-daughter of President Grant who shared some of King's spiritualist interests. She wrote to Rockefeller on Sept. 18, 1950: "I think that his love for you was greater than for any of his other men friends." Rockefeller replied: "You and I know what a wonderful friend Mr. King was. Both of our lives have been enriched and made far more meaningful and worthwhile because he figured so largely in them."[6] Their obvious fondness for him, along with the loyalty of his immediate family, were at odds with the feelings about him on the part of his personal staff, adding to how baffling his personality has to remain.

King's story should remind us that no matter how well friends may succeed in knowing someone, they are still capable of being off the mark. Although in King's intimate circle it was no secret that he was seriously troubled in 1916, and unhappy at remaining a bachelor, issues like delusions of reference, hallucinations, or electrical influences were not part of the main picture that King's friends built up. While it may be easy to make too much of the diagnostic significance of King's various troubles, it is also humanly impressive how despite the fact that his friends saw signs of the tip of the iceberg, they missed the underlying problems that King and his physicians were grappling with. But since King managed to succeed politically in spite of these difficulties, perhaps his friends' view of things was not so mistaken after all.

Chapter 7
Conclusions

For some history has been seen primarily as a matter of accumulating factual data. It took a great historiographer to insist that "to set forth historical facts is not comparable to dumping a barrow of bricks,"[1] but this lesson seems to need repeating as each generation is tempted to believe it has finally reached rock-bottom reality. Despite how important rival perspectives are in sensitizing us to areas of life which have been neglected, still history-writing has to rest ultimately on evidence which can be shared and evaluated by independent observers. Although I had long been intrigued by the subject of psychology and politics, I would never have approached any study of Mackenzie King, no matter what his oddities might have been reported to have been like, without my having had something solid to go on.

So laying out now the exact circumstances of King's having been in contact with a famous psychiatrist should at least satisfy the quest for historical thoroughness. It becomes possible to restore a hitherto lost piece of the past. One of the key sources of material has of course been King's diary. Although he knew a bit about Freud, if only due to his brother Max's prodding, it may be fortunate that King remained as relatively naive as he did; for it means that King's diary is a more direct reflection of his immediate thinking, without its being contaminated by the pseudo-sophistication of fancy terminology. King kept at his diary so conscientiously that there are times when I have tempted to treat it as if we had his free associations, and certain topics seem meaningful by virtue of their arising in close conjunction with other subjects.

But reconstructing the past becomes the more plausible as we put together a variety of sources of evidence. The hospital record, the doctors' letters, and Meyer's notes to himself, do not just supplement King's diary account but they provide different avenues of understanding. And then King's personal correspondence brings a special set of perspectives to bear, so that it is possible to understand what happened in alternative lights. Although it is hard to be systematic about exactly what I learned from talking with some who had known King personally, these people did help me make humanly understandable what might otherwise have bordered on the antiquarian.

Today psychiatry is currently in a phase where biological innovations are in the forefront of attention. We are again at a period similar to that in which Meyer found himself at the height of his career. It is notable that even with someone like King, so convinced of the reality of the spiritual dimension to life, he readily accepted that "nervousness" had a physical basis in what he thought of as "material" circumstances. Henry Cotton's emphasis on infected teeth may seem an odd by-path, but the history of science is filled with such mistaken ventures. Cotton was part of a tradition of thought in which organically oriented psychiatrists have been pushing back the frontiers of the biology of the mind. A new psychoactive drug like Prozac, for example, has recently been widely prescribed for a broad range of human troubles from depression to excess body weight. (King might well have benefited from trying it out.)

Along with the enthusiasm for what might be accomplished by means of new drugs there has in our time simultaneously been a heightened concern with how to arrange and classify the types of clinical problems that psychiatry is concerned with. It may seem like a progressive advance that homosexuality, for example, is no longer considered an illness by the American Psychiatric Association, and it is welcome that individual sexual preferences are now less likely to be stigmatized as medical "perversions." So, even at a time of advances in new pills, we still have to worry about just how relevant the whole disease model can be for the domains of psychiatry.

The most influential psychiatric manual today, which has been cited all across the Western world, is *The Diagnostic and Statistical Manual of the American Psychiatric Association*, 4th edition (known as DSM IV). The late Ronald D. Laing, who had a special flair for understanding patients who were exceptionally disturbed and although trained as a psychoanalyst in Britain went beyond Freud's own categories of thought, once wrote an interesting little piece about "God and Psychiatry." Laing irreverently said he had more trouble with the second concept than the first. He noted how the earlier manual, DSM III, lists "many" 'criteria,' which in different permutations and combinations comprise existing known mental disorders." I would like to quote Laing about them all here, in order for the reader to reflect on how many of these criteria might relevantly apply to Mackenzie King:

> refusal to maintain body weight over a minimal normal weight for age and height; magical thinking, instanced by superstitiousness, clairvoyance, telepathy, "sixth sense," "others can feel my feelings"; sensing the presence of a force or person not actually present ("I felt as if my dead mother were in the room with me"); inadequate rapport in face-to-face interaction due to constricted or inappropriate affect – what occasions people to be called "aloof," or "cold"; self-dramatizations, as in exaggerated expressions of emotions; craving for activity and excitement; overreactions to minor events; irrational, angry outbursts or tantrums; being perceived by others as shallow and lacking genuineness, even if superficially warm and charming; behavior that is egocentric, self-indulgent and inconsiderate of others, or vain and demanding; decreased effectiveness or productivity at school, work, or home; loss of interest in, or enjoyment of, sex; talking less than usual; tearfulness, and crying; marked impairment in role-functioning as wage-earner, student, or home-maker; markedly peculiar behavior (for example, collecting garbage, talking to oneself in public, or hoarding food); marked impairment in personal hygiene and grooming.[2]

This whole catalogue of indices of mental trouble should indicate the grounds on which King might look disturbed, as well as the many signs of problems which would not be applicable to him. King's tendency towards magical thinking was obviously marked even if it rarely seemed to surface politically. King also could be characterized as "aloof" or "cold", although as prime minister these proved suitable traits. His staff found him to be terribly egocentric, which helps explain why they were not more loyal to him after his death. Otherwise Laing's list of marks of emotional distress would not seem specially to bear on King. Of course one has to set aside the problem of King's sex life. And it has to be sobering to find Laing singling out "sensing the presence of a force or person not actually present," and his particular example of a dead mother, since this sounds so much like the King we have become familiar with.

It is however still an open question how psychiatry should proceed even with those who it agrees are in need of help. No one today seems to understand how many of the latest drugs manage to work, any more that the practice of electroshock treatment can be scientifically explicated; until we know more about why and under what circumstances different techniques can be effective, reliance on their use is bound to leave many of us uneasy. Over-medications, and the problems of the presence of side-effects to the use of drugs, ought not to be swept under the carpet. Nor is it a simple matter how to persuade people to take medication. Any emphasis on the role of heredity, no matter how useful from the point of view of diagnosis and classification, it not apt to be helpful therapeutically.

On the other hand long-term psychoanalytic treatment, with its ambitious aim of reconstructing childhood for the sake of attaining rational insight, which ideally should be liberating, is also not without its own draw-backs. Despite Freud's early hopes, in the end he was disillusioned about the therapeutic efficacy of psychoanalysis. And, especially since his death in 1939, a wide variety of different psychotherapeutic techniques have been experimented with in an effort to achieve better clinical results.

Meyer deserves to be remembered as someone humanistically trying to resist the temptation to reduce all psychiatric dilemmas down to any single so-called cause. It is true that in hindsight he too loyalled backed-up some of Henry Cotton's most regrettable surgical experiments. It should not be necessary to white-wash how Meyer reacted to Cotton's work in order to agree that on the whole Meyer did a remarkable job of avoiding the mistakes of either concentrating solely on the hypothesized existence of toxins or focusing exclusively on the independent force of psychological factors that Freud himself encouraged.

Today psychoanalytic psychology, after a period of great

fashionability in the States, is once again under a serious cloud as in Meyer's time. Perhaps the height of Freud's medical influence came around the centenary of his birth, 1956; in those days psychoanalysts were, at least in America, becoming regularly appointed as heads of the leading psychiatric departments. In Canada the clinical influence of Freud flourished somewhat later, and has managed to persist a generation longer than in the U.S.

In both countries, however, Freud seemed to offer an advance toward the direction of humaneness and dignity, after a period in which psychosurgeries like prefrontal lobotomy, and electroshock treatment, had been much too readily used. But the therapeutic claims for psychoanalytic therapy were so often exaggerated that the possible abuses inherent in Freud's recommended approach became medically notorious. Not long ago in the States a patient, who had been treated on a couch for depression without benefit, successfully sued a hospital on the grounds that to deprive him of available drugs amounted to malpractice. While literary critics, philosophers, and social scientists have remained attracted to the lucidity and scope of Freud's theories, and publications about his school of thought have continued to mushroom, medicine as a whole has withdrawn from what it has perceived to be the unverified ambitions that the analysts once held. Outside North America, in countries like France where Freud's influence is relatively recent, students are flocking to study psychoanalysis in a strictly academic setting. And physicians in someplace like Italy are aware how psychoanalytic therapeutic claims were once over-sold in the States, and how that backfired against Freud's profession as a whole.

Meyer was prescient in his wariness about the sectarianism of the psychoanalysts. He was exceptional in his open-mindedness, and therefore he was willing to think there might be a bit of truth in almost every theory that got advanced. If some past psychiatric practices sound too much like voodoo, it would be honest to admit that the best psychiatrists agree they are still today working in an unusually unsettled field.

Similarly to William James's having reacted to Freud as "a regular *hallucine*," Meyer too thought that psychoanalysis was dogmatic; Meyer could not accept the idea that any complex human life can be simplified into the formulas that even the most enlightened Freudians proposed. So on the one hand Meyer resisted the determinism of the biologically-oriented of his day; for he remained optimistic about what psychotherapy might be able to accomplish. At the same time he did not allow himself to go overboard in a purely psychological direction. In the 1920s some psychoanalysts were setting out not only to attempt to cure the great psychoses, but a few even went so far as to propose that psychotic reactions in patients should be evoked as a regular part of treating human difficulties. Instead of Meyer's reputation flourishing now because of the extreme tendencies he repudiated, his standing has suffered because he tried to navigate between the strictly organic and the psychoanalytic approaches.

In hindsight King was lucky that he got sent to Johns Hopkins at a time when Meyer was unquestionably the continent's leading psychiatric light. Some of the specifics of how King got treated are bound to seem bizarre today; no-one would now share the hope that extracting a tooth or taking out adenoids would be successful in relieving a "nervous" condition. But Meyer, and Barker too, were broad-minded and patient in how they approached King's troubles. For example, they touched on his sexual conflicts without intruding themselves too far; they gently tried to encourage him to be more accepting of his physical nature. But they did not attempt to infantilize King, which was one proposal of standard 1916 psychoanalytic doctrine. Meyer was practicing with King what would now be called brief supportive short-term psychotherapy. Although in a limited period of time he learned a good deal about the history and nature of King's problems, Meyer was not aiming to confront King with the idea of altering in a major way how he might live his life.

Like most people in trouble King was prone to be suggestible to the impact of physicians he could realistically consider expert. The mere fact that King had talked to Meyer, and also Barker, about his most intimate troubles may have had as much of a therapeutic impact as anything that was said to him. The relationship between King and his doctors could have been as curative as the substance of what they said to him, or the unusual-seeming procedures they undertook in the light of 1916 psychiatric thinking.

One of the difficulties in trying today to evaluate the psychiatric evidence about King is that one is obliged to have to challenge it every bit as much as one would critically approach any other set of historical documents. "Facts" never succeed in speaking for themselves, and this is as true for psychiatry as it would be for the rest of social science. One has therefore to question not only whether King had told the full truth to his physicians, but it is necessary to ask if he did remain as continent and as repressed as in 1916 he appeared to be.

For what it is worth at least one of King's later private secretaries was highly doubtful of King's abstinence, at least during the 1930s when he knew him. As I presented this former associate with King's psychiatric material from 1916, I encountered a handful of anecdotes that ran directly counter to the picture of King that we have come up with from that World War I period. King's valet supposedly complained about his having to get women's "pomade" off King's trousers ("pomade" was used then to keep a woman's hair in place) and the butler was said to have been shocked to find King in a compromising situation in his study. Either King radically changed later on or, as this private secretary was insistent on, King had simply been putting on a respectable-looking front for the sake of the image of himself he entrusted to his doctors. It might be consistent with King's having succeeded in later conquering his 1916 bout of "nerves" if he did become more tolerant of his sexual drives and was able successfully to gratify them, even if not in the conventional manner of married life.

The whole issue of marriage is in itself an aspect of the impact which psychoanalytic reasoning has had. Freud's system of thought seemed questionable to someone like Meyer just because it purported to try to answer too many questions all at once; and yet within our culture as a whole Freud's success has come precisely because of the structured nature of the propositions that he advanced. Meyer was from a psychoanalytic viewpoint too willing to live with uncertainty, what appeared to be an intellectually hand-to-mouth existence. Freud was proud of his own capacity for bringing together his ideas into a coherent body of knowledge. By his standards marriage meant theoretically the achievement of normality; successful heterosexual relations on a stable basis were intrinsic to the ideal of "genitality" that the Freudians were proposing.

At bottom Freud was by no means an advocate of middle-class conformist values; in practice he sanctioned all kinds of unusual human relationships. At least with people he liked and considered superior, as far as he was concerned all conventional rules of behavior could be broken. Sometimes he welcomed divorce; on other occasions he insisted on sexual abstinence. And with his youngest child Anna, who became his successor as leader of the psychoanalytic movement, she remained unmarried and attached to a wealthy woman friend; although Freud worried about her future there is no sign he disapproved of the kind of life she chose to lead.

Yet however tolerant of human individuality Freud might have been, as a matter of theory his system of psychoanalysis appealed in North America to some of the most conventional values. At least for the bulk of the twentieth century marriage was part of the ideal of existence which fully developed people were supposed to live up to. Fred McGregor, in reflecting on what King might have been like, was also expressing this prevalent point of view:

> The right wife might have fended off the attacks of illness and fatigue which plagued him in later years, and cheered him on his way to a much more serene old age than he did enjoy. There would have been more entertaining at Laurier House, more merriment and sparkle, a bit more prodigality, the infusion of a dram or two of humour and fun in a life that took everything too seriously. Laurier House would have lost its sombreness and Kingsmere would have been even more a paradise.[3]

McGregor's idealism about marriage was shared by King himself. In the 1940s one of his assistants straight-forwardly, in the presence of a few others, asked King why he had never married; instead of King's bridling at an impudent invasion of his privacy, or ignoring the intrusion, the Prime Minister patiently explained the particular circumstances of his life which he thought had rendered marriage impossible. This aid knew King well enough to anticipate that instead of being offended at this familiarity King enjoyed explaining about himself. Historians continue to be taken in by King's idealized self-conception of himself. "Nobody would have been surprised," it has recently been contended, "if King had married well and married long. He thought a lot about marriage, hoped he would find the ideal wife, and deeply regretted that he never did."[4]

But such reasoning follows too closely King's own failure to acknowledge how certain of his human deficiencies also help explain why he never married. As one of King's private assistants remarked to me, no woman would have seemed "good enough" for King. His family may have been preying on this propensity when they argued against Mathilde Grossert. McGregor's utopianism about what the state of matrimony could have meant to King failed to take into account the extent to which the public King and the private man were very much alike, despite the publicity which King's so-called "schizophrenic dualism"[5] has received. When McGregor was trying to explain why after the electoral debacle of 1911 Laurier might have been inclined to help other of his former Ministers, ahead of King, get back into the House of Commons, McGregor noted certain personal qualities of King's that contrasted unfavorably with that of his colleagues. The sense of superiority King harbored, however it may have helped strengthen him, could also be a personal and political liability.

Unfortunately the 1916 psychiatric file about King cannot answer all possible questions, or even be considered the rock-bottom sort of evidence that naive observers might hopefully like to take it to be. But the record does indicate he seems to have had conflicts about sexuality which are supportive of the significance of at least some aspects of Freudian theory. Whether King sometimes engaged in youthful "expeditions," or was as abstinent as Meyer thought, or been both in different phases, King would seem to have been unusually sexually dis-satisfied. And this aspect of his personality, instead of being understood as an isolated phenomena, should I think be seen in the light of his whole characteristic being.

Even with all the diary-keeping King engaged in, without the psychiatric material there would be no way of guessing at the existence of his "principle subjective disturbance...of being influenced electrically by others and of influencing others in this way." According to the standards of today's *DSM* manuals this problem would be a sign of real psychiatric trouble. Fortunately for King the doctors he saw were not unduly alarmed by what they felt was hallucinatory. Even though Meyer was no Freudian, he did think that the first and most obvious explanation of King's problems related to his intolerance of his own sexual drives.

However experts might choose to interpret King's hallucinations differently, they would appear to fit rather neatly into helping explain his later involvement with spiritualism. For example, when in 1919 King first got elected to the leadership of the Liberal party he gave the following account in his diary:

> The majority was better than I had anticipated. I was too heavy of heart and soul to appreciate the tumult of applause, my thoughts were of dear mother and father and little Bell all of whom I felt to be very close to me, of grandfather and Sir

Wilfrid also. I thought: it is right, it is the call of duty. I have sought nothing, it has come. It has come from God. The dear loved ones know and are about, they are alive and with me in this great everlasting Now and Here. It is to His work I am called, and to it I dedicate my life.[6]

I think that in any kind of crisis or turning point people who are serious get reminded one way or another of their past familial commitments. King did have genuine religious convictions. Ferns and Ostry unkindly suggested of King's relationship with Wilfrid Laurier that "the explanation of his later spiritualism" could be found in King's efforts as an "outsider to establish by psychic means the contacts he never had (and by the nature of his personality and his political outlook never could have) with a man like Laurier...."[7] Yet I think that when King wrote about Laurier and various family members being "very close" to him, it is impossible not to be reminded of how in 1916 Barker had wanted King to tell Rockefeller "about the phenomena of regarding people as near at times and of their exerting an influence upon me."

In 1916 Barker had thought, according to King, that Simon Flexner should know about this electrical issue as well. King would presumably only have hesitated to unwind about his peculiarities if he had felt uncertain about how Rockefeller and Flexner would react to the news. If King had already assimilated his troubled feelings to any sort of more or less conventional religious thinking, or even spiritualist doctrines, he would not have felt he had any "nervous" problem. (Freud tended to link the loss of religious faith to the rise of the neuroses.) In 1916 King had acknowledged in his diary that he understood that his curious convictions about influence would be "a bad sign if it becomes a fixed idea...."

Assuming King needed to absorb his 1916 beliefs about electrical influence into religious doctrines, he still required the further assistance of spiritualism in order to satisfy his thought processes in a way which was comfortable for him. At least I would propose that the now well-known commitment of King as a spiritualist, which was a secret until Blair Fraser broke the news, has to be understood not just in terms of how many other people at the time shared King's occult proclivities, but that it can be specifically traced within King's life history to his 1916 pathology. According to some branches of psychoanalytic thinking, psychosis can be closer to health than one might guess, and neurosis is sometimes thought to be less apt to be self-healing. Of course there will be those like Carl G. Jung who would argue in favor of the existence of "synchronicity," the doctrine that meaningful coincidences tend to occur "when powerful psychic components are activated."[8] Some of King's involved 1916 emotions remain, to me at least, inexplicable, although others may be able to make more sense of them. I am content to use this clinical material for the sake of establishing certain continuities within the story-line of King's life.

In later years, when King went back to Johns Hopkins for re-examination, he did not forget about his earlier troubles. In 1927, for example, he referred in a letter to Barker about "the nervousness from which I suffered at times." By then King had been functioning in high public office for years, and that sort of role has to be a highly demanding sort of testing experience. So it may not be surprising if King now chose to minimize the extent of his 1916 difficulties. As King put it, "You may recall that I then said that, except for the nervousness from which I suffered at times, I felt that I had the constitution of a lion and could go through anything in the way of work."

It is a noteworthy aspect of what happened to King, and how he succeeded in overcoming his 1916 difficulties, that neither Meyer nor Barker had tried to make any kind of rationalistic frontal assault on King's character as a whole. They made no effort to construct interpretations to dissolve his beliefs, or to change his life; they simply explained to King that his worrisome convictions were hallucinations, and he quickly accepted the idea that others did not share his view of things. King did think, in connection with "the phenomena of regarding people as near at times and of their exerting an influence upon me," that this whole thought process of his might be part of a "case that these men of science wish to study more in detail." In future years King could justify his spiritualist endeavors as part of a legitimate inquiry into a realm which science had not yet succeeded in understanding. But during seances, and at table-rappings, King would not be humanly isolated but rather sharing with others experiences which remained important to him. King's opponents under-estimated him at their peril, and we too should realize that his need for the support of human contact had limits.

The Meyerian approach had been to try and work with the strengths King brought with him. Therefore the doctors at Johns Hopkins took for granted that King was an able and promising political figure, one who might be suffering from some immediate set-backs but who could be counted upon, once he got over this particular period, to be able to find his own way. Although Meyer may have, in his notes to himself, had some doubts that King could succeed without more outside help than Meyer was then prepared to offer, Meyer did act as if King were able to make do more or less on his own.

Although King did seem acutely troubled by the fall of 1916, it has to be remarkable that he succeeded in being able to function so effectively later despite (or because of) the continuation of some rather eccentric thought processes. Here I think that the example of King's life can do something in itself for our understanding of psychological theory. However self-deceptive King was about the possibility of ever getting married, or how notoriously reluctant he was to admit he might have been wrong – about the outcome of the 1916 presidential election, for example – these peculiarities did not trip King up politically.

A tendency to exaggerate pathology can lead to missing the special resources King was able to rely on. For I do not think we have been adequately prepared for the idea that someone so privately unusual could nonetheless perform in a political democracy in such an outstanding manner. The good man, as Aristotle argued so long ago, is not the same as the good citizen; and therefore public virtues may be quite distinct from qualities that are privately admirable. Our understanding of political leadership would be enhanced if we gave up the naive idea of what normality amounts to. Freud used to like to quote Hamlet's familiar words: "There are more things in heaven and earth, Horatio, than are dreamt of in your philosophy." A proper use of psychology should make us more, rather than less, tolerant and compassionate.

I believe that King's very lack of so-called normalcy, which was so extreme as to lead some clinicians whom I have asked for advice to think in terms of a so-called latent psychosis or even schizophrenia, must have lent a special edge to his political capacities. What might look like "schizoid" detachment can be extremely helpful for a labor negotiator or political leader. Hasty retrospective diagnoses are highly suspect. But I think that King's suspiciousness about other people, whether they be servants, staff, or colleagues, could be a positive benefit to him politically. McGregor once commented on how King's "very sensitive nature could...magnify out of all proportion any sign of indifference."[9] A historian has proposed that "King's doubts about his colleagues' judgement came close to paranoia as he contemplated the mess the world was in"[10] after World War II. Neatby thought that King was "endowed with a sixth sense for danger," and that this sensitivity made him so cautious.[11] (Interestingly enough his mother was also extremely sensitive, and could entertain silly ideas about people talking about her.) Although it may not seem humanly attractive that King might have regularly proceeded on the premise that everybody else was out to do him in, some such conviction would be a basis for the political cleverness and cunning which was to be a hallmark of King's career. His choice of a political life meant that only in his retirement would he be truly lonely.

It is not possible to sustain the early hope of some political psychologists that successful democratic character can be identified with emotional health. Social scientists have not been alone with their naivete. Psychiatrists do not need to be looked upon as some sort of ideal creatures, either in their individual capacities or in their ability to predict which people are likely to perform particularly badly under severe stress.

Instead of thinking that psychology is capable of offering us any unbiased means for evaluating political character, I think we have to accept the inevitable role which surprising emotions continue to play in the lives of some of our most capable political actors. Freud himself too often liked to think he had created a science, and his ideas have often been misused for reductionistic purposes, and the belittling of human accomplishments. We ought not to be squeamish about the full range of human variety. I suspect that if King had been homosexual, or an alcoholic, or a Don Juan, to pick only a few alternatives to the life he chose to lead, people would find those choices more conventional, and therefore relatively more acceptable, than the unusual path he followed.

The 1916 psychiatric material about King should remind us how barren a dry-as-dust conception of normality has to be. If at times it sounds as if King were "crazy," I wonder to what extent we are prepared to accept a high degree of apparent irrationality in everyday "normal" life. It should be clear that the concept of neurosis can only be a starting point in understanding someone like King. He did suffer from conflicts between what he called his spiritual aspirations as opposed to his "material" side, and this fight within himself over sexuality sounds text-booky. In 1933 he explained in his diary that feelings of tension and depression could be related to "the unnaturalness of a celibate life with strong animal passions to contend with, and a highly sensitive nature."[12] The next month he was commenting several times on having had "Freudian"[13] sorts of dreams. King may have taken the companionship dogs can provide to an extreme, but then in his old age Freud too found that such animals make good friends. It does not really help much to search for labels to cover someone like King who was so remarkable in how he made use of his idiosyncracies.

At least I think what would be needed as part of a thorough exploration of King's character would have to include an investigation of his family history, the circumstances of his childhood, and the personalities of his parents and siblings, in addition to some discussion of the servants in his home. But there has already been too much unwarranted conjecturing about King, and on the whole I think psychoanalytic theory has been apt to be pushed further than the available evidence warrants. Although my own training and specialization is in political theory, I am acutely aware of the misleading appeals of what Freud, in his cautious moods, repudiated as "speculations."

So I would like to leave us with a quandry which should be instructive. We know, even though it is still not professionally widely enough recognized in political science, that every historical explanation has to imply certain psychological assumptions about human behavior. I am not referring to the most obvious sorts of examples; for instance, at a Cabinet meeting a Minister once rapped against the table with his foot "unconsciously," and King stopped the proceedings to find out what was going on.[14] In hindsight such an event has to be interesting, but more run-of-the-mill matters also require psychological interpretation.

Freud's understanding of human motives is of critical importance, and King's failure to marry cannot be considered a minor aspect of his personality. As J. W. Pickersgill once observed, King "had no wife and children, nor even much contact with other families containing young children or adolescents. He therefore had little continuous contact with the march of fashion in ordinary speech." Pickersgill worked on King's speeches, and saw the way his personality had to find expression in them: "During his last years he often expressed regret that the endless pressure of work had so limited his normal human relationships. One result was, to put it in a phrase which he would have detested, that his style and vocabulary were *frozen* in the early years of this century."[15]

Something was often felt to be humanly missing in King, and perhaps the issue of marriage can be taken to symbolize that absence. Norman Robertson, who as a high civil servant had had for years a close working relationship with King,

> took a dim view of King the man. According to Charles Ritchie, his colleague and close friend, Robertson "despised" him. Douglas Le Pan, another good friend and colleague, remembered being with Robertson at a cottage on Georgian Bay the day King passed away in the summer of 1950. "...I turned to Norman," Le Pan wrote, "and made the kind of anodyne remark about the late Prime Minister that the circumstances seemed to require. I will never forget his reply. He said quite simply, 'I never saw a touch of greatness in him.'" But what had he meant by greatness? Jetty Robertson was convinced that her husband believed that King lacked a world view, the long foresight that someone – Winston Churchill, say – had had. Others might feel that to be too charitable an interpretation, one that neglected Robertson's dislike of and resentment at King's pettiness and flawed human qualities. But whatever he meant, there is no doubt that his was a devastating and striking comment on the man for whom he had worked so long.[16]

Others of King's assistants shared the worst gloss one could possibly put on Robertson's words.

The complexities of King's mind, which observers understandably took as indecisiveness, meant that he gave out contradictory instructions to his staff. As his assistants tried to carry them out, with results that King found unsatisfactory, he failed to acknowledge any responsibility of his own.

Pickersgill was notable for being able to stand up to King, and in public succeeded in being more generous than Robertson's private remarks, but still, reading between the lines, one can see how little genuine liking King had evoked. About King's death Pickersgill reminisced:

> Throughout his career Mackenzie King had commanded respect, though it was often reluctantly given, but little

affection except for a few intimate friends. His death, however, aroused deep feeling everywhere in Canada. It was as though a whole people suddenly realized, at the same moment, that the country had lost one of its greatest citizens and that a period of history had ended. If there was not an outpouring of grief, there was a solemn feeling of awe.

Pickersgill then added:

> Although we had had such a close association for more than a dozen years, I felt no real sorrow at Mackenzie King's death. I had seen him regularly after he retired and realized that he was failing physically, but what I found sadder was his inability to adapt himself to the inevitable limitations of retirement. He missed the attention and the sense of mission which had sustained him in office. I knew he could never be happy as a private citizen. More time than he could hope for would be needed before the public began to recognize the extent to which he had transformed the country.[17]

Pickersgill was writing in 1975, just a year before Stacey's work helped ensure that King's memory would be covered with ridicule.

Looking at King with dispassion, he did have a curious combination of intuition and detachment which suited him as a conciliator even if it left his former aids a good deal less than heartbroken at his death. Perhaps if King had left a family the reaction of his former staff would seem less memorable. A political scientist has correctly pointed out that

> Given his obsessive concern with his family tree and his profound sense of his own place in history being organically bound up in the destiny of his family, how curious it is – how very, *very* curious – that King should never have married and fathered children to carry on the Mackenzie and King lines.[18]

Yet King's distance from "normal" human emotions was an essential aspect of how he was able to accomplish his particular triumphs. He was so superb and successful as a tactician, and in his ability to manage people, that his life lacks the possibility of the romance associated with failure.

It is impossible to explain how some people lack certain affects, or are particularly prone to some emotions, at least not without more research and knowledge. In King's case it does seem sometimes as if his own mysticism were an antidote to his worldly pragmatism. As political figures go King was less hollow than most; men of action are rarely as introspective as King's diaries record him as having been. It is precisely because King had been able to sustain an inner life, no matter how curious or self-serving it may seem, that psychologizing seems such a necessity in trying to come to terms with King's career.

The psychology of leadership is still relatively unknown, and the whole uncertain concept of mental health only complicates the sorts of perplexities that King's life leaves us with. King has to be unusual to the extent that he was aware, not long after the time of his 1916 consultation at Johns Hopkins, of the bearing his own psychological state had on his pursuit of a political career. As he wrote to his brother not long before he ran for the leadership of the Liberal party in 1919:

> Unless my mental health picks up within the next few months, nothing in the world would induce me to take on the strain of leadership. I have been too much run down with mental strain to cause myself to risk breaking under it. I could be of no service to the party, to the country or myself unless in decent mental and physical condition.[19]

Psychology, no matter how relevant it may be to understanding King, and the enigma he continues to pose, cannot remove all conceivable interpretive difficulties. Even with a psychiatric file about King we must still weigh and assess it, proceeding with appropriate caution and skepticism. Instead of modern psychological concepts being able by any means to settle everything, it is comforting to me as a political theorist to think that what we now have on our hands are more questions than ever. I was first drawn to Freud because of a central concern with how we ought to live. Psychology can be a rewarding approach to politics precisely because it leads to examining ourselves, and the way we are apt to think about others, with more searching sorts of demands. And King's life does, I think, successfully challenge certain stereotypes.

Psychoanalysis interested me in the first place because I thought it posed in a fresh way some old chestnuts in the history of moral dilemmas. Freud created a system of thought that posed some ancient sorts of philosophic questions. By what ethical standards should we guide ourselves? As traditional religious faith has declined, there has been a propensity to rely on social science as a substitute. Freudian theory does pose the issue of what we could possibly mean by normal behavior; for every time we categorize an act or feeling as "abnormal," implicitly we are maintaining that there is a more or less clear idea of what health itself consists in. Even though none of the questions that bringing together psychology and politics raises can have clear-cut answers, that does not make them any the less legitimate as important sources of concern.

I have therefore not undertaken to study King for the sake of any partisan purposes. It would be generally agreed that the leadership he provided during his time in public office was not of a charismatic sort. In an interesting article contrasting charismatic as opposed to "consensus leaders," a psychoanalytically oriented scholar observed:

> One of the striking characteristics of consensus leadership is the relative absence of emotional bonds between leader and follower...Centrists tend to be followers rather than leaders of opinion. They avoid substantive positions for as long as possible and, instead, concentrate their energies on procedure.

Although the author was not writing with King in mind as a consensus leader, what he proposed as lying behind such a person does fit with what we have come across. "The disruptions in self-esteem may...occur in the 'mid-life crisis.'" 1916 would seem to have been just such a disturbance for King. And some of King's key dependencies would appear to fit in with the model of consensus leadership: "the individual experienced disruption in object ties, particularly in separation from mother...."[20]

As such a consensus leader King so dominated Canadian politics for almost three decades that it is impossible to think of Canada then without his special contribution. In fact he played such an immense role in Canadian public affairs that I am inclined to think that it is a nonsensical question to ask whether what he did was good or bad for the country; it would be like questioning whether an extraordinarily long-standing marriage was successful or not. Canada and King are inconceivable without each other. Therefore I have been writing about him neither as an apologist or a critic, but as someone fascinated by the whole problem of psychology and politics.

King had correctly anticipated that his work for the Rockefellers would someday hurt him within Canadian politics. And in the spring of 1920 he was attacked for cowardice during World War I. Bruce Hutchison thought that King handled the charge "in detail which the House must have found ghastly," as King proceeded to recount to Parliament "the story of his life."[21] He read a statement into the record for *Hansard*:

> I was young, and a bachelor...When the war commenced, I was in my fortieth year. Shortly before that time, my father, a barrister and solicitor, and one of the lecturers at the Law School in Toronto, was stricken with blindness, and obliged to give up the practice of law and lecturing at the Law School. He and my mother and my unmarried sister lived together at our home in Toronto. My brother, who for a number of years was a practicing physician in this city, some little time prior to the war, after an attack of influenza complicated by double pneumonia, developed tuberculosis, and was obliged to give up the practice of his profession and for the greater part of two years to spend his time in a sanatorium. Later, he and his wife and little children took up permanent residence in Colorado. There was no one left to share the responsibilities of our home under these sad and trying circumstances, but my married sister and myself. My married sister had, as well, her own family to consider.

> On April 4, 1915, within the first few months of the war, my unmarried sister died. That left my father and mother alone. On August 30, 1916, my father died. After spending a few weeks with my invalid brother in Denver, and two or three months with my married sister, my mother came to reside with me...here in Ottawa. My mother was critically ill most of the year she was with me, and on Dec. 18, 1917, she, too, died.

King said that he thought the service he had been able to provide was "greater than any I could have performed in any other way, had there been like opportunity to take any other course." As he looked back on the war years, "so full of suffering for the whole of mankind," he felt grateful "that in that world ordeal it was given to me to share in so intimate a way the sufferings of others, and, with it all, so large a measure of opportunity to do my duty, as God gave it to me to see my duty, at that time."[22] So *Hansard* recorded King's version of the events in his family life; the private problems King had had were used by him to explain his public actions, even if he was selective enough to omit his own struggles with "nervousness" which were capped by his stay at Johns Hopkins Hospital.

It seemed to be agreed among those who worked with him that King had his human "deficiencies," but at the same time he "was a great prime minister. He knew how to direct his cabinet and how to delegate responsibility."[23] King was not fearful of having strong and capable cabinet members. As prime minister he would preside over "the completion of the evolution of Canada's status from colony to nation." And during his years in office "his political decisions did more to change the direction and transform the character of Canadian development than those of any other public man in the twentieth century."[24] King thought that it was not so much by what a leader accomplished positively that he should be judged, but by the things he prevented from happening. And by the standard of effective and lasting leadership King was to be a success. Even King's harshest critics, who thought "he succeeded in doing nothing, or as near to nothing as the exigencies of politics would permit," had to acknowledge that "in matters of detail Mackenzie King was ever a man of genius: shrewd, amoral and a nice judge of human passions and weaknesses."[25]

Today's visitor to Laurier House, or to King's estate at Kingsmere, may well wonder about the curious man who made those homes his own. The portrait of his mother hanging in his study, or the ruins he tastefully arranged on the grounds of his summer retreat, are reminders of how puzzling a man Canada's longest-lasting prime minister was. Nations, like families, live by myths, which are often incomprehensible to outsiders. In our own time King may become more interesting because of his psychology. His anxieties about electrical influence both explain certain of his characteristic qualities as well as complicate the story of his life. It may be that someday it will seem that the keeping of his diaries, instead of being a self-inflicted wound to his reputation, will become another bit of this political magician's canniness.

History has many masters, as it seeks to show us worlds other than our own. It sometimes holds up political heroes that are almost saintly:

Abraham Lincoln, for example. And it has the obligation to warn us about the presence of evil, as real as Satan, in the lives of Hitler and Stalin.

Despite the way people crave the infinite, most of human life takes place on a more mundane level, and this should seem no less real or considerable than the peaks and valleys of human experience. Mackenzie King was an uncommon man, but studying him can teach us something about our common humanity. Any such enterprise is bound to seem inconclusive, but it benefits us to bring psychology and politics together. There may be no nobler aim than that of broadening us.

Notes

Prologue

1. "The Goethe Prize," in *The Standard Edition of the Complete Psychological Works of Sigmund Freud,* ed. James Strachey, Vol. 21 (London, The Hogarth Press, 1961), pp. 211-12.

2. *The Letters of Sigmund Freud and Arnold Zweig,* ed. Ernst L. Freud, translated by Professor and Mrs. W. D. Robson-Scott (London, The Hogarth Press, 1970), p. 127.

3. W. H. Auden, *Another Time* (London, Faber & Faber, 1940), p. 118.

4. Michael Bliss, *Right Honorable Men: The Descent of Canadian Politics from Macdonald to Mulroney* (Toronto, A Phyllis Bruce Book/ Harper Collins, 1994), p. 123.

Introduction

1. Kenneth McNaught, *The Pelican History of Canada* (Harmondsworth, Penguin Books, 1969), p. 227.

2. "An Autobiographical Study," *Standard Edition*, Vol. 20, p. 72.

3. Quoted in Paul Roazen, *Meeting Freud's Family* (Amherst, Univ. of Massachusetts Press, 1993), pp. 39-40.

4. "Leonardo da Vinci and a Memory of His Childhood," *Standard Edition*, vol. 11, pp. 63-137.

5. Cf. Paul Roazen, *Freud: Political and Social Thought*, Epilogue: Woodrow Wilson (N.Y., Knopf, 1968; N.Y., Da Capo, with new Preface, 1986), pp. 300-22.

6. D. Macdougall King, *Nerves and Personal Power*, with an Introduction by W. L. Mackenzie King (N.Y., Fleming Revell, 1922), p. 249.

7. *The Globe and Mail*, March 22, 1938.

8. Quoted in George Pollock, "Psychoanalysis in Russia and the U.S.S.R.: 1908-1979," *The Annual of Psychoanalysis*, Vol. 10 (N.Y., International Universities Press, 1982), pp. 273-74.

9. Cf. Alexander M. Etkind, "Trotsky and Psychoanalysis," *Partisan Review*, 1994, pp. 303-08; Alexander M. Etkind, "How Psychoanalysis Was Received in Russia, 1906-1936," *The Journal of Analytical Psychology*, Vol. 39 (1994), pp. 191-202; Alexander Etkind, *Eros of the Impossible: The History of Psychoanalysis in Russia* (Boulder, Westview, 1997).

10. Quoted in Paul Roazen, *Erik H. Erikson: The Power and Limits of a Vision* (N.Y., The Free Press, 1976), p. 195.

11. Paul Roazen, *Freud and His Followers* (N.Y., Knopf, 1975), Part V.

12. Paul Roazen, *Encountering Freud: The Politics and Histories of Psychoanalysis* (New Brunswick, N.J., Transaction, 1990), Ch. 7.

13. Otto Fenichel, *The Psychoanalytic Theory of Neurosis* (N.Y., Norton, 1945), p. 451.

14. "Analysis Terminable and Interminable," *Standard Edition*, Vol. 23, p. 231.

15. Paul Roazen, "Nietzsche and Freud: Two Voices from the Underground," *The Psychohistory Review*, Spring 1991, pp. 327-48; Paul Roazen, "Philosophy and Psychoanalysis: Wittgenstein and Althusser," *Queen's Quarterly*, Spring, 1997.

16. Ludwig Binswanger, *Sigmund Freud: Reminiscences of a Friendship* (N.Y., Grune & Stratton, 1957), p. 21.

17. Robert C. Tucker, "The Georges' Wilson Reexamined: An Essay on Psychobiography," *American Political Science Review*, Vol. 72 (June 1977), p. 608.

18. Ernest Jones, "A Valedictory Address," *The Yearbook of Psychoanalysis* (1948), Vol. 3, p. 54.

19. For the classic pioneering article on this subject, Cf. Harold Lasswell, "What Psychiatrists and Political Scientists Can Learn From One Another," *Psychiatry*, Vol. 1 (1938), pp. 33-39.

20. Celia Bertin, *Marie Bonaparte: A Life* (New York, Harcourt Brace Jovanovich, 1982), p. 176.

21. Paul Roazen, "Memories of the Boston 'Psycho'", *Psychologist-Psychoanalyst,* Summer 1988, pp. 13-14, 45.

22. Bliss, *Right Honorable Men, op. cit.*, p. 303.

23. *The Complete Correspondence of Sigmund Freud and Ernest Jones 1908-1939*, ed. R. Andrew Paskauskas (Cambridge, Mass., Harvard University Press, 1993), p. 11.

24. Stephen Clarkson and Christina McCall, *Trudeau and Our Times,* Vol. 1 (Toronto, McClelland & Stewart, 1990).

25. Harold D. Lasswell, *Psychopathology and Politics* (Chicago, Univ. of Chicago Press, 1930; N.Y., The Viking Press, 1960).

26. H. S. Ferns, *Reading from Left to Right: One Man's Political History* (Toronto, Univ. of Toronto Press, 1983), p. 308.

Chapter 1

1. Norman Hillmer and J. L. Granatstein, "Historians Rank the Best and Worst Prime Ministers," *Maclean's,* April 21, 1997, pp. 34-39; Val Ross, "Restoration of a Tarnished King," *Globe and Mail,* Arts, May 31, 1997, pp. 1, 8.

2. Dalton Camp, *An Eclectic Eel* (Ottawa, Deneau, n.d.), pp. 136, 137.

3. C. P. Stacey, *A Date With History: Memoirs of a Canadian Historian* (Ottawa, Deneau, 1983).

4. Blair Fraser, "The Secret Life of Mackenzie King, Spiritualist," *Maclean's*, Dec. 15, 1951.

5. Interview with Carl Goldenberg, Nov. 11, 1986.

6. Interview with Dr. James, Aug. 10, 1955 (Rockefeller Archive Center).

7. J. L. Granatstein, *Mackenzie King: His Life and World* (Toronto, McGraw Hill Ryerson, 1977), p. 175. Also Bruce Hutchison, *The Incredible Canadian* (N.Y., Longmans Green, 1952), p. 82.

8. C. P. Stacey, *A Very Double Life: The Private World of Mackenzie King* (Toronto, Macmillan, 1976), p. 190.

9. Letter from Ged Martin, Nov. 5, 1986.

10. Telephone interview with Bruce Hutchison, Nov. 10, 1988; Hutchison, *The Incredible Canadian, op. cit.*, pp. 1, 2.

11. Hutchison, *op. cit.*, pp. 10, 72.

12. Camp, *An Eclectic Eel, op. cit.*, p. 133.

13. Hutchison, *The Incredible Canadian, op. cit.*, pp. 152, 157, 381, 389, 392, 2, 1.

14. Bliss, *Right Honorable Men, op. cit.*, p. 27.

15. E. K. Brown, "Mackenzie King of Canada," *Harper's Magazine*, Vol. 186 (Jan. 1943), pp. 192-200. Cf. Laura Smyth Groening, *E. K. Brown: A Study in Conflict* (Toronto, University of Toronto Press, 1993).

16. Hutchison, *The Incredible Canadian, op. cit.*, p. 9.

17. F. A. McGregor, *The Fall and Rise of Mackenzie King: 1911-19* (Toronto, Macmillan, 1962 p. 331.

18. Otto Fenichel, *The Psychoanalytic Theory of Neurosis, op. cit.*, pp. 445, 425.

19. Interview with Paul Martin, Sr., Sept. 2, 1986.

20. John Robert Columbo, *Mackenzie King's Ghost* (Willowdale, Hounslow Press, 1991), pp. 167-89.

21. Bliss, *Right Honorable Men, op. cit.*, p. 141.

22. Hutchison, *The Incredible Canadian, op. cit.*, p. 79.

23. W. L. Mackenzie King, *The Secret of Heroism: A Memoir of Henry Albert Harper* (N.Y., Fleming Revell, 1906), p. 13.

24. Irving Abella and Harold Troper, *None Is Too Many* (Toronto, Lester & Orpen Dennys, 1986), pp. 37, 39, 157, 282.

25. Hutchison, *The Incredible Canadian, op. cit.*, p. 295.

26. Bliss, *Right Honorable Men, op. cit.*, p. 203.

27. Jean E. Dryden, "The Mackenzie King Papers: An Archival Odyssey," *Archivaria*, 6 (Summer 1978), pp. 40-69.

28. McGregor, *The Fall and Rise of Mackenzie King, op. cit.*, p. i.

29. Hutchison, *The Incredible Canadian, op. cit.*, p. 4.

30. R. McGregor Dawson, *William Lyon Mackenzie King: A Political Biography*, Vol. I (Toronto, University of Toronto Press, 1958); H. Blair Neatby, *William Lyon Mackenzie King*, Vol. 2 (Toronto, University of Toronto Press, 1963); H. Blair Neatby, *William Lyon Mackenzie King*, Vol. 3 (Toronto, University of Toronto Press, 1976).

31. C. P. Stacey, *A Very Double Life, op. cit.*

32. Quoted in Hutchison, *The Incredible Canadian, op. cit.*, p. 198.

33. Hutchison, *The Incredible Canadian, op. cit.*, p. 96.

34. C. P. Stacey, *Mackenzie King and the Atlantic Triangle* (Toronto, Macmillan, 1976).

35. *Ibid.*, pp. 53-54.

36. Stacey, *A Very Double Life, op. cit.*, p. 61.

37. *Ibid.*, pp. 102, 114, 64, 181.

38. Stacey, *Mackenzie King and the Atlantic Triangle, op. cit.*, pp. 20, 13.

39. Reginald Whitaker, "Mackenzie King in the Dominion of the Dead," *Canadian Forum* (Feb. 1976), p. 8.

40. Ged Martin, "Mackenzie King, The Medium and the Messages." *British Journal of Canadian Studies*, Vol. 4, No. 1 (1989), pp. 129-30.

41. H. M. Gitelman, *Legacy of the Ludlow Massacre* (Philadelphia, Univ. of Penn. Press, 1988), p. xiv.

42. Joy E. Esberey, *Knight of the Holy Spirit: A Study of William Lyon Mackenzie King* (Toronto, University of Toronto Press, 1980). Cf. Donald Swainson, "Neurosis and Causality in Canadian History," *Queen's Quarterly*, Autumn 1982, pp. 611-17. Cf. also John C. Courtney, "Prime Ministerial Character: An Examination of Mackenzie King's Political Leadership," in *Mackenzie King: Widening the Debate*, ed. John English and J. O. Stubbs (Toronto, Macmillan, 1978), pp. 55-88; and Robert K. Keyserlingk, "Mackenzie King's Spiritualism and His View of Hitler," *Journal of Canadian Studies*, Vol. 20, No. 4 (Winter 1985-86), pp. 26-44.

43. Heather Robertson, *Willie: A Romance* (Toronto, Lorimer, 1983).

Chapter 2

1. Roazen, *Freud and His Followers, op. cit.*, pp. 378-80; Lavinia Edmunds, "His Master's Choice," *John Hopkins Magazine* (April 1988),

pp. 40-49.

2. David Paul Lumsden, "Discoursing on the Knowledge Trade and on Psychiatry As A Commodity," forthcoming.

3. William B. Spaulding, "Why Rockefeller Supported Medical Education in Canada: The William Lyon Mackenzie Connection," *Canadian Bulletin of Medical History,* Vol. 10, No. 1 (1993), pp. 67-76.

4. Michael Gelder, "Adolf Meyer and His Influence on British Psychiatry," in *150 Years of British Psychiatry,* ed. German Burrios and Hugh Freeman (London, Gaskell, 1991), p. 424.

5. Donald Fleming, *William H. Welch and the Rise of Modern Medicine* (Boston, Little Brown, 1954).

6. Charles Rosenberg, *The Trial of the Assassin Guiteau: Psychiatry and Law in the Gilded Age* (Chicago, Univ. of Chicago Press, 1968); Cf. Roazen, *Encountering Freud: The Politics and Histories of Psychoanalysis* (New Brunswick, N.J., Transaction, 1990), pp. 81-83.

7. Elliot S. Valenstein, *Great and Desperate Cures: The Rise and Decline of Psychosurgery and Other Radical Treatments for Mental Illness* (N.Y., Basic Books, 1986), p. 28.

8. Magda Whitrow, *Julius Wagner-Jauregg (1857-1940)* (London, Smith Gordon, 1993).

9. Cf. Paul Roazen, "Book Review of Whitrow's *Wagner-Jauregg, "The History of Psychiatry,* March 1994, pp. 148-50; Paul Roazen, "Psychoanalysis's Cotton Mather: Book review of Eissler's *Freud As An Expert Witness: The Discussion of War Neuroses Between Freud and Wagner-Jauregg," Contemporary Psychology,* Vol. 33, No. 3 (1988), pp. 213-14.

10. Theodore Lidz, "Adolf Meyer and the Development of American Psychiatry," *American Journal of Psychiatry,* Vol. 123 (Sept. 1966), p. 326.

11. Gelder, "Adolf Meyer and His Influence on British Psychiatry," *op.*

cit., p. 419.

12. Gregory Zilboorg, *A History of Medical Psychology* (N.Y., Norton, 1941), pp. 502-03. Cf. also Miriam Siegler and Humphrey Osmond, *Models of Madness, Models of Medicine* (N.Y., Harper, 1974), pp. 147-51.

13. John C. Burnham, *Psychoanalysis and American Medicine, 1894-1918: Medicine, Science, and Culture* (N.Y., International Universities Press, 1967), p. 6.

14. Nathan G. Hale, *Freud and the Americans: The Beginnings of Psychoanalysis in the United States, 1876-1917* (N.Y. Oxford Univ. Press, 1971), pp. 157-58.

15. Edward Shorter, *From the Mind into the Body: The Cultural Origins of Psychosomatic Symptoms* (N.Y., The Free Press, 1994), p. 136.

16. Gerald N. Grob, *Mental Illness and American Society 1875-1940* (Princeton Univ. Press, 1983), p. 112.

17. Quoted in David Paul Lumsden, "Professional Godfather: The Role of Adolf Meyer and His Students in Canadian and Chinese Psychiatry," *Culture Health*, Vol. 9, No. 2 (1992-93), p. 226.

18. Paul Roazen and Bluma Swerdloff, *Heresy: Sandor Rado and the Psychoanalytic Movement* (N.J. Jason Aronson, 1995), p. 133.

19. Lumsden, "Professional Godfather," *op. cit.*, p. 224.

20. *Ibid.*, p. 220.

21. Otto Marx, "Adolf Meyer and Psychiatric Training at the Phipps Clinic: An Interview with Theodore Lidz," *The History of Psychiatry*, Vol. 4 (1993), p. 268.

22. R. D. Laing, *The Divided Self* (London, Penguin Books, 1965), pp. 29ff.

23. Hale, *Freud and the Americans, op. cit.*, p. 17.

24. *Ibid.*, p. 18.

25. *Ibid.*, p. 438.

26. Franz G. Alexander and Sheldon T. Selesnick, *The History of Psychiatry: An Evaluation of Psychiatric Thought and Practice from Prehistoric Times to the Present* (New York, Harper & Row, 1966), p. 264.

27. Lidz, "Adolf Meyer and the Development of American Psychiatry," *op._cit.*, p. 328.

28. Gelder, "Adolf Meyer and His Influence on British Psychiatry," *op. cit.*, p. 428; Grob, *Mental Illness and American Society, op. cit.*, p. 129.

29. Anne Collins, *In the Sleep Room: The Story of the CIA Brainwashing Experiments in Canada* (Toronto, Lester & Orpen Dennys, 1988).

30. *Ibid.*, p. 164.

31. *Ibid.*, p. 67.

32. Paul Roazen, *How Freud Worked* (N.J., Jason Aronson, 1995), Ch. 7.

33. David J. Lynn, "Freud's Analysis of A.B., A Psychotic Man, 1925-30," *Journal of the American Academy of Psychoanalysis*, Vol. 21, No. 1 (Spring 1993), pp. 63-78.

34. Henry James, ed., *The Letters of William James*, Vol. II (Boston, Atlantic Monthly, Press, 1920), pp. 327-28.

35. Saul Rosenzweig, *Freud, Jung and Hall the King-Maker: The Expedition to America (1909)*, (Seattle, Hogrefe & Huber, 1992), p. 174.

36. *Letters of Sigmund Freud 1873-1939*, ed. Ernst L. Freud, translated

by Tania and James Stern (London, The Hogarth Press, 1961), p. 211.

37. Ruth Leys and Rand Evans, ed., *Defining American Psychiatry: The Correspondence Between Adolf Meyer and Edward Bradford Titchener* (Baltimore, Johns Hopkins Univ. Press, 1990), p. 56. Cf. also Ruth Leys, "Types of One: Adolf Meyer's Life Chart and the Representation of Individuality," *Representations*, 34 (Spring 1991), pp. 1-28; Ruth Leys, "Meyer, Jung, and the Limits of Association," *Bulletin of the History of Medicine*, Vol. 59 (1985), pp. 345-60; Ruth Leys, "Meyer, Watson, and the Dangers of Behaviorism," *Journal of the History of the Behavioral Sciences*, Vol. 20 (April 1984), pp. 128-49; Ruth Leys, "Meyer's Dealings with Jones: A Chapter in the History of the American Response to Psychoanalysis," *Journal of the History of the Behavioral Sciences*, Vol. 17 (1981), pp. 445-65; Craig Tomlinson, "Sandor Rado and Adolf Meyer: A Nodal Point in American Psychiatry and Psychoanalysis," *International Journal of Psychoanalysis*, Vol. 77 (1996), pp. 963-982.

38. Hale, *Freud and the Americans, op. cit.*, p. 100.

39. Leys and Evans, *Defining American Psychiatry, op. cit.*, p. 39.

40. Gelder, "Adolf Meyer and His Influence on British Psychiatry," *op. cit.*, p. 426.

41. Helen Swick Perry, *Psychiatrist of America: The Life of Harry Stack Sullivan* (Cambridge, Harvard University Press, 1982), p. 238.

42. *Ibid.*

43. Clarence P. Oberndorf, *A History of Psychoanalysis in America* (New York, Grune & Stratton, 1953), p. 84.

44. Lytton Strachey, *Eminent Victorians* (N.Y., The Modern Library, 1918), p. vii.

45. Walter C. Langer, *The Mind of Adolf Hitler* (New York, Basic Books, 1972).

46. Perry, *Psychiatrist of America, op. cit.*

Chapter 3

1. Dawson, *W. L. M. King, op. cit.*

2. Interview with Dr. James, *op. cit.*

3. McGregor, *The Fall and Rise of Mackenzie King, op. cit.*

4. Interview with Dr. James, *op. cit.*

5. H. S. Ferns and B. Ostry, *The Age of Mackenzie King: The Rise of the Leader* (London, Heinemann, 1955).

6. Dawson, *W. L. M. King, op. cit.*, p. 12.

7. *Ibid.*, p. 252.

8. *Ibid.*, pp. 252-53.

9. *Ibid.*, p. 251.

10. *Ibid.*, p. 109.

11. *Ibid.*, p. 290.

12. McGregor, *The Fall and Rise of Mackenzie King, op. cit.*, p. 10.

13. *Ibid.*, p. 59.

14. Neatby, *W. L. M. King, op. cit.*, Vol. 2, Ch. 19, and Vol. 3, Ch. 4.

15. Ramsay Cook, *The Regenerators: Social Criticism in Late Victorian English Canada* (Toronto, University of Toronto Press, 1985).

16. Dawson, *W. L. M. King, op. cit.*, p. 136. Cf. also Robert Craig Brown and Ramsay Cook, *Canada 1896-1921: A Nation Transformed* (Toronto, McClelland & Stewart, 1974), pp. 119-23.

17. McNaught, *The Pelican History of Canada, op. cit.*, p. 40.

18. Dawson, *W. L. M. King, op. cit.*, p. 220.

19. *Ibid.*, p. 223.

20. Stacey, *A Very Double Life, op. cit.*, p. 146.

21. McGregor, *The Fall and Rise of Mackenzie King, op. cit.*, pp. 22, 56, 57.

22. Raymond B. Fosdick, *John D. Rockefeller, Jr.: A Portrait* (N.Y., Harper & Bros., 1956), p. 149.

23. Dawson, *W. L. M. King, op. cit.*, p. 233-34.

24. Fosdick, *Rockefeller, op. cit.*, p. 161.

25. McGregor, *The Fall and Rise of Mackenzie King, op. cit.*, pp. 218.

26. J. L. Granatstein & J. M. Hitsman, *Broken Promises: A History of Conscription in Canada* (Toronto, Oxford Univ. Press, 1977), p. 52.

27. Ferns and Ostry, *The Age of Mackenzie King, op. cit.*, pp. 217, 212, 213-14.

28. McGregor, *The Fall and Rise of Mackenzie King, op. cit.*, pp. 218-19.

29. *Ibid.*, p. 219.

30. *Ibid.*, p. 218.

31. *Ibid.*, p. 218.

32. H. S. Ferns, "Mackenzie King on Television," *British Journal of Canadian Studies*, Vol. 3, No. 2 (1988), p. 311.

33. Stacey, *Mackenzie King and the Atlantic Triangle, op. cit.*, p. 65.

34. Hutchison, *The Incredible Canadian, op. cit.*, p. 382.

35. Quoted in Granatstein and Hitsman, *Broken Promises, op. cit.*, p. 31.

36. *Ibid.*, p. 43.

37. Ferns and Ostry, *The Age of Mackenzie King, op. cit.*, p. 22.

Chapter 4

1. John D. Rockefeller, Jr. to King, Dec. 30, 1949 (Rockefeller Center Archive.)

2. McGregor, *The Fall and Rise of Mackenzie King, op. cit.*, p. 218.

3. Horace W. Frink, *Morbid Fears and Compulsions: Their Psychology and Psychoanalytical Treatment* (New York, Dodd Mead, 1918), p. 261. See also Judd Marmor, "The Psychodynamics of Realistic Worry," *Psychiatry in Transition*, 2nd edition (New Brunswick, N.J., Transaction, 1994).

4. D. Macdougall King, *Nerves and Personal Power*, with an Introduction by W. L. Mackenzie King (N.Y., Fleming Revell Co., 1922), p. 274.

5. Hutchison, *The Incredible Canadian, op. cit.*, p. 9.

6. Quoted in Malcolm Macmillan, "The Sources of Freud's Methods for Gathering and Evaluating Clinical Data," in *Freud and the History of Psychoanalysis*, ed. Toby Gelfand and John Kerr (N.J., The Analytic Press, 1992), p. 101.

7. Henry Alden Bunker, "Symposium on Neurasthenia: From Beard to Freud," *Medical Review of Reviews*, Vol. 36, No. 3 (1930), p. 108.

8. Sander L. Gilman, *Freud, Race, and Gender* (Princeton, Princeton Univ. Press, 1993), p. 95.

9. Arthur Kleinman, *Re-thinking Psychiatry: From Cultural Category to Personal Experience* (N.Y., The Free Press, 1988), p. 7.

10. *Ibid.*, p. 14.

11. *Ibid.*

12. Jean Laplanche and J. B. Pontalis, *The Language of Psychoanalysis*, translated by David Nicholson-Smith (N.Y., Norton, 1973), p. 265.

13. Frink, *Morbid Fears and Compulsions, op. cit.*, p. 163; Cf. F. G. Gosling, *Before Freud: Neurasthenia and the American Medical Community, 1870-1910* (Urbana, Univ. of Illinois Press, 1987).

14. McGregor, *The Fall and Rise of Mackenzie King, op. cit.*, pp. 279-80.

15. *Ibid.*, p. 219.

16. Hutchison, *The Incredible Canadian, op. cit.*, p. 35.

17. Esberey, *Knight of the Holy Spirit, op. cit.*, p. 84.

18. Sigmund Freud, *The Interpretation of Dreams, Standard Edition*, ed. James Strachey, Vol. 4 (London, The Hogarth Press, 1953), p. xxvi.

19. See John C. Burnham, *Jelliffe: American Psychoanalyst and Physician* (Chicago, Univ. of Chicago Press, 1983), p. 216.

20. *The Complete Correspondence of Sigmund Freud and Ernest Jones, 1908-1939*, ed. R. Andrew Paskauskas (Cambridge, Harvard Univ. Press, 1993), p. 56.

21. (N.Y., G. E. Stechert, 1909).

22. Lewellys F. Barker, *Psychotherapy* (N.Y., D. Appleton Century Co., 1940), pp. 1, 192, 3.

23. McGregor, *The Fall and Rise of Mackenzie King, op. cit.*, p. 220.

24. Jerrold M. Post, "Current Concepts of the Narcissistic Personality: Implications for Political Psychology," *Political Psychology*, Vol. 14, No. 1 (1993), p. 101.

25. Barker, *Psychotherapy, op. cit.*, p.10.

26. Quoted in Lisa Appignanesi and John Forrester, *Freud's Women* (N.Y., Basic Books, 1992), p. 87.

27. *The Complete Correspondence of Sigmund Freud and Ernest Jones, op. cit.*, p. 57.

28. "Lewellys Franklin Barker," *The Collected Papers of Adolf Meyer* Vol. III *Medical Teaching*, ed. Eunice E. Winters (Baltimore, Johns Hopkins Press, 1951), pp. 554-57.

29. *The Complete Correspondence of Sigmund Freud and Ernest Jones, op. cit.*, p. 73.

30. Edward Shorter, *From the Mind Into the Body: The Cultural Origins of Psychosomatic Symptoms*, op.cit., p. 132.

31. Cf. Victor Tausk, "On the Origin of the 'Influencing Machine' in Schizophrenia," in *Sexuality, War and Schizophrenia: The Collected Psychoanalytic Papers of Victor Tausk*, ed. Paul Roazen (New Brunswick, N.J., Transaction, 1991), pp. 185-219.

32. Emil Kraepelin, *Dementia Praecox and Paraphrenia*, translated by R. Mary Barclay (Edinburgh, Livingston, 1919), pp. 287, 135.

33. *The Collected Papers of Adolf Meyer*, Vol. II, *op. cit.*, p. 474. I am grateful to Dr. Doris B. Nagel for pointing out this article to me, as well as the next one by Phyllis Greenacre.

34. Phyllis Greenacre, "The Content of the Schizophrenic Characteristics Occurring in Affective Disorders," *American Journal of Insanity*, Vol. 75 (Oct. 1918), pp. 200-01.

35. Hutchison, *The Incredible Canadian, op. cit.*, p. 4.

36. Gregory Zilboorg, "Ambulatory Schizophrenias," *Psychiatry*, Vol. 4 (1941), p. 153.

37. Harold D. Lasswell, *Psychopathology and Politics* (Chicago, Univ. of Chicago Press, 1977). Paul Roazen, *Encountering Freud, op. cit.*, 241-44.

38. Henri F. Ellenberger, *The Discovery of the Unconscious: The History and Evolution of Dynamic Psychiatry* (N.Y., Basic Books, 1970), Ch. 6. Cf. John Kerr, "Epilogue," in *Freud and The History of Psychoanalysis, op. cit.*, p. 368.

39. Mark S. Micale, "On the 'Disappearance' of Hysteria," *Isis*, Vol. 84 (1993), p. 516.

40. Cf. Paul Roazen and Bluma Swerdloff, *Heresy: Sandor Rado and the Psychoanalytic Movement* (Northvale, N.J., Jason Aronson, 1995), p. 132.

41. Violet Markham, *Friendship's Harvest* (London, Max Reinhardt, 1956), pp. 151, 144.

42. D. Macdougall King, *Nerves and Personal Power* (N.Y., Fleming Revell Co., 1922), pp. 129, 250, 274.

43. *Ibid.*, p. v.

44. Cf. also Charlotte Gray, *Mrs. King: The Life and Times of Isabel Mackenzie King* (Toronto, Viking, 1997); and Charlotte Gray, "Crazy Like a Fox," *Saturday Night* (Oct. 1997), pp. 42-50, 94.

45. "Five Lectures on Psychoanalysis," *The Standard Edition of the Complete Psychological Works of Sigmund Freud*, ed. James Strachey (London, Hogarth Press, 1953-74), Vol. 11, p. 49.

46. Rosemarie Sand, "Pre-Freudian Discovery of Dream Meaning," in *Freud and the History of Psychoanalysis, op. cit.*, p. 225.

47. Mackenzie King Diary, Nov. 19, 1896; and Dec. 6, 1896.

48. Eugen Bleuler, *Dementia Praecox or the Group of Schizophrenias*, translated by Joseph Zinkin (N.Y., International Universities Press, 1950), p. 472.

49. McGregor, *op. cit.*, p. 82.

50. Arnold Heeney, *The Things That Are Caesar's: Memoirs of a Canadian Public Servant* (Toronto, University of Toronto Press, 1972), p. 50.

51. Granatstein, *op. cit.*, p. 9.

Chapter 5

1. Emil Kraepelin, *Dementia Praecox and Paraphrenia*, translated by R. Mary Barclay (Edinburgh, Livingston, 1919), pp. 16, 287, 135.

2. Edward Shorter, *From the Mind Into the Body: The Cultural Origins of Psychosomatic Symptoms*, op. cit., pp. 52-53.

3. Andrew Scull, "Desperate Remedies: A Gothic Tale of Madness and Modern Medicine," *Psychological Medicine*, Vol. 17 (1987), pp. 561-77.

4. Ronald R. Fieve, *Moodswing* (N.Y., Bantom Books, 1989), p. 202.

5. Charles Kent, *Leigh Hunt As Poet and Essayist* (London, Warne, 1889.)

6. Martin, "Mackenzie King, The Medium and the Messages," *op. cit.*, p. 116.

7. Robertson, *Willie, op. cit.*, p. 13.

Chapter 6

1. Ferns and Ostry, *The Age of Mackenzie King,* op. cit., pp. 231-32.

2. John D. Rockefeller, Jr. to King, Dec. 22, 1916 (Rockefeller Archive Center).

3. Valenstein, *Great and Desperate Cures, op. cit.*, p. 37.

4. Stacey, *A Very Double Life, op. cit.*, p. 156.

5. Fosdick, *John D. Rockefeller*, Jr., *op. cit.*, p. 171.

6. Letters, Sept. 18, 1950 and Nov. 22, 1950 (Rockefeller Archive Center).

Chapter 7

1. Carl Becker, *Everyman His Own Historian* (N.Y., Appleton-Century-Crofts, 1935), p. 251.

2. R. D. Laing, "God and Psychiatry," *Times Literary Supplement,* May 23, 1986, p. 559.

3. McGregor, *op. cit.*, pp. 82-83.

4. Bliss, *op. cit* ., p. 133.

5. Whitaker, *op. cit.*, p. 8.

6. Quoted in McNaught, *op. cit.*, pp. 227-28.

7. Ferns and Ostry, *op. cit.*, pp. 174-75.

8. Anthony Stevens, *On Jung* (London, Routledge, 1990), p. 169.

9. McGregor, *op. cit.*, p. 22.

10. Bliss, *op. cit.*, p. 174.

11. Neatby, *William Lyon Mackenzie King*, Vol. 2 *op. cit.*, pp. 208-09.

12. Mackenzie King, Diary, Feb. 21, 1933.

13. Mackenzie King, Diary, March 9, 17, & 29, 1933.

14. Interview with Carl Goldenberg.

15. J. W. Pickersgill, "Mackenzie King Speeches," *Queen's Quarterly,* Vol. 57 (1950), p. 306.

16. J. L. Granatstein, *A Man of Influence: Norman A. Robertson and Canadian Statecraft 1929-68* (Ottawa, Deneau, 1981), p. 202.

17. J. W. Pickersgill, "Mackenzie King's Political Attitudes and Public Policies: A Personal Impression," in *Mackenzie King: Widening the Debate*, ed. English & Stubbs, *op. cit.*, p. 22.

18. Whitaker, *op. cit.*, p. 8.

19. McGregor, *op. cit.*, p. 330.

20. Abraham Zaleznick, "Charismatic and Consensus Leaders: A Psychological Comparison," *Bulletin of the Menninger Clinic*, Vol. 38, No. 3 (May 1974), pp. 229-30, 234.

21. Hutchison, *op. cit.*, p. 52.

22. Canadian House of Commons Debates, April 20, 1920, p. 1416.

23. Paul Martin, *A Very Public Life*, Vol. I, *Far From Home* (Ottawa, Deneau, 1983), pp. 431-32.

24. J. W. Pickersgill, "Mackenzie King's Political Attitudes and Public Politics," *op. cit.*, p. 25.

25. Ferns and Ostry, *op. cit.*, pp. 280, 332.

Acknowledgements

This book has taken so long since I first conceived it that I am more than usually worried about possibly overlooking my appropriate debts.

First of all, there are the occasions on which I was lucky enough to present some of this material publicly. With the general title of "The Enigma of Mackenzie King" I spoke at the Political Psychology Program, George Washington University (1994); the Abbey Bookstore, Paris (1992); the Canadian Psychoanalytic Society (Quebec E), Montreal (1990); the Canadian Institute of Psychoanalysis (Ottawa Branch) (1989); the International Political Science Association (1988); and the Toronto Psychoanalytic Society (1988). Also I spoke on "Normality and Politics: Mackenzie King," Dept. of Psychiatry, Toronto General Hospital (1987). The feed-back I received as my work evolved was of critical help to my thinking.

For the first time in my life I needed a research assistant, to help me on King's diary, and was fortunate in having the Department of Political Science, York University, Toronto, offer me the excellent assistance of Meghan Neylan.

I learned an immense amount from interviewing some of those who knew or worked with King, including James A. Gibson, Carl Goldenberg, John Holmes, Bruce Hutchison, Paul Martin, Sr., Edward Pickering, Jack Pickersgill, and Walter J. Turnbull. For help in reconstructing the psychiatric evidence I am grateful to Dr. Harry Hardin, Dr. Doris B. Nagel, and Dr. John Salvandy.

Work like this is dependent on cooperative librarians, and Nancy McCall, an archivist at The Alan Mason Chesney Medical Archives of The Johns Hopkins Medical Institutions was a critical help. Prof. Ruth Leys of Johns Hopkins worked on the transcription of Adolf Meyer's handwriting, and Erica Greenbloom helped with an interpretation of his idiosyncratic short-hand. Everyone I encountered at the Rockefeller Archive Center in North Tarrytown, N.Y. facilitated my work there. And I was also fortunate with the superb help I got from the staff of the Public Archives in Ottawa. The librarians at both York University and the University of Toronto have always been obliging to me, but in the case of this book I was exceptionally reliant on them.

Friends of mine who have read one of the many drafts the

manuscript has taken include Edward Andrew, Carl Berger, Ramsay Cook, Donald Forbes, John Hutcheson, David Meynell, Michael Rogin, and Anthony Storr. In addition both Michael Bliss and H. Blair Neatby have enriched with their comments different versions of the text; and Ged Martin was helpful on a specific issue. Ian Morrison and David Paul Lumsden cooperated in their individual ways. Above all Jack Granatstein has not only read through the book a couple of times, but has been a consistently supportive ally as I ventured into this whole subject.

Index